What people are saying about *Sober for Good:*

"What a gem this book is."

> — Cindy Swan-Henderlite, licensed drug and alcohol counselor, Minnesota

"*Sober for Good* is changing my life. To someone else, having two to three glasses of wine a day may not look like a big deal. But I recently became aware that I had been drinking too much — for me."

> — Beth G., California

"*Sober for Good* offers a wealth of insight and information that will help anyone who seeks personal recovery or wishes to help others to recover."

> — Fred A., 16 years sober with AA and SMART Recovery

"*Sober for Good* is a great book. I have recommended it to some of my patients who are not alcoholics, but who need help in getting their alcohol intake in control. I'm glad that I have a source for them to find help."

> — Kathy K. Isoldi, M.S., R.D., C.D.E., coordinator of nutritional services, Comprehensive Weight Control Program, New York Presbyterian Hospital

"*Sober for Good* is a revelation to me! I had no idea there were *so* many options out there for recovery. Thanks to this book I feel hopeful."

> — Kim K., new to recovery

"This is the best book of its type that I have ever read, in my carefully considered opinion. The concept and the execution are impressive."

> — John J. Boren, Ph.D., senior research scientist (retired), Treatment Research Branch, National Institute on Drug Abuse

"Gentle Bill W. — cofounder of AA — would find no quarrel with *Sober for Good* . . . I'd make this book part of any suggested readings about personal alcohol problems."

— Albert S., 9 years sober with AA

"I really enjoyed this book and feel that it would be very helpful to anyone who is going through the same thing I am. The most important part in this book for me was the realization that alcohol does not have to be a part of your life for you to have fun."

— Stephanie C., a junior in college

"Truly excellent. I wish *Sober for Good* had been available back in 1988, when I first tried to quit drinking and thought that AA was the only game in town. If more people would be told that there are many different paths to sobriety, they potentially could be saved a lot of grief."

— Alex C., SOS member in New York State

"A useful book for both DWI treatment providers and their clients. It is not often in my professional career that I run across a self-help book that is both a good read and provides helpful information. *Sober for Good* is one of those books."

— Reid Hester, Ph.D., director, Research Division, Behavior Therapy Associates, Albuquerque

"Effective remedies are treasures. This book is among them. Despite the fact that most people use it responsibly, alcohol causes more damage to individuals, families, community, and the nation than all of the illegal drugs combined."

— *Press-Telegram*, Los Angeles/Long Beach, California

Sober for Good

—

New Solutions for Drinking Problems — Advice
from Those Who Have Succeeded

Anne M. Fletcher

Foreword by Frederick B. Glaser, M.D.

Houghton Mifflin Company
Boston   New York

First Houghton Mifflin paperback, 2002

Visit our Web site: www.houghtonmifflinbooks.com.

Library of Congress Cataloging-in-Publication Data
Fletcher, Anne M.
Sober for good : new solutions for drinking problems : advice
from those who have succeeded / Anne M. Fletcher.
p.   cm.
Includes bibliographical references and index.
ISBN 0-395-91201-6
ISBN 0-618-21907-2 (pbk.)
1. Alcoholics — Rehabilitation. 2. Alcoholism —
Relapse — Prevention. I. Title.
HV5276.F65 2001
362.292'8 — dc21   00-065032

Book design by Joyce C. Weston

Printed in the United States of America

QUM 10 9 8 7 6 5 4 3

The designations of various organizations, systems, and/or products mentioned in
this book are claimed by their owners as trademarks. These include:

SMART Recovery®	Addictive Voice Recognition	Campral®
4-Point Program℠	Technique®	ReVia®
Rational Recovery®	AVRT®	DSM-IV™
RR℠	Antabuse®	

The Twelve Steps of Alcoholics Anonymous (p. 110) are reprinted with permission
of Alcoholics Anonymous World Services, Inc. (AAWS). Permission to reprint the
Twelve Steps does not mean that AAWS has reviewed or approved the contents
of this publication, or that AAWS necessarily agrees with the views expressed herein.
AA is a program of recovery from alcoholism *only* — use of the Twelve Steps in
connection with programs and activities which are patterned after AA but which
address other problems, or in any other non-AA context, does not imply otherwise.

For my sisters, Carol, Cindy, and Lois,
and for my friend Larry Lindner,
who is like a brother to me

Acknowledgments

My foremost appreciation goes to the hundreds of "masters" of alcohol problems who entrusted me with their stories. I only wish *Sober for Good* could have included quotations from all the people who responded to my call — I cannot overstate my appreciation of their willingness to help others by sharing their personal accounts. The masters included in the book spent a great deal of time completing a lengthy questionnaire, and many of them gave additional time in phone interviews and e-mail sessions. In particular, the profiled masters who open each chapter devoted hours to telling me their stories and answering my numerous personal questions.

Next, I want to thank my family — Steve, Wes, Ty, and Julia — for their patience and acceptance of the long work hours devoted to this book. No outside person ever knows how much families contribute to — and put up with in — the making of a book.

I am indebted to many researchers who supported and reviewed my work, but first I want to go out of my way to express my immeasurable appreciation to the world-renowned relapse prevention expert and alcohol researcher Alan Marlatt, Ph.D., director of the Addictive Behaviors Research Center at the University of Washington. At the outset he encouraged me to write this book, and he then acted as my consultant, friend, and conscience throughout the entire writing process, from the proposal right through review of every chapter. Not only is he a brilliant researcher, dedicated to helping people view alcohol problems in new ways, but he has been kind and generous to me throughout the development of *Sober for Good*. His enthusiasm has sustained me through the highs and lows of writing this book.

Many other experts in the field encouraged me along the way, answered questions, offered direction, and reviewed sections of this book. I was fortunate to have help with my research from John Allen, Ph.D., associate director of treatment studies at the National Institute on Alcohol Abuse and Alcoholism (NIAAA). Mark Sobell,

Ph.D., of Florida's Nova Southeastern University, was especially generous with his time — he was always willing to answer my questions and to review sections of the manuscript. Likewise, Marc Kern, Ph.D., director of Los Angeles's Addiction Alternatives, was most responsive to many queries and offered regular, thoughtful commentary. Also particularly supportive was A. Thomas Horvath, Ph.D., 1999–2000 president of the American Psychological Association's Division on Addictions. I was honored to have periodic input from the renowned researcher William Miller, Ph.D., from the University of New Mexico. I also had the good fortune to have the historian Ernest Kurtz, Ph.D., author of *Not-God,* look over much of my material about Alcoholics Anonymous.

Thanks too to the following experts, who reviewed sections of *Sober for Good* according to their areas of expertise: Barbara McCrady, Ph.D., Rutgers University; Timothy O'Farrell, Ph.D., Harvard Medical School; Tom McLellan, Ph.D., University of Pennsylvania; Jalie Tucker, Ph.D., M.P.H., Auburn University in Alabama; John Hughes, M.D., University of Vermont; Raymond Anton, M.D., Medical University of South Carolina; Robert Meyers, University of New Mexico; and Thomas Badger, Ph.D., University of Arkansas School of Medicine.

Also I want to credit the author and alcohol expert Stanton Peele, Ph.D., whose books inspired me and helped me personally; always, he has responded readily to my requests for information. Charles Bufe (owner of See Sharp Press) has also been helpful. Both of these men have tirelessly devoted themselves to disseminating groundbreaking information about the resolution of alcohol problems. Last, but not least, on the list of professional people to whom I owe thanks are Ann Bradley, NIAAA press officer; Reid Hester, Ph.D.; Deborah Dawson, Ph.D.; William Lands, Ph.D.; Esteban Mezey, M.D.; Anne Hatcher, Ed.D., R.D.; Frederick Rotgers, Psy.D.; and Rudolf Moos, Ph.D., all of whom answered questions or helped with my research along the way.

Special thanks goes to the recovery groups that helped me recruit the masters for *Sober for Good* — namely, Women for Sobriety, SMART Recovery, and Secular Organizations for Sobriety. I appreciate their willingness, along with that of Alcoholics Anonymous's General Service Office, to answer my questions about their philosophies and programs. Rational Recovery also helped me locate masters for the book and answered questions. Credit also goes to individuals who helped me locate people for the book, including Jane Brody of the *New York Times;* Emily Fox Kales, Ph.D.; George Deering, M.D.; Wendy Richardson; Stanley Fields, of the *Recovery Road Radio Show;* Betty Yarmon, with *Partyline;* and Michael McCarthy, M.D.

I will be forever grateful for the responsiveness and support of Christine Tomasino, whose relationship with me goes far beyond that of being my literary agent. She spent countless hours helping me develop the proposal for *Sober for Good,* reading the manuscript, offering professional advice, and being my friend for the nearly four years it took to write this book. I am indebted also to my sage editor, Rux Martin, whose wisdom in shaping a book is immeasurable. I am continually impressed by her ability to extract all that makes a book worth reading. Thanks too to the editor Barry Estabrook, who saw the potential in my ideas and offered helpful advice. He has been a strong supporter of my books and was instrumental in bringing *Sober for Good* to Houghton Mifflin.

Behind the scenes were special people who helped with the research, correspondence, and/or legwork involved in *Sober for Good:* Inez Thomas, Mary Stadick, Gail Zyla, Leigh Pomeroy, Kristin Woizeschke, and Britt Anderson. I thank them all for their invaluable help. My gratitude goes too to the following people from my past: George Komaridis, Ph.D.; Elaine Pitkin, Ph.D.; William Vogel, Ph.D.; Robert Wiedeman, and Chris Bettinelli.

Finally, I appreciate all the other friends and family members — including my sisters; my parents, Alan and Julia Fletcher; my mother-in-law, Ruth Keesing; and my friends Bess Tsasoe, Patty Christensen, and Bev Brubaker — who supported me and listened to the weekly trials and tribulations of taking on this incredible project and journey. Thanks also to my friends Kevin O'C. Green and Tom Frank. My special thanks go to my friend Larry Lindner, executive editor of *Tufts University Health & Nutrition Letter.* For more than ten years he has been there for me — as an editorial adviser but, more important, as a close friend and confidant who has encouraged me in my professional and personal growth. Everyone involved in *Sober for Good,* as well as those who supported me in this endeavor, should feel confident that they have played a role in helping others find a way out of a troubled relationship with alcohol.

Author's Note

Sober for Good *is not meant to take the place of professional guidance in dealing with an alcohol problem.* Anyone who thinks he or she has a drinking problem is advised to seek counsel from a physician, licensed mental health professional, and/or qualified alcohol treatment professional. Anyone with psychological distress, such as serious depression or high stress, should see a psychologist or psychiatrist. Because of the risk of serious alcohol withdrawal symptoms, anyone who has been drinking consistently should see a physician or go to a hospital detoxification unit before giving up alcohol completely.

All the people profiled in *Sober for Good* — the "masters" — have given their permission to share information about the history and resolution of their drinking problems. Unless otherwise indicated, their names have been changed to maintain their anonymity. Sometimes remarks have been edited for clarity. The information in this book was gathered over the course of the years 1997–2000; information and circumstances may have changed since that time. Any reference in the text to "now" refers to the time when the master provided me with his or her story.

Contents

"There's no *one* thing that's true. It's all true."
— Ernest Hemingway, *For Whom the Bell Tolls*
(shared by Leslie T.)

Foreword

Two roads diverged in a wood, and I —
I took the one less traveled by,
And that has made all the difference.
— Robert Frost

By allowing people who have triumphed over alcohol to speak for themselves, Anne Fletcher has given *Sober for Good* a signal virtue that many scientific studies lack. In these studies, information about individuals is often translated into numerical form and combined with like information from other individuals. Although this procedure has value, it desiccates the vibrant human experience that lies behind the numbers. We are left with an overall impression and with data that can be statistically manipulated, but we often get no sense of the people whom the data represent.

In this book, in contrast, we have full-dress, often warts-and-all portraits of people who have successfully resolved alcohol problems. Consequently, the subjects of Ms. Fletcher's research come alive for us. Here are real people who have done real things. The portraits are framed in the individuals' own words rather than in the comparatively sterile third-person narrative characteristically found in case reports. Consider Muffy G. When asked why she abstains, she responds, "Because when I drink, I tend to take off my clothes and dance on the tables, and my husband doesn't like it!"

Scientific publications are unlikely to give people who are currently involved in the struggle for sobriety the will to conquer their alcohol problems. Ms. Fletcher's study makes available at a highly personal level a phalanx of possible role models that is sufficiently diverse to serve for almost anyone. And no one should underestimate the power of a positive role model.

More than thirty-five years of experience in the field of alcohol research amply confirm for me this book's assertion that people with drinking problems are invariably told, even today, and even by professionals, that there is only one way to resolve those problems, and that is through strict adherence to the twelve steps of Alcoholics Anonymous coupled with frequent and lifelong attendance at AA meetings. The partial truth behind this assertion is that for some people, a successful resolution *is* the consequence of such a prescription, as Ms. Fletcher amply documents.

But the whole truth is that for others, this is *not* a successful pathway. For different people, different approaches are required. Neither AA nor any other formal or informal intervention is uniformly successful in combating alcohol problems — or, for that matter, any problem of comparable complexity. There is no royal road to sobriety. No one thing works for everyone.

Some people do better on their own, while others require assistance. Some do better as outpatients, while others do better as inpatients. Some find effective assistance in formal professional treatment, while others find it in the many mutual assistance groups that are now available. Some do better with a goal of moderate drinking, while others do better with a goal of abstinence. Some do better by turning their lives over to a "higher power," while others do better without taking such a step. Some feel the need for long-term group support, while others do not.

The probable reason for such thoroughgoing diversity is that people are different, and their problems are different. This home truth is gradually becoming more apparent and is beginning to replace the accepted wisdom that "all alcoholics are alike." It increasingly appears, first, that not all people with alcohol problems are "alcoholics," however the term is defined, and, second, that other than being human and misusing alcohol, people with alcohol problems do not universally share any commonalities. The many lives and many problems so well detailed here make a compelling case for this point of view.

Since the homely advice of "different strokes for different

folks" is applicable with regard to the resolution of alcohol problems, how is a given person to know which approach is the best one for him or for her? The scientific community has long considered this issue and has recently begun to approach it directly. But little of definitive value has emerged so far. At present the bottom line is that individuals must seek out the approach or approaches that are most suitable for them and their particular problems.

For those engaged in such a quest, Ms. Fletcher's book is invaluable. It empowers the consumer of alcohol treatment services. Most people who seek help from a particular program, not just from AA, are given what the British call a Hobson's choice: that program or none. As one program director put it to me, "Their choice is either to enter our program or to die." Referral to another form of treatment which might be more appropriate is virtually nonexistent. What an antidote this book offers to such a narrow perspective! It not only contains extensive descriptions of many alternative approaches, but vividly recounts different individuals' actual experiences with them. Ms. Fletcher also tells the reader where to find further information, including the treasure trove that is already available on the Internet, which will only increase over time.

In sum, if you or someone you care about has an alcohol problem and you are wondering where to turn, read this book. You will be grateful for the years of work the author spent in seeking out those who have "been there, done that" and in presenting their experiences in eminently readable form. The many possible pathways out of the quagmire of alcohol problems are given their due. The point is, there *are* choices. This book will give many the courage to make them.

— Frederick B. Glaser, M.D.
Fellow of the Royal College of Physicians of Canada,
Professor of Psychiatric Medicine Emeritus at the
Brody School of Medicine, East Carolina University

Introduction

Like all children, I was intrigued by things forbidden. And in my family, one of those things was alcohol. My parents were conscientious teetotalers, which only served to increase alcohol's allure when I hit adolescence. Although I was a good student who came from an upstanding family, I enjoyed challenging the rules. I don't remember having my first drink, but I do recall periodically drinking to excess with teenage friends and driving across state lines to where the drinking age was lower, buying malt liquor, and mixing it with cola to get it down. Eventually I grew to love the taste of hard liquor and wine.

By the time I was a young adult, my parents had relaxed their stance and occasionally enjoyed a glass of wine. But I was already learning that alcohol provided the perfect escape from the pressures of an increasingly stressful career as well as from personal angst. The several glasses of wine that I drank on Friday and Saturday evenings gradually became nightly martinis or manhattans. When other people cut themselves off at social events after a couple of drinks, I kept looking for the waiter to refill my glass. The drinking gave rise to a deep personal sadness. Still, after the birth of my first child, I secretly looked forward to the end of nursing so I could go back to my pre-pregnancy drinking habits. To sum it all up, from my early twenties to my early thirties, I drank too much.

Before becoming a mother, I knew that my relationship with alcohol was troubled. I sought professional counseling — in part to find out if I really had a drinking problem — but was told that alcohol was not the root of my sadness. Others in whom I confided also tried to talk me out of my feeling that I had a problem with alcohol. After all, I held responsible professional positions, rarely drank before five o'clock in the afternoon, had a good relationship with my husband, exercised five times a week, and ate healthfully.

But once I took the responsibility for a child's well-being, I tuned in to my own inner voice, which for years had been warning me about where my drinking might be headed. Thus I began a nearly decade-long search for ways to resolve my issues with alcohol. I had long periods of abstinence, punctuated by interludes of drinking. I saw that when I drank, my moods swung more dramatically. I sometimes forgot things my child had told me the night before. By degrees, I also saw what there was to be gained by not drinking: I liked myself better; I didn't have to think about whether I could drive in the evening when I'd had a drink or two; I was emotionally available to my family; I slept better and had more energy.

In time, like so many of the people you are about to read about, I decided that what I enjoyed about drinking was overshadowed by the costs. I didn't like the importance alcohol had assumed in my life, how inconsistent drinking was with the role model I wanted to be for my children. It simply took too much of my time and energy, and I realized that I was a much happier, more productive person when I wasn't drinking.

Along the way I tried some of the conventional solutions for alcohol problems. Though I was impressed with how helpful AA was for others and I'd benefited from the support, I'd come home from a meeting feeling like the odd one out. My take-responsibility attitude — along with my tendency to challenge the status quo and want to do things my way — didn't mesh with the program's twelve-step philosophy. I wasn't "in denial." I was looking for help but felt I had nowhere to turn. So I crafted my own rather lonely path to resolving my troubles with alcohol, with the help of some open-minded therapists who did not demand that I become abstinent or that I attend a recovery group but respected my ability to make the decision to stop drinking and encouraged me to develop my own strategies to do so.

For years after, I wondered whether I was the only person who had been able to stop drinking without using the conventional path of AA. I also felt frustrated about all the time and energy I'd spent looking for solutions, and upset that nothing that would have fit my needs much earlier on seemed to be available. I began to hear about alternative approaches to drinking problems. Every so often I read about people who had resolved alcohol problems on their own. I began to wonder whether there might be common threads in their stories. Perhaps identifying these similarities as well as the differences could help other people troubled by alcohol.

It bothered me too that the recovery stories I heard were always about down-and-out former drunks — not about people like me, who did something before their drinking got really bad. Having experienced firsthand a sense of loss after I gave up the substance that brought so much comfort and pleasure, I also wanted to know how people with very serious drinking problems — the ones who had seemingly lost it all — had managed to turn their lives around.

For answers, I decided to go out and find people who had once had drinking problems, big ones and small ones. In the spirit of my earlier books, about people who have lost weight and kept it off, *Sober for Good* stems from my fascination with how people change — how they solve difficult lifestyle and health issues that sometimes seem intractable. My hope is that these true experts can provide inspiration for all those who are still struggling. In my experience, when you're trying to overcome a problem, nothing works better than the words of people who have been there.

Sober for Good

1

A New Look at How People Really Solve Drinking Problems

If your best friend turned to you for advice about a drinking problem, what would you say? The automatic reaction of most people, nonprofessionals and treatment specialists alike, would likely be "Get yourself to AA." But is this truly the best response for that individual — is it the *only* solution? We've all heard so many things about recovery, but are they really true?

To find out how people whose lives have been troubled by alcohol have overcome their difficulties, I decided to turn to the foremost experts — those who have actually done it, people who have mastered their former alcohol problems in different ways.* I wanted to determine exactly what these "masters" did — what specific strategies they used — to get sober and stay sober. My call for information was answered by hundreds whose drinking

---

* As opposed to focusing on the label "alcoholic," I use the umbrella phrases "problem drinkers," "drinking problems," and "alcohol problems" to encompass *all* serious drinking problems. I made this decision in part because "alcoholic" is considered an outmoded term and, more important, because the term "alcoholic" is pejorative to many. At the suggestion of one of the masters, when I use the words "alcoholic" and "alcoholism," I place them in quotation marks (unless I am quoting someone else).

1

at its worst ranged from what many of us might define as a social drinker's quota to more than a fifth of hard liquor a day. (All of the 222 masters completed a seven-page questionnaire about their drinking pasts, the turning points, how they resolved their alcohol problems, and how they got on with their lives.)

Who Are the Masters?

The masters came to me through postage-paid flyers distributed in public places across the country, advertisements and listings in newspapers and special-interest magazines, postings on the Internet, and recovery groups. Some masters knew me or had heard about my work through a friend.

They come from all walks of life — they're attorneys, maintenance workers, former topless dancers, college professors, physicians, schoolteachers, homemakers, engineers, judges, former bartenders, current bartenders, nurses, and journalists. They're Christians and atheists, gay and straight, people from their twenties to their eighties who got sober anywhere from their teens through their fifties and sixties. They include husbands and wives who got sober together as well as a mother and her two grown children who all quit on their own but at different times. A quarter of them are recovery group leaders, mental health professionals, and/or chemical dependency counselors, so they know sobriety from both ends, as former problem drinkers and as experienced helpers of those who are still struggling. Gender-wise, there is close to an even split: 54 percent of the masters are men and 46 percent are women.

Along with stories of people who were rendered destitute because of their drinking, I wanted to include the experiences of people with mild or moderate alcohol problems, because little help is available for them, despite the fact that they are thought to outnumber stereotypical brown-bag "alcoholics" by three or four to one. Therefore, the stories of the masters' drinking days vary

[handwritten margin note: what about a book about how people get over Relationships that don't work out?]

from sagas of high-functioning drinkers who were able to raise families and move upward professionally despite their alcohol abuse to those of hard-core "drunks" who describe loss of jobs, health, children, and dignity. The masters' drinking at its worst ranged from a reported three to five daily drinks for some people up to two daily quarts of vodka for one man.

At the lower end of the scale, Janet C. (who believes she was "chiefly mentally addicted" to alcohol but considers herself to be an "alcoholic" nonetheless) typically had two or three single-shot martinis before dinner and one or two scotches with soda afterward — surely beyond healthy drinking, but not what most people think of when they picture the stereotypical "alcoholic." Although she felt that her drinking kept her from being a good parent to her two teenagers, she was always responsible enough to know that she "didn't dare drive" them around in the evenings.

At the other extreme, the two-quart-a-day vodka drinker, George M., attributes all of the following to his drinking: "My wife left me; I lost my career, my possessions, my teeth, and much of my eyesight; my friends disappeared. I lived in a spare bedroom in my mother's house, soiled the bed often, had drunk driving and disorderly conduct arrests, and was suicidal." (With the help of AA, he has been sober for more than five years now.) Like George, a number of other masters once abused drugs such as marijuana and cocaine in addition to alcohol. For all but five of them, alcohol was the drug of choice.

Nearly all of the masters have been continuously sober for five or more years;* the average length of sobriety for the entire group is just over thirteen years. Two thirds of them have at least a decade of sobriety.

_____

* I selected the five-year cutoff because research studies suggest that recovered problem drinkers are much less likely to relapse after five years. I made a small number of exceptions in order to include participants in SMART Recovery, a relatively new program.

Sobriety Means Different Things to Different People

For most of the masters, sobriety is synonymous with abstinence. For the vast majority, abstinence turns out to be the best policy: nine out of ten are totally abstinent.

Others have a small amount of alcohol on very rare occasions — say, when making a toast at a wedding reception. About one out of ten of the masters are near-abstinent, occasional, or moderate drinkers, which challenges the notion that one sip of alcohol will lead you back to full-blown "alcoholism." For serious problem drinkers and those who are already contentedly abstinent, however, *consuming any alcohol can be a risky proposition.*

While most people think of sobriety as total abstinence, *Webster's Tenth Collegiate Dictionary* defines "sober" not as "abstinent" but as "1 a: sparing in the use of food and drink: ABSTEMIOUS. b: not addicted to intoxicating drink. c: not drunk . . . 4. marked by temperance, moderation, or seriousness." The masters whom I call sober, then, are those who have resolved their alcohol problems and gotten on top of their drinking, usually through abstinence but sometimes through moderate or occasional drinking.

I sought the masters' help in answering such questions as these:

How important is it to admit to yourself and others that you are an "alcoholic"?

Can you recover — and stay recovered — without going to a recovery group?

If you get sober with the help of a recovery group, do you have to keep going forever?

What about treatment at places like the Betty Ford Center and hospital alcohol programs — is it necessary?

Where do you turn if you have issues about your drinking but don't really feel you're an "alcoholic"?

Is it true that you have to "hit bottom" in order to become motivated to deal with a drinking problem?

Before taking action, are most people "in denial" about their drinking problems?

Do you wake up one morning and say, "That's it: I quit"? If so, what gets you to that point, and does everything else in life just kind of fall into place afterward?

Is it helpful to see yourself as forever recovering, or can you at some point think of yourself as recovered *or* cured?

Is it true that having just a small amount of alcohol will send you right back to where you left off in your drinking, or is having an occasional drink a possibility for some people?

What if you don't have strong religious or spiritual beliefs, such as faith in a "higher power" — can you still get sober?

Do you eventually lose your longing for alcohol, or do you pine for it forever?

I had some of my own thoughts about these matters, since over the years I have coped with and resolved my own issues with drinking. But I wanted to find out what others who once struggled with alcohol had to say. What I learned from these masters is striking, and much of what they relate flies in the face of what we've been led to believe about "alcoholism."

Sober for Good examines the common threads among recovery stories of people who have resolved drinking problems in many different ways. A good deal of what the masters share about their triumphs over alcohol is supported by findings of experts whose research doesn't always make its way to the general public. I've interwoven these scientific findings with my discoveries about the masters.

Whether a drinking problem is serious or occasionally troublesome, the wisdom of the *Sober for Good* masters can help. These people offer possible solutions for those who are just wondering whether they have a drinking problem as well as for anyone who is ready to take action. They offer hope for anyone who is discouraged by the conventional route to recovery, who's looking for something different. If you're dealing with a loved one who has problems with alcohol, the words of the masters can offer insight for you as well. (Chapter 7 is specifically for family and friends of problem drinkers.)

The masters' stories show that the road to sobriety does not always have a finite course ending in storybook abstinence. They suggest that recovery takes various shapes and forms as well as twists and turns over time and can be marked by interludes of drinking again — all in the context of a serious effort to keep drinking from interfering with a happy, functional life.

Sobriety Is More Than Not Drinking

The masters' stories reveal that achieving sobriety involves much more than abandoning problem drinking — it's about taking active steps to achieve a new plane of living, to build a life with no room for alcohol abuse.

◆ Ward R. (twenty-four years)* says his "last drunk" made him realize he had two choices: "I could either work on developing a way of life in which I didn't want to drink, or I could say 'To hell with it' and continue drinking until I died." Ward made his choice by going to AA but using it in an unconventional way and by developing a life that has no room for drinking. He explains, "I am now retired and my life is full with traveling to other countries,

---

* Numbers in parentheses after a person's name indicate the number of years that person has been continuously sober.

exploring other cultures, being an active member of AARP, working on helping other seniors deal with telemarketing con artists, planning on being a volunteer deputy sheriff, being a member of a gun club, working with other recovering alcoholics, learning how to use the Internet, and remodeling a fixer-upper house I bought. I just don't have time to sit in a tavern or bar."

◆ Marisa S. (seven years, with the help of Women for Sobriety) says, "Without alcohol, I can be the person I want to be. I have gotten back into my career and have done extremely well, become passionate about my gardening and landscaping, started traveling for pleasure. I can answer the phone or the door without worrying whether I'll give myself away — 'Am I too drunk?' or 'Will people notice?'"

◆ Paul V. (nine years, through AA) says, "Since I resolved my drinking problem, there isn't really an area of my life that has been unchanged. I quadrupled my income, I became an avid hunter, I am far less moody, and my relationship with God is in good order. My perceptions of everything are better."

◆ Roxi V. (six years, with the help primarily of Secular Organizations for Sobriety but also AA) says, "I am happy and celebrate every day of my sobriety. I am a well woman." Roxi quit drinking in her mid-forties and since has gone back to school and gotten her M.S. degree. Best of all, she states, "I've grown as a person. I've become and am becoming the *real* Roxi, and I like me."

As Regina S. says, the masters have "built a life where drinking doesn't fit in." These are their stories.

2

There's Not Just One Way

How the Masters Got Sober — and Stay Sober

"**AA** works for me and works well," George M. wrote to me. "But I don't think that AA is the only way for an alcoholic to achieve sobriety. And that's not the official AA view, either. Personally, I am aware of people who have had problems with alcohol and overcome them by other means. God bless us all."

Simon D. sent me a similar message: "Although AA has been responsible for my transformation, it is not the only answer. And I am bound to take issue with those believing it to be." When I started hearing comments like these — and hearing them from AA members and non-AA members alike — I knew I was on to something.

How did the masters get sober? Let me count the ways — there were quite literally dozens of them. Although many of the masters went the traditional way of Alcoholics Anonymous, with its guiding twelve steps, many others came to terms with their drinking in nontraditional ways, including quitting totally on their own, reading inspiring books, and using less familiar recovery programs with principles very different from AA's. The message from these masters is that there are *many* ways to get sober — and stay sober.

Herb N.'s Story

"I began smoking pot at age twelve, and it just sort of took off from there," forty-two-year-old Herb N. told me. "Then I started drinking alcohol at around seventeen years old, and that became my favorite drug until I quit, in 1987." Herb drank just about daily until he was thirty-one, at which time, he says, "I quit on my own, without any help from anyone." Despite the facts that he has never been to an AA meeting, never been in formal treatment for his drinking problem, and never seen a recovery counselor, he hasn't had a drink or used any illicit drugs for more than thirteen years.

At his worst, Herb was putting away eighteen to twenty drinks a day. But toward the end of his drinking days, he was forced to cut that in half because his liver was swollen, he had stomach problems, and he couldn't down more than ten drinks without vomiting. Sure, he tried to quit — almost every month for the last ten years of his "drinking and drugging career." He elaborates: "I would last a day, a few days, or even as long as a month, but would then give in because I was so worn down by fighting off cravings."

What did he try that failed? "Most of the time, my attempts involved cutting back — trying to control my drinking. It didn't work. I also tried moving to another area, dumping some people I thought were bad influences on me, working night and day to keep my mind off booze and dope, not working at all, switching careers. At one point I was going to jump off a bridge, but I chickened out at the last minute. Every time I tried to quit, I would always end up thinking myself right back into drinking or using dope." (Long before he quit drinking, Herb overcame his drug problem.)

To please his wife, Herb went into a medical detoxification (detox) unit at one point to get the alcohol out of his system. But within a short time he was drinking again. He feels he avoided seeking additional help because his family doctor, whom he saw a few times to "scam some pills," kept telling him that the only effective way to deal with his alcohol problem was to go to AA or into formal alcohol treatment. "I objected to the religious aspects of AA, as it was described to me by my doctor, on the grounds that I am an atheist," Herb says. "The twelve steps wanted me to believe in a 'higher power' and admit that I was powerless over alcohol and drugs. But I knew that I wasn't. I wanted to learn how to fight my addiction, not give in and pray to a God I didn't believe in to relieve my suffering. All of this left me 100 percent on my own."

At the end, he says, "I felt hopeless and like I was going to die in a gutter. I tried to get my wife to take the kids and leave me so I didn't drag them down with me, but she wouldn't go." Perhaps his wife's faith that he would eventually quit drinking gave Herb hope at some level. She told him things that haunted him, and that he later used to rid himself of cravings, like "Herb, I know you, and I know this isn't really who you are. I believe you can quit if you try." Also, his previous success at giving up cigarettes gave him a bit of confidence that he would beat his drinking problem as well. "Since I had an easy time quitting smoking," he explains, "part of me held the faint hope that I could quit alcohol."

"No more deals with my subconscious"

The turning point came when Herb realized, "I didn't want my kids to see me die and then grow up to become alcoholics themselves." He also had had it with his health problems. One morning, waking up after another night of heavy drinking, he had an epiphany. "There, when I was sitting on the edge of the bed, it hit me like a ton of bricks," he recalls. "I *had* to give up all hope of ever having another drink or drug. No more little wink-wink, nudge-nudge deals with my subconscious that if the moon and earth align on a Saturday, then I'll have a little drink to celebrate — but only then."

Herb feels that what had sent him back to drinking after all his previous tries at quitting was the hope that in some way he could learn how to control his drinking and be able to drink "just a little." "After that talk with myself," he remarks, "I knew it was over. I then got busy creating my new life rather than waiting for my next relapse."

"When cravings came, I taught myself to silently scream back"

This last time, when Herb was able to stay off alcohol and drugs for good, what did he actually do to fight off the cravings that previously had gotten the better of him? Being a thoughtful, logical person, he used his head. "When cravings would come, it was like there were two voices in my mind: one loud, aggressive voice that would lobby hard to break abstinence, and the other, more passive voice that would try to hang on to abstinence for all it was worth. I taught myself to silently scream back, sometimes with profanity, at that aggressive voice — I saw it as the enemy and committed to making *it* the passive voice. When I realized I could reverse the tables on this enemy, I was able to fight off cravings for alcohol."

From his past attempts at quitting, Herb knew that when the memories of the pains of his addiction were sharp — for instance, when he recalled what a fool he'd made of himself while drinking — he had more success at fighting off cravings. He concludes, "What I realized was that I wanted to be free of the pain forever."

"I knew my addiction was over for good that day"

During Herb's first week of sobriety, while he was home in bed going through withdrawal from alcohol, his wife and two young daughters cheered him on and told him they believed in him. The first day back on his job at a logging camp, he entered an empty meeting room where fellow workers had just held a party — empty except for some leftover beer. "There I was, all alone with a keg of cold, free beer, and me eleven or twelve days clean and sober. To my surprise, I experienced only a very mild discomfort. I think the unconscious part of me that wanted to drink was scared to death to talk to me about drinking any of that beer, so it whimpered once or twice and quickly shut up. I didn't feel like the king of recovery or anything like that. I just knew for sure my addiction was over for good that day, and it was calm and quiet in my head."

Herb proceeded to learn all he could about addictions, and he has spent the last decade helping others become sober. Although he has taken many counseling courses, he is largely self-educated about recovery, having become "sort of a self-help junkie." After recovering, he worked in a detox unit and lived for more than three months on skid row to understand his clients better. For a while he ran his own recovery course for people who wanted to do it on their own, but he now works as a counselor, mainly for hard-core drug addicts, for a clinic sponsored by the Canadian government. His work with alcohol and drug abusers leads Herb to say, "AA's twelve steps are great for some people, and they find comfort and relief in their surrender and powerlessness. But my brain doesn't work that way. I wanted to learn how to fight my addiction."

Trying to Get Sober in a One-Track World

Herb N. is among a number of masters who were told over and over that if they wanted to solve their drinking problem, they would have to go to AA. Some of them, like Billy R., just proceeded to get worse. Before getting sober using Rational Recovery techniques, Billy made several serious attempts to stop drinking, only to relapse with every try. "Each time," he attests, "I was told in no uncertain terms that AA was the only way to recover and that looking for another way was just a waste of time, because AA was the only thing that worked. It finally came down to this: I had a choice between continuing to drink or going back to AA. I chose to continue to drink for a long time." Then, when he was in the hospital detox unit one last time, he saw a notice about Rational Recovery on the wall. "It was the first time I was informed that there was an alternative to AA," he explains. He has been sober for more than five years now.

Rosa L. declares, "AA works for many people, and I am grateful for those people that it is there. I am also very angry at the recovery community and treatment centers for not allowing space for other programs and for not telling their clients about other approaches." Rosa got sober ten years ago with the help of the recovery group Women for Sobriety.

As Billy's and Rosa's experiences suggest, it can be hard to find any kind of help in the United States that doesn't embrace a twelve-step approach, from local AA groups that meet in community buildings and churches, to residential treatment centers for "drying out," which usually incorporate the twelve steps, to outpatient treatment programs with chemical dependency counselors who typically encourage clients to attend AA meetings. In fact, the National Treatment Center study conducted by the University of Georgia found that *more than 90 percent of 450 representative U.S. alcohol treatment programs surveyed were based on the twelve-step approach.* Popular culture reinforces the notion that AA is the only way to go. Not long ago, a "Dear Abby" column concluded a test for assessing alcohol problems with the advice, "If you answered yes to four or more of the questions, you are in trouble. Run, do not walk, to Alcoholics Anonymous." Twenty-one-year master Rick N., who quit drinking on his own but was told by treatment professionals that he was "doomed to fail" if he did not follow the twelve steps, recalls a public television series on alcohol problems hosted by Bill Moyers that he felt delivered the same one-sided message: that "the only answer to the problem is a 'spiritual awakening' plus lifelong attendance at twelve-step recovery groups."

Physicians seem to do no better at suggesting alternatives to

AA. Lev W. told me, "I knew I had an alcohol problem and felt hopeless. When I turned to an M.D. for help, asking, 'What works?' he said, 'Peer support and belief in a higher power.' I responded, 'What do you do with a loner and an atheist?' to which my doctor replied, 'Wait until they are not.'" Lev finally quit drinking on her own after she woke up one morning with a bad hangover and unpleasant memories from the night before and said to herself, "I can't do this anymore."

AA's book *Alcoholics Anonymous*, also known as the "Big Book," however, suggests a more flexible approach in its advice to members who are trying to help another person with a drinking problem: "If he thinks he can do the job in some other way, or prefers some other spiritual approach, encourage him to follow his own conscience. We have no monopoly on God; we merely have an approach that worked with us."

The Perils of Forced Attendance

The masters told me some disturbing stories about being coerced to attend AA — a common practice by courts and employee assistance programs in the United States. For instance, Cheryl T. laments, "Going to AA is mandatory if I am to retain my nursing license. I would not attend meetings if not required; they are of little or no benefit to my personal recovery program. SOS is a program that better suits me."

More disturbingly, I heard from Ted B., a physician who became concerned eight years ago when he noticed that his nightly seven or eight shots was more than other friends or family members were drinking. He recalls, "I began discussing ways to handle this and was thinking about seeing a therapist when my wife told a colleague, who then told the hospital administrator — who was a recovering alcoholic — that I was drinking a lot." The upshot was that, under threat of losing his medical license, Ted was sent to a treatment program that required a four-month stay, followed by five years of regular attendance at AA meetings.

After treatment, Ted was subjected to the humiliation of periodic random urine tests to see whether he was using drugs, and he was monitored by two colleagues who had to write monthly reports on how he was doing. Although non–twelve-step readings were forbidden at the treatment center, Ted read about Rational Recovery and SMART Recovery after he was discharged and found that their approaches were much more appealing to him. Even though he told his monitors that he felt worse after attending AA meetings, however, he was required to attend them.

Ted now sees that his abuse of alcohol was linked to longstanding depression, which, to his dismay, did not go away after a year of abstinence from alcohol. The depression almost immediately lifted, however, when he happened to go off a blood pressure medication (in the drug family known as "beta blockers") that he had been on for fifteen years. It soon became obvious that his gloomy state of mind — which is a known side effect of beta blockers for some people — had been caused by the drug. Now, seven years after his ordeal, Ted enjoys having one or two drinks about five times a week. He adds, "I have no urge to drink heavily since I stopped taking beta blockers."

Some people feel that ordering individuals to go to twelve-step programs is at odds with AA's own precepts — the program is meant to operate by attraction. Vincent A. affirms, "When I was an AA meeting chairman, I always had qualms about signing papers of people who were ordered by the courts to attend meetings. I felt it was a violation of AA traditions." (According to *Resisting 12-Step Coercion,* by the alcohol expert and attorney Stanton Peele, Ph.D., and Charles Bufe, as of the year 2000, four higher U.S. courts had ruled that mandating attendance at twelve-step programs violates First Amendment rights because the programs are considered religious activities, which the state cannot legally require individuals to attend. In general, the courts have decided that simply offering a nonreligious alternative to twelve-step programs is acceptable.)

Profiled master Herb N. feels fortunate that he is free to use any model he wants. He says, "It's not that I'm against the twelve-step model, but I don't like it for me. I did all the work, and I'll take all the credit for my success or the responsibility for my failure."

The Many Ways in Which Masters Overcame Drinking Problems

Herb N. is far from alone. In the final analysis, of the 222 masters included in *Sober for Good,* 125, or 56 percent, resolved their drinking problems in an unconventional way. I call them the nontraditional masters. Another 97 masters, the traditional ones, went the AA route to recovery. The two thirds of the masters who have enjoyed a decade or more of sobriety are divided equally between traditionalists and nontraditionalists, suggesting that long-term sobriety can be achieved in many different ways. (For a summary of the masters' methods, see page 20.)

There are big differences in how the nontraditional masters overcame their drinking problems. Herb is part of a subgroup of thirty-nine people whom I call "loners" — individuals who have maintained their sobriety solo, without ongoing formal help like that from a recovery group. These loners include twenty-five masters who, like Herb, quit completely on their own. Seventeen of them have ten or more years of sobriety, and all but two have never had a relapse. Other *Sober for Good* loners came up with their own solutions after trying several programs, after reading a helpful book, or after going to an alcohol treatment center such as Hazelden, then deciding they could maintain sobriety without a recovery group.

These people challenge the prevailing notion that problem drinkers can't recover on their own. On the contrary, dozens of studies confirm that many people quit drinking without help. An analysis of two surveys involving more than 12,000 randomly

Before You Quit

Before giving up alcohol or cutting way back independently — or by any route, for that matter — anyone who has been drinking heavily should be prepared for the possibility of withdrawal symptoms. Although serious withdrawal symptoms occur in only about one out of ten people, it is definitely recommended that you consult a physician, because withdrawal can be physically dangerous.

Symptoms of withdrawal typically begin within four to twelve hours after someone stops or reduces alcohol intake, peak in intensity during the second day, and go away within four to five days. The symptoms commonly include hand tremors, sweating, a fast heartbeat, and agitation. Other possible problems include nausea, vomiting, insomnia, increased blood pressure and body temperature, and psychological problems such as depression, anxiety, anger, and increased irritability.

While withdrawal can often be managed outside of a hospital setting by a physician, a formal inpatient detoxification program at a hospital or residential treatment center is likely to be necessary for people with severe drinking problems.

chosen adults, published in the *American Journal of Public Health* in 1996, revealed that three quarters of those who had recovered from alcohol problems had done so on their own. Master Ann N., who is also a substance abuse counselor, is on target when she says that "sixty percent of alcoholics get sober without *any* help." Some studies suggest that *the number of people who resolve alcohol problems independently may actually equal or surpass the number who resolve alcohol problems after receiving formal assistance.*

Yet individuals working in traditional addiction treatment have largely ignored or viewed with skepticism the possibility of self-recovery — perhaps because it challenges the idea that alcohol problems can be resolved only through intensive treatment and long-term recovery group support. As master Jean A. says of her early recovery, "The message that I was getting was that I (and *all* alcoholics) was not strong enough or good enough to get or stay sober on my own — that I needed AA for the rest of my life."

You may wonder: Were these people who quit on their own really "alcoholics"? Research does suggest that those who quit drinking independently tend not to have severe alcohol problems. But people with less serious drinking problems account for most of the alcohol problems in our society, and these are the very people who are unlikely to seek conventional help for their drinking. Knowing that it's possible to do something independently should be encouraging if you're not inclined to seek treatment or go to a recovery group.

The masters show, however, that even people with severe drinking problems can get sober on their own. Of the twenty-five masters who quit by themselves, eleven said they drank the equivalent of more than a pint of hard liquor a day — and six of these people consumed a fifth or more. (That's seventeen or more daily drinks.)

Another forty-six of the nontraditional masters achieved sobriety with the help of groups other than AA, which many people do not know about. They include Secular Organizations for Sobriety/Save Our Selves (SOS), SMART Recovery, and Women for Sobriety (WFS). Still other masters counted as nontraditional include those who were initially helped by AA but who left the program because of something they didn't like or because they didn't use AA's tenets; they now maintain sobriety on their own.

A handful of nontraditional masters resolved their alcohol problems through psychological counseling, through religion (not related to AA), or with the help of Moderation Management, a group that helps people with less serious drinking problems learn to drink in a controlled fashion. Strategies taught by Rational Recovery, which currently refers to its educational approach as "Self-Recovery Through Planned Abstinence," were used by another four masters as their major recovery tools. (RR used to have self-help groups across the country, with which some masters were involved. But RR has changed its focus to an individual self-recovery approach.)

Last among the nontraditional masters are twenty-five people who followed multiple paths — that is, they employed a variety of strategies to overcome their drinking problems. Take Jessica C., who used a combination of residential alcohol treatment, AA, WFS, psychological counseling, and reading on her own about alcohol recovery. She says, "By being willing to try everything that might help, I found the approach that was right for me. I got something out of everything I did. I was able to develop a personalized recovery program over time."

Similarly, Ralph C. uses a combination approach. He recovered six years ago with the help of an inpatient Veterans Administration hospital program (based on the twelve steps), followed by weekly aftercare meetings, which he still attends. After a short time he added SOS meetings, which he liked because their philosophy was close to his own. In addition to his support groups, Ralph says, "I've done a lot of reading about alcohol recovery — my 'program' is made up of bits and pieces of what I've read, plus bits picked up in my weekly meetings."

The masters' stories of their recovery methods not only illustrate diversity and creativity but also show that *sobriety is not static*. In other words, many of the masters are doing different things now to *stay* sober from what they did in the beginning to *get* sober. For instance, four of the masters who quit drinking on their own have now decided to go to AA. One of them, Rebecca M., says, "I may go to AA once or twice a week if life is overwhelming. But if all is calm, it may be once a year."

In contrast, Vincent A., who initially benefited from AA because it offered supportive friendships when he stopped drinking

Summary of the Masters' Recovery Methods

Because of the eclectic nature of many of the masters' recovery methods, it is difficult to classify masters according to one method. Most of those who switched approaches have been classified according to what they are doing now.

Recovery Method	Number of Masters
Traditional recoveries (twelve-step)	97
Nontraditional recoveries	125
Sober on their own	25
Secular Organizations for Sobriety (SOS)	18
SMART Recovery	13
Women for Sobriety	15
Went to A.A., but quit	12
Multiple paths	25
Treatment center, then on their own	5
Psychological counseling	3
Religion	4
Moderation Management	1
Rational Recovery techniques	4

twenty-four years ago, stopped going because he felt like a hypocrite attending meetings and saying that the twelve steps changed his life. Now he attends SMART Recovery meetings about two times a month. He concludes, "AA can be great when it works, but it doesn't work for everyone. There are alternatives that are just as effective, and people need to hear about them."

One Program, Different Outcomes

As I was reading about each master, I was struck by the stark contrasts in their experiences with AA.

For some, like Sally O., AA has been a source of strength and hope. "When I went to my first AA meeting, I heard three sober alcoholics share their experience, strength, and hope with me. *I never wanted to leave,*" she wrote. "It is now forty-one years later, and I have not had a drink since that first night in 1957. The only reason I went to AA was to stop drinking — little did I know what miracles would occur in my life. The fellowship and warmth of AA took away my compulsion and obsession with alcohol."

But for others, like Marisa S. (seven years), who got sober with the help of WFS, SMART Recovery, personal counseling, and many different books on recovery, AA's effect was anything but positive. "AA was repeatedly presented to me as the only option, but I did not fare well there. I tried with all my heart to make it in AA but kept sinking into despair and relapsing," she said. "The turning point for me was when I decided that I didn't have to go the AA route, stopped doing what everyone told me to do, and started trusting my own judgment (which I was told repeatedly not to do) and doing what made sense to me. I needed to believe and trust in myself, to learn to take responsibility for my life, and to make healthy choices. I think our treatment system does us a terrible injustice when it acknowledges and legitimizes only AA."

How can it be that some people find AA so helpful while others experience it as not helpful? Louise L., who got sober ten years ago with the help of SOS, has a good answer: "People think that for everyone who's an alcoholic, there's one master plan. That doesn't work for diabetics, so why should it work for alcoholics? I realized that there is no rule book for staying sober. I had to find what was right for me."

In 1990 a prestigious panel of experts convened by the Institute of Medicine (a division of the National Academy of Sciences) released a report after critically reviewing available research and experience in the United States and other countries about various approaches to treating alcohol problems. One of the group's major conclusions — suggested by the title of its 600-page tome, *Broadening the Base of Treatment for Alcohol Problems* — was that treatments for drinking problems need to be diversified. In particular, the report stated that there was a need for more options for people with mild to moderate alcohol problems. Despite the fact that this report came out more than a decade ago, the strong tendency in this country is still to treat all people with alcohol problems the same way and as if they are all the same.

The masters make it clear that while AA does work for many, what doesn't work is trying to fit all people with alcohol problems into the same mold — that is, sending them all in the same direction to resolve their drinking problems. Herb N. feels that if he had had access to alternative recovery programs that are available today, "I might have saved myself years of struggling with my alcohol problem."

It's All About Choice

What does appear to work is giving people options for overcoming their drinking problems. Experts believe that we are most likely to change when we feel we have been given alternatives. Finding an alternative to AA became the turning point for Sarah N., who had been through numerous twelve-step treatment programs before she sobered up more than seven years ago. Finally, she says, she found a treatment program that referred her to Women for Sobriety, which, she says, "put me on the road to recovery."

I was surprised by how many of the masters themselves seemed to be unfamiliar with alternatives to AA. Comments from more than half of them indicated that they had never heard of or never been advised to check out Rational Recovery, Women for Sobriety, SMART Recovery, Secular Organizations for Sobriety, or Moderation Management. Annie B. (thirteen years) says, "When I quit, I didn't know about the options." So she did what most people do — she went to AA. After about ten meetings, she decided it wasn't for her, stopped going, and went it alone for about a year, until someone told her about WFS, which became her niche after two meetings.

As the masters indicate, alternatives to AA *are* available, but they are often difficult to find. Altogether, there are more than 50,000 AA groups in the United States. Nationwide, the estimated number of nontraditional recovery groups — including those of SOS, SMART Recovery, and WFS — is no more than 1,000. In each of two large university towns where I spent time while writing *Sober for Good,* I was able to locate only one alternative recovery group to AA, and neither was widely publicized or known to local referral sources. (The appendix, "A Consumer Guide to Recovery Options," explains how to locate the various groups, how to find them via the Internet, and how to obtain their literature if you can't find a group nearby.)

Alternative recovery options are constrained in part by managed health care, which tends to limit the range of professionals and treatment programs for which a subscriber can seek reimbursement. For instance, you may be able to find a therapist who does not encourage AA attendance and who will help you with your alcohol problem using other strategies, but your health plan may not cover that therapist's services.

Is AA the Best Way?

"AA'S PATH TO RECOVERY STILL SEEMS BEST," reads a headline in a *Time* story on the causes of addiction. But researchers tell a different story. The 1990 report by the Institute of Medicine concluded that "Alcoholics Anonymous, one of the most widely used approaches to recovery in the United States, remains one of the least rigorously evaluated." Not much has changed since this report was issued more than a decade ago.

Only three controlled studies in which problem drinkers were randomly assigned to various treatments have involved AA, and AA was not found to be more effective than other approaches studied. However, it should be noted that all three studies involved people who had been forced to attend AA meetings and so do not necessarily reflect what happens when individuals attend voluntarily. (At this writing, well-designed studies comparing the efficacy of alternative recovery groups such as WFS, SMART Recovery, and SOS with each other or with AA have not been published in research journals.)

Some other studies suggest that people who go to AA, keep going to AA, and get involved by doing things like actively participating in meetings and getting an AA sponsor to help them tend to remain sober. One study of more than 8,000 people who had been through treatment programs found that those attending AA one year after treatment were 50 percent more likely to be abstinent than those not attending AA. But it is not known whether the AA participants remained abstinent because of the program itself or because of some quality they possessed that may have attracted them to AA in the first place. Perhaps those who stick with AA prefer group support, and any recovery group would do.

Master Vincent A., who has been active in SMART Recovery as well as in AA, told me he has observed that in both groups, "The people who come regularly sober up and stay sober." He goes on, "AA saved my life. But it would be interesting to find out exactly what people mean when they credit AA with their recovery — the steps, the AA community, or the practical advice. What helped me stop was the mutual support and practical advice rather than the twelve steps."

Whatever the case, it's hard to argue with AA's many success stories, as the historian Ernest Kurtz, Ph.D., the author of

Not-God: A History of Alcoholics Anonymous, pointed out. He once stated, "There exists no 'proof' of the efficacy of Alcoholics Anonymous — this despite descriptions by hundreds of thousands of members of Alcoholics Anonymous who attest that AA has saved their lives and made it possible for them to live lives worth living." However, the large number of people who get sober using AA may be a reflection of the fact that it is larger, older, more available, better known, and therefore more utilized than other recovery methods. The fact remains that there is no evidence that AA is better overall for recovery than any other approach.

The sad truth is that few people seek help for their drinking problems, period. Indeed, of the almost 14 million Americans (more than 7 percent of adults) estimated to have serious problems with alcohol, it is believed that only one in ten receives any form of treatment. Thus, it's safe to assume that the vast majority of alcohol abusers never set foot in a recovery meeting of any type. Of those who do seek help, many don't stick with it. Some years ago, an unofficial interpretation of AA membership surveys — which may or may not reflect the current state of affairs — suggested that about half of those who went to AA for the first time stayed in the program for less than three months; by twelve months, the number of dropouts appeared to be more than 90 percent.

So what's the solution? Master and recovery professional Rick N. (twenty-one years) says, "There are probably about as many ways to defeat alcohol problems as there are people who want to recover. The more choices we can offer, the more people can be helped."

As Herb N. advises, "Keep an open mind and try to find as much information as possible on recovery. Pick out bits and pieces that fit *you*. There are *many* roads to recovery, in spite of what you hear."

3

It's Not How Much You Drink

How the Masters Faced Up to
Their Alcohol Problems

How did the masters know when they were drinking too much — when they had crossed the line from "just having a good time" to having a problem? Was it when they went from a nightly six-pack of beer to a twelve-pack? A half-bottle of wine over the course of an evening to a full bottle? A pint of gin every Saturday and Sunday to a fifth each day? While the amount of alcohol and the regularity of drinking certainly provide important clues that something is amiss, the masters' stories suggest that their awakening had more to do with recognizing what drinking was doing to them and those around them. As Karen M. (fourteen years) puts it, "It's not so much the frequency of drinking but how it affects your life when you do."

We always hear about how people with alcohol problems are blind to them — in denial — and can't begin to recover until they admit to themselves that they are "alcoholics" with an incurable "disease." Although many masters do use these terms, others were able to face up to their problems with alcohol without *ever* seeing themselves as "alcoholics" with a "disease." *At some point, however, regardless of what labels they used and how much they drank, virtually all of the masters saw the connection*

26

between alcohol and problems they were having in their day-to-day lives.

Liz B.'s Story

When Liz B. first contacted me about participating in this book, she wrote, "I'm not sure how serious my drinking problem was, because I was never officially diagnosed. But I know it was a problem for me and my relationships." She couldn't recall exactly when she became aware of her troubled involvement with alcohol, but she noted, "For a long time before I quit, I knew in my heart of hearts that I had a problem. To this day, my husband still argues with me about whether I was an alcoholic, but I never wanted to label myself that way because of the stigma."

It doesn't matter how Liz B. defines her drinking past. Fifteen years ago, an accumulation of events led her to see that alcohol was causing trouble in her life, enough so that she decided to quit drinking the same way she had quit smoking two years earlier: cold turkey and completely on her own. Now, at the age of fifty-five, she announces, "I'm proud of what I've accomplished. My health is good, and I like being in control of myself and not being embarrassed by what I said or did. I like the admiration I get from family and friends for overcoming booze. Giving it up also helped me to be the kind of role model I wanted to be for my two boys."

Before she quit, Liz typically drank four or five glasses of wine a day, spread over the course of several hours — a far cry from stereotypical "alcoholic" drinking. And she drank that way — no more, no less — just about every day from the time she was thirty until she was forty. Liz had grown up in a family plagued by alcohol-related problems, however, and began to see that drinking was causing similar troubles in her own life. (Both parents were heavy drinkers; her father in particular became verbally and physically abusive when he drank, was unpredictable, and would explode out of the blue.) Liz chose to do something about her drinking before she lost what she wanted to keep most: her marriage and her family.

Like many young people, Liz partied her way through college, often drinking to get drunk. "When I drank, I thought I was funny and clever and fun to be around, but I really made a fool of myself," she says. She struggled with a painful stutter that became worse when she drank, but she would keep right on talking.

"I never connected my partying with the problems"

After graduating and getting a rather sophisticated job involving a lot of travel, Liz did ease up on her drinking for a number of years. Still, the warning signs were piling up. While on a business trip, she had a painful encounter, which she didn't realize was a wake-up call. "I met an adorable guy at a cowboy bar," she explains. "We danced, he asked me to go back to his apartment, and I slept with him." On their next date, she wasn't even sure she would recognize him because she had been drinking that first night. Sometime between the two dates, Liz got pregnant and wound up going through the difficulty of seeking an abortion, in the days before the procedure was legal. She notes, "I don't think I ever connected my partying with having these problems."

Eventually Liz met her husband, and she is delighted to say that she has been married to him for twenty-nine years — but not without tension caused by her use of alcohol. "For many years, he hated my drinking — it would ebb and flow as a topic of conversation. I saw it as a control thing; I didn't want him controlling me," she explains. As young stay-at-home mothers, Liz and her friends would "drink wine in the afternoons like some women would drink coffee." Following these daily afternoon parties, she would typically have another glass or two of wine, then become tired and cranky.

Liz remembers dinner parties where it was a treat to drink expensive wine. "It was the taste, not the feeling, that appealed to me," she says. "But I would continue to drink until I was wobbly, my head ached, my words slurred, and I'd be tired. My husband became very disapproving of my behavior." She also recalls picking fights with her husband, not being able to let things go, over-reacting to small incidents — all of which she slowly began to connect with her drinking.

"When my son played back the tape, I could hear a slur in my words"

"I don't know if other people's telling me that I had a drinking problem had much of an impact," Liz reminisces. "I had to come to see the problem myself." What finally began to open her eyes was an incident with her eight-year-old son that occurred two years before she quit drinking. He had tape-recorded an interview with her for a school project. "When he played back the tape," she remembers, "I could hear a slight slur in my words, and that really bothered me." This made Liz painfully recall her father's drunken behavior and both of her parents' slurred speech and "boozy breath" when they kissed her goodnight during her childhood. "I didn't want my boys to have to deal with that from their mom," she explains.

But she didn't quit right away. "I recall shooting my mouth off at a dinner party, lighting into my husband. I could be a mean drunk. I knew this behavior was connected to my drinking, but it was a gradual awareness. I couldn't predict what I would be like. I wasn't in control of my behavior because of my drinking — just like my father.

"Obviously, a number of things have to come together at the same time," Liz reflects. The final straw occurred when she and her husband hosted a Fourth of July party where there was plenty to drink. "I was rowdy and hyper. My husband and I got into an argument after it was over — he was angry about the way I had acted. It was then that he sort of issued me an ultimatum." When I asked Liz what that ultimatum was, she said it was more of a feeling she got than a direct threat. "He seemed angrier than at other times. Maybe for the first time I was scared, scared that something really drastic would change — like he would leave or something." She went on, "It was so tedious, one more fight about my drinking. I probably had just come to realize that alcohol was eventually going to destroy my family — if not through divorce, through polarization. My husband wouldn't respect me and I wouldn't respect myself. It just wasn't worth the hassle it was causing. I asked myself, 'Is drinking worth more than my family?' It wasn't. I felt I had a lot to lose: my husband, my boys, the respect of others. I finally decided I loved myself more than the alcohol." The next day, she made up her mind that she had had her last drink.

When It All Comes Together

Before you can do something about a problem, you have to admit to yourself that there is one. At some point, the masters faced up to their troubled relationship with alcohol, less by thinking about the *amount* they drank and more by *making the connection between drinking and problems in their lives.*

Clearly, Liz had come to see that alcohol was a common thread running through many of her problems:

making a fool of herself
stuttering, which got worse with drinking
being promiscuous and having unprotected sex
repeatedly arguing with her husband about her use of
    alcohol
picking fights
not being able to let things go
overreacting to small incidents
having unpleasant physical consequences of drinking —
    wobbliness, headaches, fatigue
seeing behavior in herself like that of her heavy-drinking
    father — lack of predictability, volatility, slurred
    speech

Thus, while Liz has never seen herself as an "alcoholic," she did finally put together the relationship between alcohol and her accumulating problems. Other masters did the same thing.

◆ Marguerite E. (nine years) told me, "My life just stopped working one day. Through a series of unfortunate events, all due to my drinking, I came to realize that alcohol was the one common denominator in all the events, and I stepped back to look at that."

◆ Paul V. (nine years) said that when his drinking was at its worst, his circle of friends was dwindling and he was distancing himself from his family. Also he had kidney pain, a drunk driving arrest, bad grades, and broken relationships. Paul's point of awakening came when he too began to recognize that alcohol was the common denominator.

◆ Before Jackie D. (ten years) saw the light, she says, "I had attributed all my problems in life to other things: trauma, the world's not fair, money. Suddenly it became crystal-clear that if I took alcohol away, I could handle all the other stuff."

At this point, following the example of the masters, pause and make a list of the current problems in your life. Then ask yourself, "Is alcohol connected to any of them? Is my drinking a common denominator in my troubles? Could I handle my problems better if it weren't for the way I use alcohol?"

How Much Alcohol *Is* Too Much?

So how do you know when you are drinking too much? There is no definitive test, and masters like Liz B., who usually drank no more than four or five glasses of wine a day, illustrate how people who don't drink huge amounts can have a significant

A Wake-Up Call: Questions from the Masters

Do you drink to get drunk — or at least to catch a buzz — every time?

Do you use alcohol as an escape from life and its problems?

Do you notice that you drink more than others?

Do you consistently drink more than you intended?

Do you feel that something is missing when you're faced with the thought of going for a day without having a drink?

Are you unable to drink just one?

Do you repeatedly have pain in your life caused by alcohol, but you continue to drink?

Do you ever feel that you would be more loving if you did not use alcohol?

Are you ever mad at yourself, knowing that alcohol keeps you from being who you truly are?

Does drinking depress you?

Are you tired of regretting your actions?

Have you ever avoided taking a medication because you can't drink while taking it?

Do you have a huge hole in your spirit that you are trying to fill?

Do you sometimes have physical problems because of your drinking — insomnia, night sweats, stomach pains, or nausea?

Do you ever think, "I cannot drink alcohol successfully"?

Does alcohol give you courage to say outrageous things?

problem. Although many experts would agree that the defining factor in whether you have a bona fide problem is less the volume and frequency of your drinking than what alcohol does to you, the amount of alcohol you consume can surely be a warning sign. Obviously, if you are regularly drinking at least a fifth of hard liquor or the equivalent every day — as did more than ninety of the *Sober for Good* masters when their drinking was at its worst — you are drinking far too much. It is highly unlikely that someone can drink like that on a regular basis and

Do you have drinking friends and nondrinking friends? Do you try to keep them separate from each other?

Do you depend on alcohol to help you relax, chill out, face problems, herald joy?

Does alcohol instead of reason make your decisions?

Do you sometimes feel that alcohol keeps you from being present in your life?

Do you ever drink even though you feel lousy because you drank the day before?

Do you use alcohol to avoid responsibility and uncomfortable feelings?

Is the desire for, procurement of, and consumption of alcohol a main focus of your life?

Does your desire for alcohol get in the way of your daily activities: working, taking care of children, eating properly?

Does drinking lead you to do things you wouldn't do sober, such as driving recklessly, spending too much money in nightclubs, or avoiding your responsibilities?

Do you drink because you feel you *need* to?

Has there been a decay in your value system as a result of your drinking?

If alcohol is not available, do you make it available?

Does it ever feel like you are having a great love affair with alcohol?

If you find yourself answering some of these questions with a yes, it may be a signal — not a definitive answer — that alcohol is causing problems and interfering with the quality of your life.

not be physiologically addicted. But most people who have problems related to alcohol don't come close to drinking that much.

How much someone can drink without experiencing difficulties depends on the individual. In general, larger, more muscular people can handle more alcohol without untoward consequences than smaller people can. Women are more susceptible than men to the effects of alcohol, apparently because of differences in body composition and because women tend to metabolize alcohol more slowly. Of course, even regular drinkers who don't have a serious alcohol problem can wind up being able to handle more alcohol than their counterparts who don't drink regularly, because they have developed a tolerance for drinking larger amounts.

It has been widely publicized that light to moderate drinking is associated with a decreased risk of heart disease, with moderate drinking considered to be no more than two drinks a day for men and no more than one drink a day for women. (See "What Is 'A Drink,' Anyway?" below.) More than four drinks on any one occasion for men and three drinks for women can impair thinking and increase the risk of alcohol-related problems such as accidents and injuries. Accordingly, U.S. government guidelines indicate that men may be at risk for alcohol-related problems if they drink more than four drinks per occasion (or more than fourteen drinks a week) and women if they drink more than three drinks per occasion (or seven drinks per week).

Simply stated, the more a person drinks, the greater the number of both physical and behavioral problems he or she is likely to have. The more you drink, the greater will be your risk of cirrho-

What Is "A Drink," Anyway?

Each of the following contains approximately the same amount of alcohol as the others and therefore constitutes "one drink":

1 cocktail with 1½ ounces of 80-proof hard liquor (a fifth is 25 ounces, or seventeen drinks)

1 regular beer (12 ounces)

1 5-ounce glass of wine (a typical 25-ounce bottle has five drinks)

1 12-ounce cooler (wine/malt or spirit-based)

1 3-ounce glass of sherry or port

8 ounces of malt liquor

sis of the liver, high blood pressure, stroke, and cancers of the breast, liver, larynx, mouth, and esophagus. A number of experts agree that it can be helpful to keep daily records of alcohol intake, noting the amount and time of each drink. This can help you assess whether you are drinking too much for safety's sake or for your health.

Labels Aren't Important

It's understandable that Liz B., with her daily four to five glasses of wine, might not see herself as an "alcoholic." But how could anyone like Jeanne F., who at her worst drank as many as twenty-four beers in a day, not recognize herself as such? Rather than label herself with the "A-word," Jeanne describes her former drinking problem as follows: "Sometimes I drank until I blacked out. Sometimes I had just a few drinks. I did not need alcohol every day." You might be tempted to say that people like Jeanne are just playing games with themselves. Why not call a spade a spade — stop using euphemisms and own up to the fact that you're an "alcoholic"?

While we've been led to believe that admitting you're an "alcoholic" to yourself and others is a prerequisite for recovery, a good number of masters do not use this label to describe themselves. How *do* they describe their drinking problems? Here are some of their interesting responses:

◆ "Not knowing when to stop once I began." — Liz B.

◆ "I used to have problems in my life because I drank too much." — Murray K. (six years, became sober by using principles taught by RR and SMART Recovery)

◆ "I realized that I was irresponsible with alcohol and said, 'I won't use it anymore.'" — Bobby P. (six years, quit on his own)

◆ "I didn't consider myself an alcoholic while I was drinking heavily; now, I think I was an alcoholic during that period. I don't consider myself an alcoholic now." — Ned G. (fifteen years, quit on his own)

◆ "I was a 'crutch drinker' — I drank every day, especially when problems rose up." — Marie E. (twelve years, spiritual recovery)

◆ "I had a physiological need that was hard to satisfy. I had to keep on drinking once I started." — Pete S. (nine years, quit on his own)

◆ "I was a chronic problem drinker." — Ben H. (eleven years, quit on his own)

What's fascinating about these personal descriptions of drinking problems is that some bear a close resemblance or are identical to definitions *other* masters use for "alcoholism." Although none of these masters see themselves as "alcoholic," some would at one time have "failed" those quizzes available for determining whether you have a serious drinking problem (see pages 32–33) because of the serious nature of their troubles. Marie E., for example, used to drink at least a six-pack of beer or a quart of wine each day and would get the shakes when she tried to quit.

Studies indicate that labeling yourself as "alcoholic" has nothing to do with whether you will be able to resolve a drinking problem. Master Tom W. says that sometimes he tells people, "I used to drink heavily and quit," without using the word "alcoholic." "When I do this," he adds, "I think they hear me better." Jonathan E. confirms Tom's impression; he first recognized his problem with drinking after listening to a psychologist talk about "alcohol-troubled people" at a Rotary Club meeting.

Because the word "alcoholic" is laden with values, it threatens many people, and they avoid seeking help. Liz B. maintains that one of the reasons she never considered going to a recovery group was that she didn't see herself as an "alcoholic." During the one- to two-year period in which Janet C. knew she had an alcohol problem but didn't do anything about it, she says she recalled a recovering cousin talking about AA and thinking, "I don't want to say I'm an alcoholic and have to go to all those meetings!" According to Dr. Mark Sobell and Dr. Linda Sobell, a respected husband-and-wife alcohol research team at Florida's Nova Southeastern University, "One of the most consistent themes for why alcohol abusers do not enter or delay entering treatment is the stigma related to being labeled an 'alcoholic.'"

But while the familiar AA introduction of "Hi, I'm Sue, and I'm an alcoholic" may be seen by some as self-deprecating, to others it can be helpful. (Although most people follow this practice at AA meetings, labeling yourself an "alcoholic" is not actually a requirement for participation in AA.) Master Krista O. notes that her experience with AA helped her to see that "alcoholism strikes all kinds of people, including my kind: the well-brought-up, educated, happy-childhood kind that had no reason to be an alcoholic." Heath F. adds, "For me and many others in AA, the connection between feeling bad and abusing alcohol never came about until after we admitted 'the problem.'" In other words, for some people, using the description "alcoholic" can help in seeing that many of the problems in their lives are caused by their drinking.

One of the difficulties with the word "alcoholism" is that it's used to describe all kinds of drinking problems, from small to large. Medical or mental health professionals often try to assess the extent of an alcohol problem by distinguishing between alcohol abuse and alcohol dependence. This distinction is established by the widely used professional guidebook known as the

DSM-IV (*Diagnostic and Statistical Manual of Mental Disorders, Fourth Edition*), which has not used the term "alcoholism" in years. In general, alcohol *abuse* is considered risky or harmful drinking without physical addiction. Alcohol *dependence* — the term professionals now commonly use in place of "alcoholism" — is meant for more severe problems, which usually include increased tolerance for alcohol and withdrawal symptoms when drinking is stopped.

However, the *DSM-IV* definitions of and distinctions between abuse and dependence are confusing, and most people just wind up using the catch-all term "alcoholic" to describe all alcohol-troubled individuals. Again, some drinking problems are relatively mild and others are severe, and many fall in between. Although there is no consensus about the meaning of the word "alcoholic," most lay people, many health-care professionals, AA members, and most of the masters *do* use the term. In fact, 85 percent answered yes to the question, "Do you or did you consider yourself to be an alcoholic?" However, the masters who resolved their drinking problems in nontraditional ways are less likely to use the A-word to describe themselves than are those who recovered with traditional twelve-step programs. This is particularly true of the loners like Liz B. — people who got sober and stay sober without formal support. Just six out of ten of them describe themselves as "alcoholic."

It doesn't matter what you call yourself or your relationship with alcohol as long as you recognize when drinking is getting in your way.

All People with Drinking Problems Are Not Created Equal

As master Oliver G. puts it, "There are different levels of affliction." Tom W. adds, "It is not the same problem in all people — there are degrees of alcohol problems."

Accordingly, some alcohol problems are easier to resolve than others. At the severe end of the spectrum, I heard from

◆ Clay R., who has been through no fewer than "fifty rehabs, detoxes, and hospitals" and finally quit eight years ago by going to a Salvation Army rehabilitation center when he realized he was going to have to panhandle to continue drinking.

◆ Sally O., whose four-year-old son was tragically killed by a truck while she was "having a party" and who went to her first AA meeting in ninety-degree weather wearing a filthy bathrobe, slippers, and a winter coat. (She's been sober for forty years now.)

◆ Theron J., who "lived on the streets" for the better part of a decade, went to jail four times, held fifty-three jobs in ten years, and was behind the wheel in a drunk driving accident in which his best friend was pronounced dead at the scene but lived. (Theron is now an attorney with sixteen years of sobriety.)

All three of these masters at one time drank a minimum of a quart a day of hard liquor.

Once again, such extreme cases do not represent the majority of people with alcohol problems. As Marc Schuckit, M.D., director of the Alcohol Research Center at the San Diego VA Medical Center, suggests in his book, *Educating Yourself About Alcohol and Drugs,* most people with serious drinking problems have jobs, families, and places to live; they are "likely to attend our place of worship, be respected in the community, and be highly productive." In other words, most serious problem drinkers are more like Liz B. or the following masters, who didn't drink vast amounts but who nonetheless had notable problems.

◆ Harriet B., who rarely drank more than two or three martinis but recalls driving home after an evening out with no memory of part of the drive; who was "rude, discourteous, and uncivil" to people after drinking; and who "was inattentive to crisis" in her daughters' lives.

◆ Ned G., who at his worst drank between three and five "heaping jiggers" of whiskey (with occasional beer and wine) every night, spread out from 5 to 10 P.M. He had "no overt symptoms, no hangovers in the morning," and says that drinking never interfered with his job. He realized that alcohol was interfering with his life, however, when he backed out of a trip to China because he was told alcohol wasn't allowed there. "I knew then that I had a real problem, because I really wanted to go."

◆ Rose S., who at her worst would drink three or four large glasses of wine or several gin and tonics, which was "enough to become intoxicated." Sometimes she drank daily, but more often just two or three times a week. A main consequence of her drinking was anger, frequently expressed as rage toward her husband. She also had one drunk driving arrest.

Some alcohol problems are intermittent, while others are chronic. Some are acute — say, after an emotional crisis. And contrary to the notion that alcohol problems are progressive, some stay the same, as was the case with Liz B., who drank the same amount for ten years. Sometimes alcohol problems even lessen before they are fully resolved, as happened with Rose S., who says, "Unlike the classic pattern, I drank less and less after my peak period of drinking. By the time I quit, I was drinking only socially, infrequently, and mostly without any problems." However, Rose gave up alcohol altogether after a dinner party at which she became irrationally angry with a friend. "I saw what I did with alcohol and anger and knew I had to give it up totally or some truly horrible thing might happen," she explains.

Big-Time Warning Signs

The alcohol researcher Mark Sobell emphasizes the following symptoms as warning signs of a very serious drinking problem.

Blackouts are episodes of amnesia that occur while you are drinking. Blackouts often reflect heavy consumption of alcohol within a short time period, which in turn suggests a high tolerance for alcohol. Experiencing blackouts is not the same as passing out from drinking or having unclear memories about events; the latter experiences are by no means benign, but they do not necessarily represent the same degree of problem as blackouts. The particularly scary thing about blackouts is that when you have one, you are actually still conscious and might do something embarrassing, dangerous, or illegal, which you will have no memory of but could be held responsible for.

Withdrawal symptoms occur when you are physically dependent on alcohol. That is, your body has adapted to having a steady supply of alcohol. If you stop drinking, your body goes through a readjustment, called withdrawal. The first withdrawal symptom most people experience is tremors — uncontrollable little twitches, most noticeable in the fingers and usually when you wake up in the morning, when your blood alcohol level has dropped. Other withdrawal symptoms include sweating, a fast heartbeat, and agitation. More dangerous withdrawal symptoms, which can occur in severely alcohol-dependent people in the absence of proper medical attention, include seizures, hallucinations, and delirium tremens (DTs), which involve a psychotic state of confusion.

Withdrawal symptoms can be avoided by using prescribed medication properly (say, in a hospital detox unit) or by drinking more alcohol. Needing early-morning drinks (or drinking to avoid withdrawal symptoms at any time of the day) is definitely a warning sign that serious problems have developed. (Morning drinking should not be confused with having a bloody mary at brunch, drinking before noon on holidays, or drinking several hours after you wake up just because you feel like having a drink, which is certainly not a healthy habit but is not the same as drinking to avoid withdrawal symptoms.) *continued*

Big-Time Warning Signs, continued

Abnormal liver function test results, determined by taking a blood sample, may suggest liver dysfunction because of excessive drinking. (Test results can also be abnormal because of other factors.) For instance, elevated levels of the enzyme gamma-glutamyl transferase (GGT) are often a sign of heavy drinking. But normal liver function test results don't necessarily mean that you're off the hook: some people who drink heavily have liver damage that does not show up in test results. If your physician does tell you your liver test results are abnormal, don't jump to the conclusion that you have cirrhosis, a serious disease that can be caused by heavy drinking. Diagnosis of cirrhosis requires a biopsy.

U.S. government guidelines suggest that positive responses to one or more of the following questions may be indicative of alcohol dependence:

◆ Are there times when you are unable to stop drinking once you have started?
◆ Does it take more drinks than before to get high?
◆ Do you feel a strong urge to drink?
◆ Do you change your plans so that you can have a drink?
◆ Do you ever drink in the morning to relieve the shakes?

From "The Physicians' Guide to Helping Patients with Alcohol Problems," National Institutes of Health publication no. 95-3769.

The idea that serious drinking problems do *not* always worsen, or follow a predictable course of events, is supported by findings of two large, ongoing studies conducted by George Vaillant, M.D., of the Harvard Medical School, who has followed hundreds of men with alcohol problems over the course of their adult lives. Dr. Vaillant found that some abused alcohol all their lives but never got any worse, and some returned to nonproblematic drinking. The alcohol researchers Linda and Mark

Sobell add, "The more common pattern can be described as persons moving into and out of periods of alcohol problems of varying severity, with problem periods separated by periods of either abstinence or drinking without problems."

There is no way of knowing whether you have a drinking problem that will worsen with time and could have dire consequences. And there is no clear line that indicates when a drinking problem becomes a very serious drinking problem, or what is commonly called "alcoholism." However, some symptoms should not be taken lightly and do suggest that an alcohol problem probably warrants professional consultation (see pages 41–42).

Disease or Not — and Does It Matter?

To face up to their drinking problems, did the masters need to understand the cause? Did it help to view their unhealthy relationship with alcohol as a "disease"? The disease model views "alcoholism" as similar to diseases like high blood pressure and diabetes, which result from an inherited biological component combined with environmental influences. People who subscribe to this idea tend to see "alcoholism" as a disorder that is progressive and that can be arrested (through abstinence) but not cured. Master Matt D. expresses some of these popular beliefs: "Alcoholism is a disease or illness or a condition that combines genetic, environmental, personality, and biologic factors making a person allergic to alcohol and unable to metabolize it in a normal manner. A psychological and physical craving for alcohol as well as the denial of problems associated with the abuse of alcohol seem to be part of the behavior."

Although the disease concept of "alcoholism" has dominated alcohol treatment for many years, not everyone accepts it; only 60 percent of the masters indicated that they fully subscribe to this idea when I asked them about it. Others saw their problem as more of a bad habit. For some, it just doesn't matter. Ralph C., who resolved a very serious drinking problem more than six years ago, cuts to the chase when he says, "I just feel so much better sober than when drinking that the cause isn't important."

Some masters take issue with the disease theory because they feel it can be used to absolve people of responsibility for their behavior, as Liz B. explains: "I have no patience for people we're supposed to feel sorry for because it's a disease. There is something you can do about it. You can't always blame your problems on other things." Cheryl T. agrees: "I think too many folks waste too many years obsessing on the diagnosis of alcoholism. Seems like everyone wants a label that allows them to play victim and shirk responsibility."

Doesn't the fact that alcohol problems tend to run in families support the disease idea? After all, eight out of ten masters answered yes to the question "Do/did other people in your immediate and extended family have drinking problems?" More than sixty of them clearly stated that their mother, father, or both had suffered from the problem. Some research does suggest that genetic inheritance plays a role in the development of alcohol problems. According to the government journal *Alcohol Health & Research World,* adoption studies indicate that children of "alcoholics" who are raised in nondrinking homes continue to face an increased risk of "alcoholism." Other studies have shown that the identical twin of an "alcoholic" has a much greater chance of becoming "alcoholic" than the fraternal twin of an "alcoholic" does.

But having parents with drinking problems does not prove a genetic link; drinking habits may be shaped by observing or identifying with parents. For instance, children who see a father cope with stress or depression by turning to the bottle may in turn do the same thing. Certainly if you have a family history of alcohol problems, it makes sense to be on guard about your drinking, as Liz B. was, but it doesn't mean you're doomed.

There's little doubt that the disease idea has helped remove the stigma from "alcoholism," suggesting that it is no more "immoral" than diabetes or cancer. Says master Paul V. (nine years), who believes in the disease theory, "It was like I had found a ray of hope when I realized that I might be a good person with a bad problem rather than just a bad person." Removing the moral connotation may also encourage some people to seek treatment for their drinking problem. (Traditional masters were much more likely to view "alcoholism" as a disease than masters who resolved their drinking problems with nontraditional means.)

As the landmark 1990 Institute of Medicine report concluded, a single cause for all alcohol problems probably will never be identified; there likely are different causes in different people, and people can be effectively helped without knowing the causes. The master and alcohol treatment counselor Rose S. sums up nicely with this view: "Alcoholism is *like* a disease and it's definitely a bad habit, but it's a condition that, like many things human, is the result of conscious choices as well as compulsions. But I believe that one can *change*."

The Myth of Denial

Contrary to the popular notion that people with active drinking problems are "in denial" about them, the majority of the masters had long been aware that they had serious alcohol problems by the time they finally recovered. In fact, nine out of ten answered yes to the question, "Did you go through a period of time when you knew you had a serious drinking problem but couldn't or chose not to do anything about it?" Of those who gave a time period, the average was a little more than six years.

Like Liz B., who was alarmed by her slurred speech on her son's recording several years before she quit, most of the masters *gradually* got in touch with the connection between alcohol and their problems. It took some time for them to actually do something about it.

Sarah N. admits, "I knew I was in trouble with alcohol from age twenty to age thirty-two and did nothing. I knew exactly what was happening — no denial here! — and just didn't care. In fact, the self-destruction was part of the allure." Likewise, from his early forties until he was forty-seven, Ralph C. says, "I admitted — only to myself — that I probably was alcoholic but had no desire to quit. I couldn't even imagine one day without a drink."

Some masters had the opposite problem: they knew their drinking problems were serious but had a difficult time convincing others. When Rosa L. told her husband, his response was, "Aah, you don't drink that much." Six months later, when she tried once again to convince him, he told her that it was summer, and it made sense that she would drink at least a six-pack of beer a day. Heather F. adds, "I can't tell you how many times I worried out loud about my drinking — to my doctor, my psychologist, even to my husband. But because I seemed like a together person, no one saw what I knew to be a serious drinking problem."

At least some of the masters did go through a period of denying to themselves and others that they were in trouble with alcohol, however. Even after they admitted that they had a drinking problem, some failed to see or didn't much care about the extent of the adverse consequences of their drinking. Sometimes, as was the case with Ralph C., denial took the form of reluctance to tell others about their drinking problem even though they knew they had one. Many masters went through periods of trying to convince themselves that they could drink moderately, only to find that they were putting off their inevitable need to swear off alcohol completely. Becky E. says she drank heavily from age twenty-two to age thirty-four, noting, "During much of that time, some part of me worried I *might* have a serious problem. But I kept trying to limit myself and drink like a 'normal' person."

Even if you are able to admit to yourself that you've got a serious drinking problem, as most of the masters did long before they got sober, it does not necessarily mean you are ready to do something about it. You may well be at a point where, despite your recognition of untoward consequences, the pleasure you derive from your beer, wine, or liquor overshadows the down side of your drinking. However, becoming aware of the link between your alcohol intake and problems in your life just might mean that you're *beginning* to be ready.

4

You Don't Have to "Hit Bottom"

How the Masters Reached the Turning Point

For years drinking kept winning out, despite the masters' awareness of their troubles with alcohol. To this day, many of them will admit that at some level they long for what any seasoned drinker knows as the pleasures of the bottle. When I asked, "What do you miss about heavy drinking?" they responded with words like "The rush. The glow. The secret world. The liquid courage to meet new people, be in new social situations. The sense of oblivion from drinking when life got overwhelming. The illusion of elegance — sipping wine with dinner, having a glass of champagne at the rail of a cruise ship. Drinking energized situations, and there was an excitement that was addictive in itself."

So what did it take to turn the tide — to finally take action and do something about the drinking? For many masters, it was a process of taking stock — of weighing the pleasures of alcohol against the pain and problems it caused and arriving at the conclusion that drinking just wasn't worth it anymore. Another deciding factor for a number of masters was defining what they had to be sober for: they looked at how alcohol interfered with what was really important in their lives and what drinking might cause them to lose. You might be thinking, "Don't you *have* to lose everything in order to recover — don't you have to hit bottom?" On the contrary, *many masters reached a turning point without having their lives fall apart or losing all that was dear to them.*

Jackie D.'s story

Like every other master, Jackie D. got something out of drinking. "I was a *very* organized and responsible person," she says, "and alcohol allowed me to mellow out or get wild and crazy." But in the end, the gratification from her nightly bottle of wine or six to eight hard-liquor drinks was offset by the negative effects of her drinking. Despite experiencing numerous alcohol-related problems, however, Jackie never hit bottom in the classic sense of losing everything. She explains, "My 'bottom' was simply recognizing that my life was not what I had intended and that alcohol was the reason why. It was, 'How can I not look at this anymore?' It's a miracle that I was able to see that as early as I did."

In short, Jackie recognized that drinking was standing in the way of the two things she wanted most in life: a loving relationship and a meaningful career. So, at the age of thirty-two, she decided to swear off alcohol for good. Now sober for ten years — with the help of professional counseling, a "free-thinking" AA group, and support from her husband — she can boast, "Alcohol is no longer a part of my life, and I like it that way."

Jackie describes her former self as a "high-bottom drunk," elaborating, "I was successful in school and work and justified my drinking by the seemingly okay outward appearance I was able to show." As early as seventh grade, she experienced her first drunken episode, when she and a friend took liquor from their parents' cupboards to a school dance and got "bombed." From that time on, she says, "I got away with it. I was an honors student. My double life started early." By college, her heavy drinking was, in Jackie's words, "well established." She adds, "I always drank more than other people; when they stopped, I kept drinking. But I still had the grades and seemed bright and confident."

She graduated from college with a degree in textile design, secured a good position in the textile industry, and moved up the professional ladder. Her double life continued. She says, "I never drank on the job, but I drank every night until I passed out. I fell into bed with men I didn't know and wouldn't have chosen had I been sober. My memory started to fade, and I had to write everything down. I had black moods and depressed, suicidal thoughts. I alienated friends who were afraid to confront my drinking. I found myself avoiding events where no alcohol would be served. I felt completely alone and isolated."

"Drinking was the one big lie"

After a short-lived marriage, Jackie went through six months of soul-searching — in her head and on paper — which helped her to see that having a meaningful relationship was very important to her and that alcohol was standing in her way. "Being an analytical person," she says, "I spent several months writing a personal ad to find a mate, trying to articulate what I brought into a relationship (both good and bad) and what qualities I needed in a man to complement or contrast with mine." In the process of her soul-searching, she asked herself, "What is the most important value in my life?" The answer was honesty. "I was painfully honest in other areas of my life, and I admitted to myself that drinking was the one big lie." She realized that she would either have to find a man who drank like she did or meet someone who wouldn't put up with her drinking. In going through this process, Jackie began to prepare herself for the fact that she might have to give up alcohol. But she kept drinking.

The personal ad netted nearly two dozen responses, and after three months Jackie met the man who had the "basic traits" she was looking for: "Ethical — Committed — Loyal — Giving — Open — Gentle — Sensitive — Healthy — Self-sufficient — Intelligent — Humorous — Playful — Sensuous — Surprising." Three months later, he confronted her about her drinking. Jackie explains, "Glenn said he could see something in me that he liked a lot, but he couldn't take my drinking. It was what I didn't want to hear but wanted to hear. I knew he was right, but I was afraid to stop." In the end, she feels, it came down to a choice between love and alcohol — she had to face the fact that she couldn't continue to drink and have a loving partner with qualities she admired.

"Alcohol had crossed the line"

During the next two weeks, Jackie almost sabotaged this new relationship by getting drunk and sleeping with a business colleague, her ex-boss. "I had always had a rule not to mix business with drinking, but now alcohol had crossed the line into my career," she says. This violation of her own rule — which she describes as "the final push to realizing how tired I was of not being able to trust myself" — coupled with the recognition that she might ruin her newfound relationship prompted Jackie to take the first step to do something about her drinking.

She decided to go to a social worker with expertise in alcohol problems, who was recommended by a friend. Before she could go for counseling, however, she had to get a physician's referral, and the doctor showed her the following quotation, which also led Jackie to take stock of alcohol's role in her life. It read:

> Until one is committed, there is hesitancy, the chance to draw back, always ineffectiveness. Concerning all acts of initiative, there is one elementary truth, the ignorance of which kills countless ideas and splendid plans: that the moment one definitely commits oneself, then providence moves, too. Whatever you can do or dream, you can begin it. Boldness has genius, power, and magic in it. Begin it now.*

---

* This quotation is commonly attributed to the German writer and scientist Goethe, but it appears to be an amalgamation of the insights of a number of different authors.

"I wasn't going after what I wanted in life"

When I asked Jackie why these words were so powerful, she said, "They made me aware that I had not followed through on the dreams in my life. I had never made a commitment to be what I wanted to be. As long as I was drinking a bottle of wine a night or half a fifth of Jack Daniel's, I couldn't be honest with myself." She elaborates, "I wasn't going after what I wanted in life: finding a stable relationship, following through on my desire to do artwork and to be self-employed as a writer, being able to be by myself and really relax, and having a better relationship with my father. Alcohol got in the way of all these things."

When Jackie finally did go to counseling, the therapist did not insist that she stop drinking but suggested that they'd probably get further if she did. The therapist also offered Jackie options for dealing with her alcohol problem, including going to AA, Rational Recovery, or SOS; but mostly she offered her the opportunity to continue the self-analysis she had already started on her own. Within two weeks of starting therapy, Jackie made up her mind to quit drinking and change her life.

At this point Jackie decided to give Alcoholics Anonymous a try and proceeded to shop around, visiting different meetings until she found a few she really liked. As an agnostic, she feels she got lucky, because her second meeting was specifically for agnostics and atheists, one of only four such AA groups in the large city where she lived. She notes, "I had found, completely by accident, the nonreligious AA I needed! The attendees were rationalists, physicists, bikers, mystics, humanists, and anyone who felt alienated or ostracized by traditional AA. It allowed pagan, scientific, or Buddhist beliefs, or whatever worked for its participants. The only requirement for membership was a desire to stop drinking."

While this became her home group, Jackie found other AA groups she liked, including a women's group and one that met at a hospital, and she continued to go to AA meetings at least several times each week for three years. (For more than five years now,

Jackie has not felt a need to go to regular AA meetings, but she wouldn't hesitate to go back if she had a desire to drink.)

Professionally, Jackie slowly worked her way out of the corporate world and gained the confidence to do her artwork. Although it took her five or six years to be able to earn a living as a freelance writer, which was another of her dreams, she has accomplished this goal and has written books and landed her own newspaper column. She has also cultivated a wonderful relationship with her father. (Her mother died many years ago.)

Jackie finds it amazing that Glenn, whom she eventually married, has stuck by her through it all. "I really was a mess the first year, but I think as the real me emerged, he saw more of that person he only glimpsed while I was drinking." (They've been married now for more than eight years.) She concludes, "Alcohol is so much not a part of my lifestyle, I can't imagine ever going back. I have too much to lose now. My life is terrific! When I drank, alcohol clouded my choices. Now I have choice in everything I do. Choice, in my mind, is the opposite of being stuck. Choice is freedom."

On Hitting Bottom

Jackie D. represents the many masters who feel that their lives did not have to fall apart in order for them to reach a turning point with their drinking. In fact, four out of ten of the masters either answered no or were ambivalent when asked, "Do you feel that 'hitting bottom' (reaching a point of complete crisis) was necessary for you to be ready to resolve your alcohol problem?"

We're often led to believe that a problem drinker will keep right on drinking until the consequences are catastrophic. Master Booker T. expresses that conventional view: "Most of us almost kill ourselves before we quit." It's not uncommon to hear people say of someone who is not ready to get sober, "He hasn't hit bottom yet."

Masters who recovered by going to twelve-step programs

were much more likely than others to feel they had to hit bottom before getting sober, which may reflect hearsay from AA meetings. However, in his book *Not-God,* Ernest Kurtz points out that in AA's early days, "hitting bottom" did not necessarily refer to losing everything. Instead, it had more to do with a "sense of being 'really licked' and hopeless." Although current AA literature states that "few people will sincerely try to practice the AA program unless they have hit bottom," it also suggests that you don't necessarily *have* to sink that low.

As master Rose S. points out, believing that life has to deteriorate totally before you reach a point of readiness can actually get in the way of your recovery by creating a self-fulfilling prophecy. She explains, "The idea that one has to hit bottom keeps some alcoholics digging."

Master Cheryl T. offers a more useful view of what it takes to reach a turning point: "The so-called bottom is different for everyone. The bottom is more a point of realization that alcohol is interfering with the pursuit of happiness." Rosa L. adds, "For some, hitting bottom is lying in the gutter, homeless. Others say that alcoholism is like you are going down in an elevator, and you can decide when to get off." Indeed, there are steps you can take — as Jackie did — to "get off the elevator" before a drinking problem escalates to more serious proportions.

The Turning Point

What exactly tipped the scales so that the masters *finally* took action, which in most cases meant giving up alcohol altogether? To find the answer, I asked, "What was the turning point when you were finally successful? That is, what were the events and circumstances that motivated you to do something about your drinking once and for all?"

Typically, people gave multiple responses to this question, for usually more than one event turned them around. Their answers were varied and highly individual, having to do with everything from religious experiences to suicide attempts to reading a book. After sifting through the masters' many turning points, I found that the top five had to do with the following:

#1: A general feeling of being worn down by the battle
The most frequent responses to the turning-point question referred to being sick and tired of the struggle with alcohol. People had simply had it with drinking, and it just wasn't worth it to continue. Betty B. told me, "I could not stand to live one more day like that." Of the end of her drinking days, Roxi V., who had been cited for drunk driving, says, "I knew that I was a valuable person but that alcohol was causing *all* my problems. I'd had enough of anything controlling my life." Bruce E. woke up one morning and resolved that he could no longer live as he was, likening the experience to that of "a prizefighter who had been beaten up so badly that he couldn't get off the stool and come out for the next round — who then throws in the towel."

#2: Concerns about family and children
Phil Q., who wasn't quite ready to quit drinking when a judge sent him to a treatment center, said that his feelings about his nine-year-old son played a powerful role in his decision not to go back to the bottle after he completed treatment. Anthony G.'s turning point was "wanting to have a better life and my love for my son. I realized what my drinking was doing to my family and what it would do to the son I loved so much."

#3: Embarrassing or frightening incidents
Becky E. made a promise to herself to quit drinking after "a blackout, a fall, broken furniture — with no memory of the event." She said, "My terrified housemate found me and couldn't figure out what was wrong with me. I scared myself and was ashamed that my best and oldest friend found me like this." The turning point for Marguerite E. was when she slept with someone

during an alcohol-induced blackout. "I woke up in my car with my pants off and my best friend's husband next to me with his pants off. At that moment I knew my life was not working."

#4: Medical problems or health concerns related to drinking

"Observing health problems in drinking cronies" helped turn Cal T. around. When one of his friends was diagnosed with alcoholic pancreatitis, Cal says, "I saw myself heading there." Kathryn N.'s turning point occurred on a plane, after she had been up all night drinking and packing, when she thought she was having a heart attack. She says now that she was probably experiencing tachycardia (rapid heartbeat) compounded by fear. But this incident spurred her to tell her husband she was an "alcoholic."

#5: Breakup or serious problems with a significant other

Maddie M.'s turning point came when her partner of seven years informed her that she was in love with someone else and was leaving: "I knew with absolute certainty and clarity that if I continued to drink, I would drink myself to death." Zoe A. told me, "My marriage was failing after only two years. When I went to a counseling session with my husband, all the feedback shouted, 'Get into treatment fast! You have a serious problem!'"

Where would profiled master Jackie D.'s turning point fall among these? Perhaps it would be in the last category, since she would have had serious problems with her significant other if she had not quit drinking. Maybe her turning point was embarrassment when she got drunk and slept with a colleague — when her secret drinking life spilled into her professional life. Or maybe she was simply worn down by her double lifestyle and feeling bad from alcohol use. Then again, it might have been the meaningful quotation that made Jackie face the fact that alcohol was interfering with what she really wanted out of life. In fact, a string of events probably led Jackie finally to take action.

Studies of the process of resolving drinking problems confirm that readiness to change is seldom a sudden event, although it sometimes appears to be spurred by a distinct incident — the proverbial straw that breaks the camel's back. Consider the case of Nancy B., who took her last drink after attending a party at which she bumped into a "previously alcoholically drinking friend." He told her he had quit because alcohol had caused so many problems in his family's lives — his parents' deaths, his two brothers' disastrous lives, and his own divorce — and "it just didn't make sense to keep on drinking." At that moment, Nancy says, "I put down my glass of wine, and I have never had a drop again." It would appear that that one incident led her to quit, when in fact, she says, she had already spent several years hating her husband, her job, herself, and her life because of her drinking. She also notes that her decision to give up alcohol had a lot to do with her son's stay at a rehabilitation program for a serious drug problem. The program's rules were that no alcohol would be in the home and no drinking would occur within eight hours of seeing a participating child, which forced Nancy to cut back from her daily habit of drinking a fifth of bourbon. When she put down her last glass of wine, many things had come together.

Taking Stock

One way to avoid hitting bottom — or to bring yourself back up if you're already there — is to follow the masters' lead by taking stock of the pluses and the minuses of your drinking, then deciding whether continuing to drink is worth it.

In one form or another, master after master told me how he or she went through a stock-taking process, weighing the positive aspects of drinking against the negative consequences. Jackie D. actually took stock several times before she quit drinking: when she wrote her personal ad for a mate and saw how alcohol led her to choose the wrong men; when she slept with her colleague and woke up to how tired she was of her secret life; when the doctor gave her the quotation that made her recognize that alcohol kept her from making choices consistent with her goals.

One crucial final event also helped her take stock. Just before she quit drinking, she was one of three company managers involved in reprimanding a supervisor who was found drunk on the job. When offered the choice of going through alcohol treatment or resigning, the supervisor resigned. Jackie asked herself, "If I were in the same position, would I do the same thing? Was drinking more important than my livelihood? My answer was a definitive *no.*" She adds, "This story may illustrate my own vision of what my bottom might have looked like! It was so close to home — a strange case of my double life coming full circle, and it smacked me in the face with a bit of reality."

Here's how some other masters arrived at the conclusion that the negative consequences of drinking overshadowed the pleasure it brought:

◆ "What I miss about drinking is losing my scruples," says Harriet B. (nine years). "It was fun to be outspoken, naughty, and blame it on the booze. Normally quiet, I became the life of the party. Besides, I was widowed and divorced, and I didn't know one man who didn't drink, socially at least." As she contemplated such "pros" of her drinking, she asked herself, "My health seems good — but will it stay so? How much better could I feel if I quit? Would I feel better physically? Have less anger at life? Raise my self-esteem? Be happy? Would I be a better person as a nondrinker?" The costs of drinking finally tipped the scales when Harriet felt that alcohol caused her to be rude to people, to forget things she shouldn't, and to be inattentive to her children's problems.

◆ "When I drank, it was to open up, because otherwise I was shy and reserved," says Billy H. (fourteen years). "It was a morale booster for singing auditions, job interviews, and meeting new people." The turning point for him came when, "in a stupor," he decided to travel cross-country with a total stranger, who became obsessed with him and followed him everywhere upon their return. "Very scary!" he exclaimed. "I wasn't enjoying the alcohol and what it did to me or the problems it was causing in my personal life. I like being in control, and I was losing that when I drank."

◆ "Most of all, I miss sitting in a barroom with light streaming in and watching the light change to dark while drinking beer and talking with friends," Jack B. (fifteen years) recalls longingly. "I miss gazing at the night sky after a bout of drinking and seeing the stars through an alcoholic prism and feeling so damn good about life and the world. And, stupid as it may sound, I miss staggering home from a just-closed tavern and hearing the crunch of snow under my feet or feeling the hot night air on my face." But the costs were too great. Jack neglected to eat and slept fitfully "at best." He was frightened by several blackouts during which a whole day or night was lost to his consciousness. (He once fell off a bar stool and smashed his face and glasses on the floor but had no recollection of it.) In the end, he says, "Fear was the motivator." After being abstinent for a while, Jack is now a moderate drinker.

A number of studies of those who have successfully stopped or moderated their drinking suggest that going through a stock-taking process is critical to recovery. The *Journal of Substance Abuse* describes one study in which people who had resolved alcohol problems were given a choice of ten possible reasons for quitting or reducing their alcohol intake. It didn't matter whether they had quit or reduced drinking on their own or had help through formal treatment or AA: the most frequently endorsed reason was that they had "weighed the pros and the cons of drinking and not drinking."

Heather F., who went through a series of relapses before deciding to quit for good, did exactly that as she tossed and turned after her last night of drinking. "I kept thinking about how much I loved my bourbon, wine, and gin. My drinks truly brought me more pleasure than anything at that point in my life, particularly when I was depressed. But then I thought of my family — how I had forgotten important things my little boy told me when I was drinking, how I couldn't drive my kids to activities in the evening because I'd had a few, how I didn't want to be this kind of a role model for them." She also reflected about alcohol's effect on her sleep — she woke up with night sweats and was not able to go back to sleep — and the depressive effect alcohol had in the morning, when the drinks had worn off. She decided that quitting was the gift she would make to her family on Christmas, two days later.

As Becky E. advises, "Make a list of the positive features of your drinking and examine them in a brutally honest way. Then make a list of the negative features and examine *them* in a brutally honest way." The costs don't have to outnumber the benefits; they just have to be more powerful.

Getting Beyond Ambivalence

Dorothy C. captures the conflict between wanting to quit and wanting to drink in her description of the ten-year period during which she knew she had a serious problem but felt unable to change. "It was like I had two personalities: I wanted to be sober, but my choice was to drink. I had feelings of being a no-good mother, yet I wanted to be a good mother. I left my two children, whom I loved deeply, because the alcohol had become more important."

Herb N. (profiled in chapter 2) nicely describes how he resolved his ambivalence: "I wanted the pain to stop and consciously knew that meant I had to stop using alcohol and drugs.

However, unconsciously I knew I wanted to drink and drug forever. People aren't used to going against their gut feelings, and
that's what makes quitting difficult. So I had to learn to align my
conscious and unconscious to fight for the same goals."

It all boils down to this: *in order to do something about their
drinking, the masters had to see that the short-term pleasure provided by alcohol was not worth the long-term problems it caused.*
As master Randall N. attests, "The temporary relief drinking afforded me became smaller as my drinking progressed, in proportion to the increasing pain and harmful effects caused by it." Harriet B. sums up, "The brief 'joy' of alcohol is not worth the loss of
real freedom."

Defining What You Have to Be Sober For

"We have to find something we want more than we want a
drink," says Lois S., adding, "Many times it's right in our everyday lives and we don't see it."

Some masters decided that what they had to be sober for was
preventing or avoiding something they didn't want to happen or
didn't want to lose. After long recognizing that she had a serious
drinking problem, Judy K. decided to quit drinking when someone made her think about what might happen if she didn't give up
alcohol. She had had a scary blackout, which led her to her first
AA meeting, where she met one-on-one with a veteran member.
The turning point came when this woman asked Judy, "Do you
beat your kids?" (Her two children were ten and eleven years old
at the time.) Shocked, Judy answered, "No! I would never do
that!" to which the other woman responded, "If you keep drinking, I guarantee you will start." Judy's reaction? "I guess at that
moment I had to decide which or who I loved more. The booze
lost out."

Like Judy and Jackie D., many other masters realized that
their love and concern for family and significant others gave them

something to be sober for. Here's how some of these people describe their turning points:

◆ Milton S. (five years, religious recovery): "One day when I was drunk and smoking a cigarette, the hot ashes fell off and landed in my son's shoe and burned his foot. Naturally he told his mom, who said, 'Tell your dad to quit smoking.' He did tell me, 'Dad, quit smoking.' All of a sudden it hit me: 'What have I done? Forgive me, son.' At that moment I recognized that I had a problem and vowed to my son I would never smoke or drink again." And he hasn't. To this day, if Milton has an urge to drink, he says his son's name to himself.

◆ Herbert Z. (six years, SOS recovery): "When my wife suggested I buy wine by the case instead of by the bottle — which I read as a suggestion that I go ahead and commit suicide — I felt that I was on the brink of being 'dead' as a husband and a father. Then my nine-year-old son asked me to my face, 'Daddy, you're a drunkard, aren't you?' That shocked me, and I sought help within the week."

◆ Babz L. (eleven years, AA recovery): "I was planning on moving back home from grad school to be with my five-year-old son, and I didn't want him to have a drunk for a mom." Today she says, "I love being there for my three kids and mothering them as I wanted to be mothered."

◆ Harriet B. (nine years, quit on her own with the help of several books): "I did not want my small grandchildren to grow up thinking of Granny as a lush." When she first stopped drinking, one of the things that helped her stay sober was spending former "booze bucks" on new clothes and gifts for her grandchildren.

It doesn't have to be just kids and relationships that give you something to be sober for. A dream of early retirement became the motivating force for Cal T. and Clare J., husband-and-wife masters. Early in their sobriety, they started taking long walks and talking about what they really wanted from life. "Every night we'd walk and visualize how we would become financially independent, and we started building our way there. We calculated how much we spent on drinking and saved that money. We kept our starter house rather than move upward. This goal is what replaced our drinking life," they explain. By the time they were in their early fifties, they were retired, financially independent, and doing what they wanted in life.

As the renowned University of New Mexico alcohol researcher William Miller, Ph.D., points out, the essential question is this: What do you care more about than drinking? He acknowledges that in some cases the answer seems to be "Nothing." But with exploration, people can usually find something more important to them than alcohol.

Dorothy C. lost just about everything before she swore off drinking. She describes her drinking days like this: "Problems, my dear, would be a book in itself. There was fighting. I lost my children, spent money to the extreme, was put in a paddy wagon, set the bed on fire, took pills hoping for an overdose to kill me, and was disappointed when I didn't succeed." But even Dorothy had something to be sober for — she wanted her kids back. Her wish came true when she complied with her husband's ultimatum: "Stay sober, and you can come home to your children." She told me, "I desperately wanted to be with them and realized the terrible loss after I left them to drink." She has now been sober for decades.

Imagining Life on the Other Side

What does it take to make the grass of sobriety look greener? For starters, you might imagine what life can be like on the other side. Jackie D. explains how she went through this process: "The negatives of my drinking were obvious, but I had trouble articulating any positives of getting sober. I had to believe that not drinking would be better, though I couldn't exactly say why. I think that perhaps for the first time in my life, I had to act on faith instead of on logic."

Here are five key questions to help you imagine life on the other side:

Would life work better for me sober? Phil Q. says he gained a lot with sobriety: "I'm calmer. I'm more rational. I make better decisions. I'm not chained to that habit anymore. I lost a whole bunch of phobias." He adds, "Life works infinitely better for me sober."

Is my drinking pattern compatible with my values? Calvin A. says, "The turning point came when I could no longer square my behavior with my values. For years I was able to say that I was just a fun, wild, crazy guy. But at the end my staying out all night, my disregard for my wife and family, my ignoring my job and other behaviors — too personal and private to mention — caused me such anguish that I felt I had to change or go crazy."

What might I lose if I keep drinking? Homer D., who quit drinking at the age of sixty-five, says that in addition to wanting to preserve his health, fear of losing his driver's license was and is a real motivator. Jackie A. adds, "Think about the possibility of really losing the confidence and trust of those who are closest to you. Are you willing to lose your job, have your career suffer?"

What do I want in life that alcohol keeps me from having? Jackie D. advises asking yourself this question, then says, "Set these things up as long-term goals." Arnold C. adds, "When tempted to drink, ask yourself, 'Will this promote or hinder the achievement of my goals in life? Is this self-enhancing or self-defeating?'"

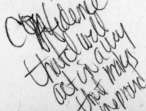

Psyching Yourself Up: Tips from the Masters

"Take a long, hard look at all the things you give up to drink. Then make a list of things you do when drinking that you wouldn't do when sober." — Robert H. (six years)

"Talk about your desire to quit drinking with close friends, family, or a professional; talking about it makes it real and possible." — Susan L. (ten years)

"Realize that you really aren't as clever, sexy, compelling, witty, or fun as you think you are when you're drunk. You're much better than you think you are when you're sober." — Phil Q. (fourteen years)

"Do you think that God, Buddha, or your own brain wants you to trash your wonderful self with alcohol?" — John V. (thirteen years)

"Volunteer at a detox; watch videos about how bad booze is; read books on the subject." — Bryce G. (five years)

"Find others who are successfully living sober lives." — Melinda J. (eight years)

"Examine your spiritual life. What questions are unanswered? What are you really longing for?" — Zoe A. (ten years)

"Realize that there is a whole lot to life and that drinking is just a small part of it." — Billy R. (five years)

What might I get back if I give up drinking? Heather F. knew what life was like "on the other side" because of several long periods of sobriety. When she finally quit for good, she says, "I got back sound nights of sleep, which I lost when I drank. It's nice to wake up with a clear head, no pain, no fogginess. Things taste better to me, like my big ice cream cone each night, my really good coffee that didn't taste nearly as good 'the morning after.' I'm so glad

I can drive my children around — anytime, night or day. And orgasms are better without alcohol taking the edge off them! Life just seems to coast more easily. And best of all, there is no more of that awful morning-after remorse: Why did I drink that much? I won't do it again . . . What did I say? Did anyone notice?"

Ironically, it may turn out that the very things you fear losing will be your returns in recovery. Take the case of Sara F., who, when asked what she misses about drinking, said, "I guess it would be the loss of control. Being in control is hard work. But this is also what I treasure most about myself now: being in control of my actions and my life." Then there's Becky E., who misses the ability to relax and socialize easily, which came with drinking. "But," she adds, "these are exactly the things that led to trouble." What she likes about not drinking is that "when I relate to people and they relate to me, it's the real me, not the alcohol."

Doing It for Yourself

Although Jackie D. was given an ultimatum of sorts by her future husband, she stresses that her recovery was voluntary. "I did it for me," she says. Indeed, quite a few masters gave a clear message that ultimately, *you have to want to do something about an alcohol problem for yourself, not because someone else is on your back.* When I asked them if they felt that resolution of their alcohol problem was voluntary, nearly nine out of ten masters said yes. Violet F. replied that for her, quitting drinking was "absolutely" voluntary, adding, "I stopped for me and remain sober for me. This isn't something one can do for someone else."

Some of the masters shared how their failed past attempts had been at someone else's urging. For instance, before Calvin A. resolved his drinking problem by receiving inpatient treatment and turning to other sober people for support in AA and SOS groups, he had made an insincere attempt to quit drinking to placate his wife. Elena G. says, "Years of nagging by my husband and son didn't work until I finally decided to do something myself. Only I could have stopped me."

Jackie A., who was coerced into sobriety, is one of the exceptions. She is one of the minority of masters whose turning point came from a mandate by the law or a profession, a formal alcohol intervention, or an ultimatum from someone else. Jackie A. quit drinking after her seven children arranged a formal intervention. However, she too feels that her recovery was voluntary, adding, "I shifted my thinking from 'I can control my drinking myself' to 'I can decide to stop myself.'" It may be that intervention came just at the point when she was ready to change.

None of this is to say that loved ones' concerns should not influence your decision to do something about your drinking. *But ultimately you have to want it for yourself.*

When Others Interfere

Although some masters were pushed into their decision to change by well-intentioned loved ones, others found that loved ones got in the way of their decision to take action. Jackie D. had a hard time telling her family of her decision to stop drinking: "Most of them drink regularly, and on some level I knew that my admission would make them have to look at their own behavior. They said things like, 'Oh, you're not an alcoholic — it's just a bad habit. But if you really think you need to call yourself one and go to AA, okay.' It felt like a bit of a put-down, but I soon learned it is a common reaction of denial."

Some people even went so far as to try to sabotage efforts to stop drinking. When Sally C. first got sober, she found that the toughest part was dealing with people who told her she needed a drink to loosen up. Some made fun of her for being a "teetotaler" and went so far as to put alcohol in her soft drinks without telling her.

When Sharon P. was newly sober, her roommate shook up a

beer and sprayed it all over Sharon's face and clothes. Although the members of her social group did their best to "tempt and tease" her, Sharon used such acts of sabotage to strengthen her resolve. She maintains that "their negativity inspired me to stay sober. Needless to say, none of these people are my friends today!"

Taking a Break

If you've been drinking heavily for a long time, it might be hard to fathom what life can be like without a drink in your hand. To let yourself reexperience sober life and its bonuses, a number of masters suggest taking a break from drinking for a while. Annie A. says, "Set a goal of quitting for six months, just to prove to yourself that you can, and really pay attention to how you feel during that time." Russ N. suggests that a two- to four-week break might be enough, if all the while you "look back at your life, then look ahead at your future." Clay R. advises, "Try for *any* period of abstinence and *honestly* compare how you feel — health, personal pride — after and before."

Vincent A., who was a morning-till-night drinker, says that experiencing three months of abstinence and then trying to drink again was the turning point for what now adds up to twenty-four years of sobriety. His three months off from drinking were spurred by attending an AA meeting. "Up until then," he declares, "it never occurred to me to stop completely. Duh!" When New Year's Eve came, he decided to have a few drinks, which led to two more months of drinking. "Before I had experienced a couple of months of abstinence, my behavior seemed normal," he says. "But this time I had some perspective. I could see that my drinking was out of control, and the contrast was so stark with the three months sober that I went back to AA meetings."

After Tom W. took two or three weeks off from drinking, he says, "I realized that I didn't want to drink anymore. I could see more clearly the reasons not to start again." One event that led him to this point was his disgust with himself as he stood by the side of the road urinating with a flask of whiskey in his hand, which was inconsistent with his values. "I was trying to follow my wife in an understanding of Christianity but felt like my love for alcohol was leading me where I didn't want to go. So I quit for a short period and in doing so realized I wanted to quit for good." After quitting on his own, Tom has remained sober for twelve years.

Trying Again and Again

What if you've tried and failed many times to quit or taper off your drinking? When I asked the masters for their advice about this, George M. responded:

a) Never,
b) Never,
c) Never give up.

In fact, "Don't give up" was one of the ten most frequent suggestions from the masters for people who want to quit drinking. As Jane R. puts it, "Never stop trying. If one thing doesn't work, try something else." One third of the masters told me that they had seriously tried to solve their drinking problems at least three times before they were finally successful. (One in five tried to quit five or more times.) Helen H. tried to quit drinking "a million times by myself and about three or four times in a group." When she found Women for Sobriety, the program that eventually helped her, she made a commitment to go to meetings despite the fact that she continued to drink in between them for the first three months. Emerson A. says he made many attempts before he was successful. "I was in and out of AA and counseling for eleven years. The first two years I attempted 'controlled' drinking. The last nine years I was periodically abstinent for two, three, or eight months — then I'd fall back to drinking for several weeks. Finally I was sick and tired of being sick and tired." Now sober for twenty-six years, he still attends AA meetings once a week.

Experts emphasize that most people make many attempts to stop drinking before they are really successful. And trying is worth it. Verner S. Westerberg, Ph.D., of the University of Mexico's Center on Alcoholism, Substance Abuse, and Addictions, says, "Trying does matter — going to treatment, going to AA, anything that is positive and moving toward something else and away from drinking."

I was surprised to find, however, that as many as four out of ten masters said they were successful *the first time* they made a serious attempt to solve their drinking problems. The key word here might be "serious." As Jackie D. says, "I made several not-too-serious attempts, which lasted a week or so."

Instead of dwelling on past failures, it's more productive to learn from your past, treating past recovery attempts as a rich library of experiences to shape your future. Then, when you feel ready to try sobriety once again, use the concepts that worked in the past and don't repeat things that were not helpful.

Doing Something in the Meantime

While two thirds of the masters quit cold turkey when they were finally successful, many went through periods of on-again, off-again drinking or attempted to drink moderately before quitting for good. As Marisa S. states, "I tried cutting back, found this to be very difficult, and wound up in enough trouble that it eventually became clear that I needed to be abstinent. Once I had an established goal of abstinence, I still didn't do well for quite some time. I would get small chunks of abstinence which gradually grew larger and larger, punctuated by bits of problem drinking."

Although many people believe that anything short of total abstinence is failure, a number of masters made progress by using productive strategies in the interim — even before they were ready to give up alcohol.

◆ Marisa S. (seven years) cut back on her drinking "dramatically" for three years before she became abstinent. During this time, with the help of a therapist, she says, "I started reading about alcoholism and thinking about my use of alcohol and what I wanted for myself. Instead of the 'shoulds' that used to rule my choices and put me in a drinking mode, I began learning to take care of myself rather than everyone and everything else. I started thinking about what I actually liked doing and went out of my way to pursue some of my own interests — like gardening. I also made a point of putting myself in situations where I wouldn't drink as much." Marisa began exercising to relieve stress instead of using alcohol for this purpose, which she found helped her to drink less. And even though she had not quit for good, she explored various types of recovery groups, including AA, SMART Recovery, and Women for Sobriety. "All these things caused me to drink less and ultimately to give up drinking," she says.

◆ Karen M. attempted controlled drinking for three years before quitting completely fourteen years ago. During this period, because of depression, she saw a psychiatrist, who did not insist that she quit drinking but who did help her make a conscious effort to drink less. "She suggested alternating my wine with a glass of water or soft drinks. She said I needed to be sure not to drink on an empty stomach and suggested that I observe a sober friend of mine who was in AA to see if she left parties before everyone else did, which she did." The therapist also encouraged Karen to go to AA. Karen says, "I originally went to AA to find out how to drink less — not to stop." Still active in AA, she says that she often sees people at meetings who continue to drink, noting, "They may not have quit yet, but they are learning techniques that could eventually help them."

◆ Louise L. (ten years) says that in the process of resolving her drinking problem, she relapsed for just one night every three months for the first two years. Despite these relapses, she had taken a huge step in the right direction. From the age of eighteen on, she says, every time she had a drink, "nothing short of getting drunk and falling down would do." For six years toward the end she drank a nightly liter of black Russians. During the time when she was relapsing every three months, she saw a counselor, distanced herself from the father who had abused her as a child, and avoided clubs that she associated with drinking. After each relapse she would return to the Friday SOS meeting that she had been attending regularly. She recalls, "People there were never judgmental but asked the hard questions: What was the trigger, and how could I avoid it? What was I going to do the next time?" At the end of two years, she was ready to quit drinking for good.

Cutting back or moderating their drinking didn't work as long-term solutions for any of these people. Until they were ready to quit, however, all three took important interim steps — with the help of a professional — to limit the amount of trouble alcohol was causing in their lives. Psychologists call this idea "harm reduction." Alan Marlatt, Ph.D., editor of the book *Harm Reduction: Pragmatic Strategies for Managing High-Risk Behaviors,* says, "Such user-friendly approaches make it easy for people with alcohol problems to get on board, get involved, and get started."

The point is that *doing something about drinking does not have to involve an all-or-nothing resolution — doing anything is better than doing nothing.* Cutting back on drinking to lessen its harm should not necessarily be the long-term goal; nor is a harm-reduction approach to be used to kid someone with a severe drinking problem that he or she will be able to drink moderately someday.

Since this type of approach can be risky — especially for people with serious drinking problems — it is wise to seek guidance from a professional who is familiar with harm-reduction strategies. One way to find such a person is to check listings in the yellow pages for psychologists, psychiatrists, social workers, or alcohol counselors with experience in this area. Then make phone calls — anonymously, if you prefer. Say that you are trying

Reducing Your Risk Before You Quit

Always have a designated driver; when you don't have one, do your drinking at home rather than in a bar, or take a taxi.

Always do your out-of-home drinking with a responsible friend who can guide you if you start to get into trouble.

Carry a condom to increase the odds of safe sex if you get into an intimate situation.

Limit your drinking to a specific time late in the day, and do everything you can to stay busy until that time arrives.

Do your drinking in a safe place — not, for instance, where you know you have a tendency to get into fights.

Measure your drinks rather than pouring directly from bottle to glass.

If you are a hard-liquor drinker, switch to beer or wine. (Do this only if this helps you consume less alcohol — it doesn't work for everyone. For drink equivalents, see page 34.)

Alternate alcoholic with nonalcoholic drinks, or keep one of each in front of you and alternate sips.

Don't buy huge quantities of alcohol at a time. For instance, avoid opaque boxes of wine that prevent you from seeing how much you've drunk.

Try going to recovery group meetings, to see what they're like and to get some ideas about managing life better.

to find a licensed counselor who will assist you in your efforts to drink less and decrease the problems alcohol is causing in your life. (See pages 268–72 for more guidelines on how to find a therapist.) Don't be put off if you encounter people who tell you that you're in denial and can choose abstinence only. *Just keep trying*.

Replacing the Pleasure

After taking stock of their drinking and finally dec‍
indeed brought more pain than enjoyment to their liv‍

ters did not downplay the pleasures they had experienced in the bottle. "Let's not pretend drinking isn't really nice," Phil Q. reminded me. "One can never forget going for the click, that wonderful moment when the lights go down and everything seems under control . . . that feeling of absolute serenity that only good, experienced drinkers can achieve." But for him "the click" started to come back early in his sobriety, from watching his little girls swing high on a swing set or reading them a story that none of them wanted to end. After many years of alcohol-related insomnia, Phil can now say, "Sometimes the click comes when I put my head on the pillow and find sleep waiting for me. This new click is almost the same as before, but in some ways it's even better."

5

It's Not Necessarily One Day at a Time

How the Masters Made a Commitment to Sobriety

I'd always heard that if someone wants to quit drinking, the best way to do it is one day at a time. After all, how can anyone who lives for his next drink possibly imagine swearing off alcohol forever? Much to my surprise, a profound pattern that runs counter to the day-at-a-time philosophy emerged from the masters' responses to my questions about how they resolved their drinking problems and how they stay sober. Here's what they told me, time and again:

> "I made a strong decision to quit for good."
> "I accepted that I could not drink moderately."
> "I told myself that I would not drink again."
> "I said, 'That's it; I quit.'"
> "My basic tenet was 'Don't drink.'"
> "I accepted that I couldn't handle alcohol."
> "I put the cork in the bottle."

AA member Chad V. (seventeen years) said it best. At the end of the questionnaire he returned to me, he attached a note saying, "We try to make this more complicated than it really is: *Don't drink*. I can do almost anything in my life except drink." From there he went on to explain how great his life is now that he has accepted that he will never drink again.

That's when it hit me: these masters were telling me that they have truly accepted the fact that drinking is no longer an option. It's over. As Elise C. puts it, "There's a point at which you close the door and realize you can't reopen it." In essence, after concluding that the benefits of drinking were not worth the price they were paying, many masters made a commitment *never* to drink again. While AA talks about doing this a day at a time, numerous people told me that in order to become sober for good, they needed to make a *long-term* commitment to changing their relationship with alcohol.

Richard D.'s Story

As Richard D. completed the drinking history questionnaire I sent him, he probably wasn't aware that he commented about his commitment to give up alcohol forever no fewer than *nine times*. For eight long years before he finally made this commitment, he knew he had a serious drinking problem. During this time he often asked himself, "What's wrong with me? Why can't I drink two beers and go home?"

Now that he has been sober for more than seven years, Richard can say, at the age of forty-seven, "I am closer to the man that I want to be. Each month that goes by, I think less and less of my drinking life and more and more about how natural and wonderful my life is without alcohol. I have made a conscious choice that I will remain alcohol-free for the rest of my life. Alcohol and drugs make no sense to me. I am aware of the allure, but nothing can touch or compare to living a sober life!"

Like so many masters, Richard says, "Drinking started as adolescent experimentation, then progressed to acceptable social inebriation, then to unacceptable social inebriation." His drinking lessened while he was finishing his college degree, but escalated again when he got married and his wife became pregnant. "On the nights I was at home, I might have just two or three beers. But often I'd go out drinking to escape everything, and then it was always six to ten beers." After his daughter was born, he says, "My wife got into healthy eating and raising our daughter properly, and I got into spending after-hours time and a lot of money in bars. She had her rules in her house, and I had mine out of the house — in the bar. We were always mad at each other." This conflict between lifestyles continued for years, with regular confrontations about his drinking.

After several moves, a lot of marital problems, the loss of his job, and some very rough financial times, Richard started his own landscaping business and began serious physical training, working up to running four miles at a time and bicycling twenty-five miles. Yet his drinking continued, despite his wife's constant complaints. When she finally hurled the challenge that he wasn't capable of stopping, he quit for a year, to prove her wrong. "But the relationship got no better," he explained. "I saw no point and started drinking again, typically five or six beers on weeknights and two cases [forty-eight cans or bottles] over the weekend."

Finally, when his wife left him for a "vacation" but didn't return for more than three months, Richard was shaken up enough to start going to a mental health counselor and attending "nonstop" AA meetings. He also got an AA sponsor. But soon, he says, "I grew tired of listening to other people's stories, how their lives were shot, and how they would always be alcoholics." He adds, "I was into taking responsibility and getting on with my life."

For the next year or so, the marital conflict continued, and Richard went back and forth between drinking and not drinking. "I could go days, weeks, even months without drinking, but then I'd start again." With the end of the marriage in sight, his wife asked him to move out, and his drinking picked up again. They eventually got divorced, and Richard married Lucy, a woman he met one night when they were both drunk. He says of this new relationship, "We became the best drinking buddies and would go out to bars every night, all weekend. We egged each other on."

Despite their good times and the love they felt for each other, Richard and Lucy fought a lot when they were drinking. While under the influence, Richard fell prey to "beastly anger." His relationship with alcohol came to an end when, after three days and evenings of drinking, he became physically violent with Lucy during a fight, pushing her to the floor with enough force to bruise her face. Nothing like this had ever happened before. Lucy had him arrested. He describes his ordeal — and his farewell to drinking — as follows: "That night, November 29, 1992, my life totally changed. I have never taken a drink since. I sat in jail for eleven days before I could bail out. Within two weeks, I was at Rational Recovery [RR] in California. Twenty-eight days there gave me the information and the tools to live my life alcohol-free."

Richard had read about RR months earlier in a *USA Today* article. "No matter how much I drank, I always knew that one day I was going to quit. I just didn't know when. At the time I read the article about RR, I stated to myself that when I decided to stop drinking, I would contact them." When he got out of jail, he asked everyone he could think of how he could find out more about RR, but even counselors couldn't help him. Finally Richard found someone who had a copy of *The Small Book,* by Jack Trimpey (at the time, the organization's guidebook), which had RR's phone number listed in the back. He contacted the organization and left home to take part in a twenty-eight-day residential program (which no longer exists as part of RR).

During his stay, he got confirmation of what he had known all along: "That it was up to me to make a commitment. It helped me see that the consequences of my drinking were not worth it. I also saw that alcohol had no natural part in my life and that it kept me from doing so many other things that I wanted to do." In short, RR helped him to see that "not drinking made more sense than drinking." At that point, he declares, "I made a commitment to myself that I would never drink alcohol for the rest of my life. And I will not!"

Richard never attended another recovery group meeting. He periodically goes to self-improvement seminars, and he stresses that a big factor in his recovery was learning to manage anger and conflicts and how to communicate better.

His wife, Lucy, still drinks — sometimes too much, but usually just a couple of drinks at a sitting. Richard is adamant that her drinking does not tempt him. "I really can't describe how natural not using alcohol is to me now," he asserts. "I could care less if others around me are drinking. They have made their choice and I have made mine. It is, as Sherlock Holmes would say, 'Elementary, my dear.' I choose not to drink!"

The Abstinence Pledge

Richard D. is just one of many masters who worked his way through periods of sobriety, relapse, and attempts at cutting back, only to wind up taking a pledge of abstinence. In fact, comments about making a commitment to a life without alcohol were among the five most frequent responses to my two main questions about how the masters resolved their drinking problems and how they stay motivated. For some, realization of the need for such a commitment was the turning point in recovery; for others, the realization evolved as they were finding their personal route to recovery — be it quitting on their own, finding a recovery group that was right for them, or going through counseling.

Indeed, the vow of abstinence cut across recovery methods:

◆ "I made a million vows to *control* drinking; I made only one vow to quit. There was no 'approach' per se. Not drinking, for me, consists of just that: not drinking, not under any circumstances, not playing games or making deals with myself."
— Becky E. (ten and a half years, quit on her own)

◆ "The underlying cause for my past relapses was that I had not fully committed to being a sober individual. Sobriety becomes part of who you are, and to drink would be a violation of yourself — that's when you don't drink anymore." — Sarah N. (seven years; a former moderator for Women for Sobriety)

◆ "I have made a personal commitment to lifelong abstinence." — Billy R. (five years, recovered using RR principles)

◆ "I met a counselor who gave me some literature. I went to my car and read the material. There was one sentence that said something like this: 'There is only one way out of the problem and that is to quit now and forever.' This sank in immediately and I knew instantly I was done drinking." — Pete S. (nine years, quit after one session with a chemical dependency counselor)

◆ "My turning point was when I recognized that I was unsuccessful at cutting back for any length of time. When I was finally successful, I recognized that temporary abstinence would not allow me to resume drinking at a moderate level." — Duane L. (five years, involved in SMART Recovery)

◆ "I made a promise to myself before I became pregnant that I would give up drinking and never drink again so I would always be there for my child." — Sara F. (ten years, quit on her own)

◆ "I was in and out of AA for almost ten years. My turning point came after my retirement party, where I had had three beers, spoke a few words, slurred my words, and embarrassed myself. Driving home, I heard a voice speak to me, saying, 'Armas, who are you kidding? You can't drink.'" Armas wept when he told me, "At that moment, I knew I'd never have another drink." — Armas J. (twenty-one years, quit with the support of AA and a spiritual group)

I believe this commitment to abstinence represents a paradigm shift in thinking. Simply stated, a paradigm is a key premise from which you operate. A paradigm shift is a wholesale change in this premise — a totally new orientation to how you approach something. The paradigm shift for these masters occurred when they stopped seeing themselves as people who might eventually be able to control their use of alcohol, if only they tried a little harder, and began to see themselves as people who no longer drank. They started to regard themselves as nondrinkers, making an inner (and sometimes outward) commitment never to drink again and to change their lives accordingly.

Research conducted by Sharon Hall, Ph.D., and colleagues at the University of California in San Francisco supports the significance of committing to not drinking. In studies done with problem drinkers as well as with smokers and drug abusers, these researchers found that people from abstinence-based programs who made a commitment to total abstinence were more likely to remain abstinent over the course of the next six months than those who made less serious or vague commitments.

These abstinence pledges were made by masters who were seriously dependent on alcohol — drinking the equivalent of nearly a fifth or more of hard liquor a day — as well as by people who at their worst drank no more than five or six drinks a night. The commitment never to drink again was voiced by people who consider themselves "alcoholics" as well as those who do not. Comments about the importance of committing to abstinence forever did come more frequently from those who resolved their drinking problems in nontraditional ways. However, one in five traditional masters stressed this as well. It's also of interest that those who maintain sobriety on their own were much more likely to stress their commitment to long-term sobriety than those who have or had formal support in recovery.

Most surprising, I heard about this commitment from people who are *not* totally abstinent. Ned G., for instance, allows himself to drink moderately when he travels to foreign countries.

When he is in the United States, however, he is committed to strict abstinence. (He was completely abstinent for the first nine of his fifteen years of sobriety; since January 1, 1983, he has never taken a drink in the United States.) Then there's Oliver S., whose alcohol problem has been resolved for sixteen years and who "occasionally sips microbrews for taste comparison." Over and over, he shares his commitment not to return to abusive drinking. He says, "I simply stopped. Drinking was no longer an option. I made up my mind that I had no choice — I could not drink ever again."

The clinical psychologist Marc Kern, Ph.D., director of Addiction Alternatives, a private practice in Los Angeles, says of his experience working with many problem drinkers, "I've found that people who are successful with moderate drinking after having had serious problems with alcohol make a profound commitment to lifelong vigilance around alcohol." A recent study of people who resolved serious alcohol problems, reported in the journal *Psychology of Addictive Behaviors,* suggests that those who elect abstinence tend to make a commitment abruptly, whereas those who become moderate drinkers resolve to change their relationship with alcohol more gradually.

The point is that whether you ultimately elect abstinence — as the vast majority of the masters did — or you choose moderate or occasional drinking, commitment is involved. It's a commitment to living your life without having alcohol rule it.

Forever or a Day at a Time?

What about the philosophy of taking sobriety in short segments? Isn't it just too difficult to accept *never* having another drink? Amy P. says, "I'm an exception to the rule in that I don't stay sober one day at a time. I gave up alcohol forever. That is my commitment, that is my crusade, and even though AA does not think my attitude works, it works for me."

AA's book *Living Sober* does indeed say, "Although we realize that alcoholism is a permanent, irreversible condition, our experience has taught us to make no long-term promises about staying sober. We have found it more realistic — and more successful — to say, I am not taking a drink *just for today.*"

Given this emphasis and the fact that ninety-seven of the masters recovered by going to AA, I was surprised that so few of them — eleven in the entire group — said anything about the importance of taking sobriety a day at a time. Perhaps the philosophy of facing sobriety moment by moment is not as important after you have been sober for a long time, as most masters have been.

However, some masters went out of their way to stress that from the start, the day-at-a-time philosophy wasn't an option. Herb N., profiled in chapter 2, says, "I had to think in terms of never instead of one day at a time when it came to the ultimate unconscious question every alcoholic in the world has to ask him- or herself: 'How long will I quit for?' The cravings will stay alive as long as that unconscious question has not been resolved."

Similarly, Ward R., who has used a potpourri of methods to stay sober, including AA and SOS, states, "The toughest part of life in early sobriety was accepting the fact that my drinking days were over. In my opinion, the attempts of some programs such as AA to evade this by substituting a don't-drink-for-today-only approach is not the way to go. My goal became total abstinence for the rest of my life."

Former AA member Jackie D., profiled in chapter 4, offers a broader perspective on the day-at-a-time approach: "At AA they say, 'Seek progress, not perfection.' That's the crux of the one-day-at-a-time thing — that you're getting somewhere each day, not just with your drinking but with other aspects of your life."

It's up to the individual to decide whether it's easier to face this reality one day at a time — at least in the beginning of sobriety — or to bite the bullet and, like Richard, commit to not drinking over the long haul.

Making Sobriety a Priority

Part of the "abstinence pledge" for some masters is a commitment to making sobriety a priority. (Although this is a tenet of the recovery group SOS, masters who recovered by other means talked about it as well.) Randall N., who quit drinking on his own with the help of *The Small Book,* nicely captures the way he made sobriety a priority with his description of how he resolved his alcohol problem: "I accepted the fact that alcohol was my *primary* problem and my other problems would remain or get worse with continued drinking. I also accepted the idea that sobriety had to be the most important thing in my life — that physical and mental pain, even death itself, would be better for me than continued drinking. I recognized and accepted the fact that I had to abstain from alcohol in spite of myself. That is, not taking a drink even though my whole body, mind, and spirit were aching for one." Now, Randall indicates, he doesn't miss alcohol at all and almost never feels an urge to drink.

His advice for people struggling with an alcohol problem? "Do whatever it takes, if it's not illegal or immoral — do anything, but don't drink." Similarly, the WFS moderator Jessica C. advises, "Put sobriety first — change anything in your life that endangers it: relationships, jobs, hobbies, places, habits." With time, consciously making sobriety a priority may be unnecessary, as is the case with Richard D., who declares, "I have not subscribed to the 'sobriety priority' for years. After a couple of years, I found that people, relationships, jobs, hobbies, places, and habits changed, and my life automatically moved on without much effort."

Taking Responsibility:
The Paradox of Powerlessness

Isn't accepting the fact that you can never drink again tantamount to admitting that you're powerless over alcohol? One could argue that this supports AA's first step, which reads, "We admitted we were powerless over alcohol — that our lives had become unmanageable." Surprisingly, however, nowhere in the masters' ten most frequent responses to key questions about recovery did the subject of powerlessness appear — even though ninety-seven of them had had traditional twelve-step recoveries. On the contrary, like Richard D., a number of masters stressed the importance of *taking responsibility* for their drinking problem — accepting that it was up to them and in their power.

◆ Jackie D., who recovered with AA, says, "I never bought into the AA powerless thing. I don't think I'm powerless. I had too many years of not taking charge of my life, and I don't want to lose that now. Becoming sober felt like taking control — the more I saw the results of staying committed to sobriety, there was a power in it. As long as I stayed sober, I was in control of my behavior, my responses to people and things, and able to make choices rather than have circumstances make the choices."

◆ Rick N., who went to AA for several years before finding that cognitive-behavioral approaches (see page 103) were far more helpful for him, says, "I think I always knew that one day I would quit drinking and that I had the natural ability to do so when ready. It was this core value, this powerful belief in choice and in self-determination, that made quitting possible."

◆ Sarah N., who recovered with the help of Women for Sobriety, says, "I had found the twelve-step recovery model to be incomprehensibly passive. I'm too much of a do-it-yourselfer for that kind of thinking to be helpful. The WFS focus on individual responsibility and encouragement to pursue anything that worked *for me* outside its program made *me* responsible for my recovery."

There is, however, a way to reconcile AA teachings with a take-charge, take-responsibility view. Acknowledging lack of power over drinking can empower some people to move on with their lives. In *Research on Alcoholics Anonymous,* Stephanie Brown, Ph.D., of the Addictions Institute in Menlo Park, California, writes, "Recovering alcoholics acknowledge that they have no power over alcohol and are, in turn, empowered by this truth and their acceptance of it . . . It is precisely the deep acceptance of loss of control — surrender — that forms the foundation for empowerment and deep internal change of individuals in recovery."

Several masters, including some who are not AA members, confirmed that accepting their powerlessness over alcohol in some way actually helped them take charge. For instance, after making many attempts to control her drinking and after trying AA, SOS, and RR and finding all of them unsatisfactory, Jackie A. got sober on her own when she "accepted that I couldn't handle alcohol but that I had to handle quitting *by myself.* I shifted my thinking from 'I can control it *myself*' to 'I can decide to stop *myself.*' I think I made an unconscious commitment of some kind."

Note that Jackie A. talks not only about commitment but also about *acceptance* — a concept some might view as more helpful than the notion of powerlessness. Acceptance has to do with admitting to yourself that alcohol is a problem for you, acknowledging that you need to commit to abstinence (or to modifying your drinking substantially), and recognizing that sometimes "that's just the way life is." From there, you can take charge and do whatever you need to do to get on with your life in a healthy and positive way.

Believing in Yourself

Part of making a commitment to sobriety is believing in yourself. As some masters suggest, *if you think you can get sober and stay sober, you will.* Phil Q. notes, "Most of us have tremendous power and resources within ourselves if we dig hard enough. For me, it was a matter of digging." Neil H. advises, "Put any idea that you can't quit out of your mind. You acquire great strength with each passing day. You can, if you are determined." As Violet F. puts it, "Success leads to more success."

Recognizing your past accomplishments and success at overcoming other obstacles can build confidence in your ability to handle new challenges and may give you some clues to strategies that would be useful when you decide to deal with your drinking. Take it from some of the masters who have tackled multiple challenges in life:

◆ Liz B., who beat a two-pack-a-day cigarette habit a number of years before she quit drinking, says that becoming a nonsmoker gave her the confidence to give up alcohol and eventually to lose thirty pounds. "I felt that if I could do one thing, I could do almost anything else."

◆ Heather F. says, "Because I had overcome an obsession with food and binge eating, I knew deep inside that someday I would be able to lick my drinking problem."

Another strategy for enhancing belief that you can take hold of an alcohol problem is to follow the example of successful role models. As master Joey S. encourages, "If I can do it, you can do it too." Simon T. suggests that one person is all it takes: "Talk to someone who has quit — see what their life is like and how they did it." Leo Hennigan, M.D., says that what helped him make his commitment was "finally realizing that the serene, happy people at AA were those who had given up alcohol completely. The role model is what made the difference, the recovered alcoholic." Rafael P. essentially discovered the same thing. Although he didn't use AA's philosophy, he went to AA meetings in early sobriety for support, met some people who were an inspiration, and thought, "If they can do it, so can I."

Making an Outward Commitment

A number of masters told me that it helped them to make an announcement or commitment *to others* that they were quitting drinking for good.

◆ Jackie D. explains, "At first I committed outwardly to my boyfriend and to my therapist. Then, a few weeks later, I began to tell family and friends."

◆ Clinton F. waited for a while after quitting (on his own) before telling others. "After I felt I had it under control, I let all my friends and associates know that I quit."

◆ Amy P. stresses, "I have never kept my alcoholism a secret from anyone. Everyone at work knew where and when I was going for treatment. They all were incredibly supportive. It is a fact of my existence, and as long as I can talk about it and get support, I think my chances of going back to drinking are less."

Experts affirm that the more you verbalize your plan to others, the more your commitment will be strengthened. This does not mean that you have to tell the world of your decision to do something about your drinking. Certainly you can use a recovery group to make an outward commitment, like Thomas V., who, six years into sobriety, still regularly attends both AA and SOS meetings. He maintains, "It's useful for me to be reminded that I've made a commitment to abstinence and to be around people who care whether I honor that commitment."

More privately, you can make an outward pledge to one or two close persons — a spouse, your parents, a supportive boss, your minister, a therapist. Richard D. says, "I told my wife, daughter, parents, and one friend. That was it. I saw or felt no need to shout out to the world 'I'm sober for life!'"

The Masters and Smoking

Commitment to one positive lifestyle change seems to lead to another, as suggested by the seventeen masters who quit smoking before they got sober and the sixty-one who indicated that they gave up cigarettes after they gave up alcohol. Sixteen others quit smoking at an unspecified time, while nine licked both bad habits at once. *That adds up to 103 smoke-free former drinkers.* (Another seven indicated that they want or are trying to quit.)

An estimated 70 percent or more of alcohol-dependent people smoke, and smoking appears to kill more people with serious drinking problems than alcohol itself. The two together are deadlier than either one alone.

Here are the experiences of some masters who gave up cigarettes after they became sober:

◆ Clinton F., who used to consume up to seventeen drinks and four or more packs of cigarettes every day, said he quit drinking first because drinking scared him the most. "One year later I quit smoking, at first using nicotine gum, then just going cold turkey." After he quit smoking, he proceeded to lose 180 pounds.

◆ Heath M. says, "Abandoning cigarettes became a snap thanks to attending a smoking cessation program about four years into sobriety."

◆ Lilith V. says, "When I finally quit smoking, it was the hardest thing I'd ever done — difficult enough that I don't think I'll ever risk going through it again. The bottom line was that I had kicked booze and drugs and bad men; I wasn't going to let another addiction kick my butt!"

Some masters used the same strategies to quit drinking and to quit smoking. For example, Rafael P. used strategies of "stubbornly denying the urge" and "quitting-for-life thinking" to give up cigarettes a decade after he stopped drinking. Eighteen months after George M. sobered up, he used AA principles to beat a three-pack-a day habit. He notes, "I realized it was dumb to quit drinking but still kill myself with smoking." Jackie D. quit smoking after about seven years of sobriety. She explains, "I used the same strategies as

The Masters and Smoking, continued

I did for quitting drinking, particularly the one-day — or, in my case, one-hour or one-minute — at-a-time idea. Eventually I began to be aware that, as with alcohol, ridding myself of the cigarette addiction had a freeing effect — I didn't have to think about getting cigarettes, where I could or couldn't smoke. And I started to exercise, which made me aware of how much healthier my lungs were."

John Hughes, M.D., an expert on smoking and drinking affiliated with the University of Vermont, warns that a small percentage of resolved problem drinkers will experience a craving for alcohol when they quit smoking. "If this happens, then these people need to be closely monitored by a therapist when they try to stop smoking," he says. "Or they might want to increase attendance at a recovery group or counseling or temporarily take a medication that helps keep them from drinking, such as Antabuse or ReVia." (See pages 92–94 for more on such medications.)

As is the case with drinking, when you're ready to quit smoking, be persistent, because it may take a number of tries. A recent national poll conducted by the Hazelden Foundation suggested that on average, former smokers try to quit about eleven times over the course of more than eighteen years before they give up cigarettes for good.

Grieving Over the Loss of Alcohol

Compared with most masters, Richard D. had it easy when he first made his commitment to lifelong abstinence. He states, "Although for the first two weeks I was really wondering if my old twenty-five-year habit of drinking would be stronger than my desire to be a sober human, it turned out that I had no problems. I had already done the tough part." Nevertheless, as some masters have stated, parting with alcohol can be very painful, and it's perfectly fine to allow yourself to grieve over your loss.

Jackie D. recalls, "The last night that I drank, I bought a nice bottle of wine, and I wept. Not drinking completely scared me. I believed life wouldn't be worth living without it. I couldn't imagine what I'd look like not drinking. I thought I would never again be happy, never sleep again, my boyfriend wouldn't like me anymore. Alcohol was who I was." Similarly, Frank L. remembers, "In the beginning, I grieved, I cried, I felt guilty. I also wondered if I would be less of a person without alcohol, if I would lose some of my drive, my ambition — and what would replace it."

Giving It Time

The good news is that although many of the masters found things difficult when they first committed to sobriety, not drinking has gotten much easier with time. Consider their responses to the following questions:

On a scale of 1–5, to what extent do you still battle with the urge to drink?

1	2	3	4	5
Frequently feel an urge				Never feel an urge

Ninety percent of the masters responded with a "4" or above.

On a scale of 1–5, to what extent do you miss drinking?

1	2	3	4	5
Miss it a great deal				Don't miss it at all

Eighty-six percent of the masters responded with a "4" or above.

On a scale of 1–5, to what extent has it gotten easier *with time* to abstain?

1	2	3	4	5
It's no easier			It's so much easier, it's almost no effort	

Ninety-one percent of the masters responded with a "4" or above. (172 people gave a "5.")

Can Drugs Help with the Commitment to Sobriety?

A number of prescription drugs now on the market, or soon to be on the market, can indeed make a commitment to sobriety easier. Because the masters quit drinking years ago, however, they had access to just one of them: disulfiram. While many of them tried this drug, only four credited it as a key factor in recovery.

Three primary drugs (listed by generic name and brand name) are used to treat alcohol problems:

Disulfiram (Antabuse). Available by prescription in the United States for about fifty years, disulfiram is probably the most familiar drug used for alcohol problems. It acts as a deterrent to drinking because it produces unpleasant symptoms such as nausea, vomiting, headaches, flushing, and palpitations if you drink alcohol while taking it. Although it does not appear to increase the proportion of people who maintain total abstinence, there is evidence that when disulfiram is combined with psychological counseling, it may lower the amount of alcohol consumed and decrease the frequency of drinking in recovery. Because of the unpleasant consequences, however, people are not always compliant about taking this drug when it is prescribed. In short, there does not appear to be enough evidence of its success for disulfiram to be routinely prescribed for alcohol-dependent people, but it might be helpful for someone who wants to increase motivation to remain abstinent. Disulfiram may also help someone get through a particularly tough time, such as a business trip involving a lot of exposure to alcohol. Because it has some potentially serious side effects, such as liver problems, people on the drug should be carefully monitored by a physician. And when you are taking disulfiram, it's important to avoid all sources of alcohol, including foods, mouthwashes, and over-the-counter medications that have alcohol as an ingredient.

Naltrexone (ReVia). Approved by the U.S. Food and Drug Administration in the mid-1990s, naltrexone is relatively new to the scene of alcohol treatment. This drug appears to block the urge to drink and to reduce the

pleasurable effects of drinking, inhibiting the experience of the i
indicate that naltrexone may help promote abstinence as well as play
in preventing slips from becoming full-blown relapses. Because it reduces
the severity and frequency of drinking episodes, it may be suitable for people
who are trying to reduce their drinking gradually or who are attempting
moderate drinking. Its side effects may include nausea and headaches. Since
naltrexone can also pose some risk of liver damage when given in high
doses, it should be used with caution or not at all by people who have liver
problems. (Nalmefene, which is similar to naltrexone but may be more powerful, is another drug under study for Food and Drug Administration approval.) There is a Web site devoted to naltrexone treatment for alcohol
abuse: www.recovery2000.com.

Acamprosate (Campral). At this writing, acamprosate has yet to be
approved for use in the United States, but the drug has gained attention as a
successful treatment for alcohol problems in Europe. The way in which it
works is not well understood, but it may decrease the intensity of craving for
alcohol after you give it up. Research suggests that acamprosate can be very
effective in reducing the frequency of drinking and also may enhance abstinence. Several studies have indicated that alcohol-dependent people who
receive acamprosate along with counseling can go longer without taking a
drink, have more abstinent days, and have lower dropout rates than people
given a placebo. A recent review of medications for treating alcohol problems in *Alcohol Research & Health* concluded that acamprosate's potential
appears to be the most widely established of those studied. Possible side effects include diarrhea and headaches.

The bottom line is that all three of these drugs can make it easier to
maintain a commitment to sobriety, but they don't usually work all by themselves. As an expert and researcher on medications for alcohol problems
from the Medical University of South Carolina, Raymond Anton, M.D., affirms, "There is no magic bullet, but the anti-alcohol drugs can help if you
combine them with other approaches, such as group support and counseling.
People who are able to maintain longer periods of abstinence have a better
chance of staying away from alcohol long-term — these medications can

Can Drugs Help?, continued

help you accomplish that." According to Dr. Anton, "Recent data suggest that some alcoholics may benefit from longer-term use of these medications to assist in the maintenance of sobriety and/or to inhibit slips from turning into relapses."

Basically, these drugs can buy you some time to get accustomed to living sober. However, physicians who don't specialize in treating alcohol problems may not be familiar with them, particularly newer drugs like naltrexone. Thus, you may want to ask your physician about these drugs, and to take some information along. For more about these medications, visit the Web site of the National Institute on Alcohol Abuse and Alcoholism (NIAAA); see page 291.

Finally, antidepressants or anti-anxiety medications are sometimes prescribed for recovering problem drinkers. Research findings are somewhat mixed as to the effectiveness of these drugs in alcohol recovery, but they appear to be somewhat helpful for people who are also experiencing psychological difficulties such as depression or certain anxiety conditions (generalized anxiety disorder, social phobia, or post-traumatic stress disorder). When taking antidepressants or anti-anxiety medications, always check with a physician before consuming alcoholic beverages.

Here's how some masters describe the way sobriety became easier — and was worth it — as time passed:

◆ "It was a daunting, overwhelming circumstance to have to start life all over at age thirty-one. After a while it became an adventure, and that helped. Everything I have in life now is directly as a result of sobriety." — Don D. (eighteen years)

◆ "At first I found it difficult to go anyplace at which alcohol might be available. I was almost afraid to go into a restaurant that served drinks. But I kept focusing on my goal of 'total abstinence for life,' and with time it became easier. Today I travel frequently with two companions who are heavy drinkers, but that doesn't bother me a bit. I have no compulsion. There isn't a sonofabitch big enough to make me drink again." — Ward R. (twenty-two years)

◆ "At first it was hard to go and do things I had done before without having a drink. I constantly felt weird and out of place. In a year or so, I was not feeling bad. I had done almost everything once sober instead of with a drink. I had survived and lived." — Helen H. (eighteen years)

◆ "I kept believing that, like an LSD trip, the worst feelings and thoughts would go away or get better. And as the emotional ups and downs of the first year started to even out, I began feeling better both physically and mentally. I had proof that my life was better." — Charles S. (fourteen years)

For many of the masters, the promise to maintain sobriety marked the beginning of a new way of life. Richard D. says, "I miss nothing! Ever since I made my commitment to myself, the rest has been very enjoyable."

6

Be Your Own Expert

How Seven Different Masters Found Their Way with Seven Different Approaches

When I asked the masters how they found the right approach for them, quite a few indicated that it was a matter of researching and exploring the options, then trying different approaches until they found one (or more) that fit. Through a trial-and-error process, many wound up matching themselves to a program or approach that suited them as individuals. Here's what a few had to say about how they found *their* right approach:

◆ "I found the approach that was right for me by studying, researching, asking questions, and going to many alternative support groups. I proactively sought out a philosophy that suited my approach to life." — Jac C. (eight years, sober with the help of SOS)

◆ "It was trial and error. For me there weren't one or two 'just right' approaches." — Phoebe M. (eighteen years, quit with the help of AA but stopped going after the first year or so). Besides going to AA, she says, "I did lots of reading, talked with my minister, attended conferences relating to chemical dependency, went to therapy, and talked to different professionals and to those with similar problems. I have borrowed from many sources of wisdom."

◆ "I tried AA a couple of times, but the focus on powerlessness was not right for me. I saw a skilled acupuncturist who taught me to change my focus, behavior, and thought patterns. I read books about how other people recovered and lived healthy lives. And I had the support and example of my husband and a new friend who had been sober for years." — Tammie A. (seven years, eclectic recovery)

◆ "Three years before I quit drinking, I called around for a non–twelve-step approach until someone told me about SOS and Rational Recovery. I tried them both. SOS was all right, but RR ideas helped me more." — Regina S. (six years, now a SMART Recovery coordinator)

Wouldn't it be great if you didn't have to go through what so many masters went through to find *your* way to get sober — if you could sit down with an experienced counselor, someone who was unbiased and familiar with all the options, who would ask you a bunch of questions about your background, and who would then match you up with a recovery approach that is ideal for you? It turns out that not long ago, a huge, very expensive study called Project MATCH was funded by the National Institute on Alcohol Abuse and Alcoholism to assess whether there's a reliable way to predict whether people with certain characteristics will respond better to one form of treatment than another. The results suggested that the three different treatment approaches tested (one was a twelve-step–based approach; the other two were promising psychological strategies) were equally effective and therefore interchangeable, regardless of differences between the individual participants. Some experts have criticized the study's design, however, saying that it wasn't a true test of matching individuals to programs that might suit them.

The bottom line, according to Dr. Alan Marlatt, is that "there are no clear guidelines for matching people to recovery approaches." He concludes, "Therefore, it's up to the consumer, and consumers need informed choice about what the options are." It all comes back to this: like the masters, you have to shop around to find the method of resolving your drinking problem that's right for you.

This chapter tells the stories of seven people and the approaches that led them to sobriety, from brief intervention and counseling to recovery programs and formal treatment. The appendix provides information about each program, including how to obtain its literature and find its Web site — both of which can be useful avenues for someone who wants to benefit from a certain approach but who cannot or does not want to take part in meetings.

Brief Intervention
How Lester Y. found his way

For Lester Y., who once drank a case of beer a day plus whiskey and Scotch, the turning point came when he went into the hospital for minor surgery and discovered that he had the beginnings of serious alcohol-related liver problems. "The doctor pulled no punches," Lester remembers. "He was astounded at the quantity I drank and told me, 'The way I see it is this: stop drinking now and live a relatively normal life, or continue and be dead in less than ten years.' I had to take a long, hard look at myself. Finally, admitting that I was an alcoholic, I stopped drinking in October of 1981. I truly believe that had it not been for the doctor's blunt assessment and my wife's love and support, I would not be the person I am today." Lester has maintained sobriety on his own.

Is brief intervention for you?

Like Lester, some masters were able to beat their drinking problems after very brief contact with a professional who pointed them in the right direction. A number of studies have found that this kind of short-term approach, known as "brief intervention," is as effective for some people as more intensive types of treatment.

It is usually initiated by a physician or other health professional who is not an addiction specialist. Typically this person offers a clear message to a problem drinker about how and why it would be wise to lower alcohol consumption. The advice is presented in the context of concerns related to the individual's health, social, or family problems. A suggestion is usually given about cutting back or abstaining, at least for a while, to see if the problems subside. The final goal can be moderate drinking or abstinence. The patient might be given educational material about alcohol problems and self-help. Follow-up might include phone calls and another office visit or two to see how things are going. If this doesn't work, the adviser usually recommends more intensive types of treatment. (Despite Lester's experience, this type of intervention is generally most effective if it is done with empathy and optimism rather than by confrontation.)

Brief intervention is thought to work best for people whose alcohol problems are not particularly severe and who have not received previous treatment. However, as is obvious from Lester's story, this approach sometimes benefits people with more serious problems.

Unfortunately, physicians are not typically trained in brief intervention strategies. Moreover, health-care providers don't always pick up on alcohol problems in high-functioning problem drinkers — the very people who are apt to benefit from brief intervention. For instance, Heather F. says that she went through an entire pregnancy with a physician who pooh-poohed her concern when she tried to talk about her drinking. Before that, she had spent several years in therapy with a psychologist who minimized the severity of her drinking problem. Years later, she said of her routine visits with her internist, "I'd go in for a physical, thin as a rail, and they'd be puzzled that my blood pressure was high — yet they *never* asked me about my drinking habits. I wonder if my drinking problem would not have gotten so bad if someone had addressed it head-on earlier."

Contrary to the popular notion that long-term treatment of alcohol problems is best and that lifelong attendance at recovery meetings is needed to stay sober, many people do not need these approaches, as suggested by a growing body of evidence. Moreover, expensive treatment is not necessarily more effective than less expensive treatment.

Individual Counseling
How Marjorie A. found her way

"I began drinking when I was sixteen and quit when I was twenty-five," Marjorie A. told me. "At that time, I was drinking to get drunk daily — a bottle or two of wine, sometimes with five to six beers or shots of vodka or cognac. I was aware that I was abusing alcohol for about five years before I quit, but I had surrounded myself with friends who supported my addiction. Nothing was working; my life was a mess, I felt out of control, and I was constantly depressed. The turning point came when I had a particularly embarrassing sexual incident with my boss — I had hit a crisis point where I had to try something to make my life better."

This experience led Marjorie to a counselor for women who had posted a notice on a bulletin board. Up front, the therapist told Marjorie about the various tools she would give her: keeping a journal, helping her take responsibility for her choices, focusing on the positive things that happened each day, and using affirmations that eventually would help her feel good about herself.

100

In their first session, the therapist (who happened to have experience with alcohol problems) also suggested that Marjorie consider thinking about the role that alcohol played in her life. They examined this over the course of the next several sessions. "We looked at the parts of my life that were out of control — like my relationships with men, work, friends, and my family — and identified some of the reasons things weren't working. We kept coming back to alcohol."

She goes on: "So we talked specifics, like quantity, regularity, triggers for drinking — all of which helped me to focus on the daily role alcohol played. I began to see how and why I used alcohol and the effects of this use." The therapist then suggested that Marjorie consider not drinking for a limited time — six weeks — just to see how that felt. "I was horrified and angry," she says. "I insisted that the problem was my parents' divorce, my mother's alcoholism, my dysfunctional childhood. But I decided to give it a try, thinking that not drinking for a while would be easy. However, my first sober day and night illuminated what I'd known all along: I was an alcoholic, from a family of alcoholics, and I could never drink again."

A recurrent theme in Marjorie's journal was that she was looking for peace. She and her therapist examined ways she could achieve it: stay sober, learn how to deal with her feelings, resolve outstanding issues with her family, examine her relationships with men, and explore the possibilities for more meaningful work. Since all of her friends were heavy drinkers and her leisure activities revolved around alcohol, Marjorie had to adopt a new lifestyle. For about ten months she remained in once-a-week therapy, which she paid for out of her own pocket, since her medical insurance did not cover the cost.

"I needed to learn simple things like what to say when I'm offered a drink, how to deal with people around me when they drink," she explains. To break out of the old lifestyle, Marjorie spent many solitary nights with her journal and good music. She changed her diet to a healthier one and began to cook and bake for herself. She had one close friend who decided to quit drinking at the same time, and they would get together and cook or watch movies or talk. Sometimes Marjorie went to movies alone or for long walks on the beach.

She reflects, "I literally stopped doing everything I used to do — going to clubs and bars and seeing the people I used to see. Almost immediately I began to feel centered and relaxed, and I liked that feeling. I did miss the high of drinking, but I tried not to focus on the negative stuff. I just kept listening to that inner voice that said I deserved better."

With the help of the therapist, after talking at length about what her dream job was and how she could find it, Marjorie quit her job as a waitress and eventually wound up in a professional career. Her relationships with men became healthier. She confronted family members about past hurts — after using her journal to practice by writing out her feelings, her expectations, and what she was going to say. When she reached the point where she and her therapist felt that she had completed all the work she needed to do to stay sober and live a productive life, she stopped going to counseling. She has been sober now for eleven years.

Cognitive-behavioral versus insight-oriented therapies

Having counseling with someone other than a chemical dependency (CD) counselor was one of the top three ways in which the masters resolved their drinking problems. (Having CD counseling wasn't far behind.) Most of the masters used counseling along with other approaches. But for some, like Marjorie, counseling was the primary route to recovery.

When most of us think of counseling, we tend to think of psychoanalysis, or what is sometimes called insight-oriented psychotherapy. The premise of this type of psychotherapy is that your symptoms (in this case alcohol abuse) stem from underlying, at least partly unconscious psychological conflicts that you need to uncover and resolve through interpretation and insight. But this "classic" kind of psychotherapy has not been found to be particularly beneficial all by itself for the resolution of drinking problems, in large part because it doesn't place primary emphasis on controlling alcohol use, as suggested in the textbook of the American Society of Addiction Medicine (ASAM), *Principles of Addiction Medicine*. Continued heavy drinking can undermine therapy. For example, Marjorie had been in psychotherapy two or three times before she went to counseling for alcohol problems. She says, "Because I was drinking, I wasn't very focused. Drinking would come up in counseling, but it wasn't the main focus of therapy, and I wasn't ready to quit."

As you'll see in chapter 10, a number of masters found it helpful to deal with issues from the past at some point during their recovery. But it's safe to say that most therapists and counselors who work effectively with people with alcohol problems first help them control alcohol use and focus on current life problems. Then, once some control has been exerted, it becomes easier to deal with other issues.

Marjorie's therapist used some techniques from cognitive-behavioral therapy, one of the more popular research-based forms of psychological counseling, which can be effective for people with alcohol problems. Cognitive-behavioral approaches regard problem drinking largely as the result of learned thinking and behavior patterns that can be altered. To "unlearn" a set of responses, such as relying on alcohol to cope with troubles or reduce anxiety, a problem drinker must identify the factors that precipitate drinking and break those connections by responding in new ways. Cognitive-behavioral counselors often help people deal with deficiencies in other areas of their lives by learning such things as how to form and maintain healthy relationships, be more assertive, refuse drinks, handle cravings for alcohol, manage stress, improve conversational skills, and handle criticism. Other parts of this here-and-now type of counseling might be acquiring new job skills, finding new leisure activities, and learning new ways to deal with negative thoughts, feelings, and emotions.

Should You Go the Recovery-Group Route?

Of the more than two thirds of the masters who took the recovery-group route, some used groups as their sole path to sobriety and others used them as follow-up and aftercare support when they completed formal alcohol treatment programs. A number of masters use (or used) combinations of recovery programs, and many found counseling to be helpful in conjunction with groups.

Obviously, the advantages of recovery groups include support, inspiration, and practical insights from others with similar experiences. As one woman put it, "There are some things that other people with alcohol problems just get that nonalcoholics don't. You have a sense that you are with people who have been there, just like you." With their peer pressure to stop drinking and stay sober, groups also foster accountability — it's incongruent for someone to keep showing up at a group, only to go home and open a six-pack of beer. (Although most recovery groups encourage abstinence, typically they allow people to attend while still drinking — as long as those people show up at meetings sober.)

Recovery groups also have a number of advantages over formal alcohol treatment or counseling: they cost little or nothing; they allow people to receive help without having their alcohol problem become part of their medical record; and people come and go as they please rather than being locked into a formal commitment.

One drawback is that people in recovery groups can be dogmatic, asserting that the group's way is "*the* way" or bashing other approaches. And while recovery groups stress anonymity and confidentiality concerning what goes on in meetings, there is always the risk that someone will not respect these parameters. Certainly in small communities in which most people know when and where meetings occur, total anonymity can be an illusion.

Is the counseling route for you?

Those who prefer an individualized approach, who like their privacy, and who are not necessarily "group people" tend to be best suited to psychological counseling as the primary route to recov-

Any recovery group is going to attract people at different stages of recovery, and the presence of down-and-out drinkers who are still trying to find their way out of their problem can be depressing for members who are further along in recovery. At some meetings, you may find that the only thing you have in common with the people there is your drinking problem, which can sometimes make you feel even more alone.

Anyone checking out recovery groups should be aware that even though there are separate groups for people with drug problems, such as Narcotics Anonymous (NA), drug abusers (and people with problems such as eating disorders) often show up at AA, WFS, SMART Recovery, and SOS meetings. Master Anne H. says, "When I first joined AA, there seemed to be more straight 'alkies' in the membership. Now there are a lot of people who were pretty hard-core drug users. Though I understand intellectually that alcohol is a drug too, my lifestyle was more that of an alcoholic than that of a drug user. A fine distinction, perhaps, but there's just a feeling of difference."

Finally, you should be aware that most recovery groups are not led by alcohol professionals. No one should put so much faith in the program that the need for professional help with issues like physical abuse and depression is ignored.

If you decide to try the recovery group route, shop around, trying out all the different programs to which you have access. Once you find a program you like — be it AA, SOS, WFS, SMART Recovery, or something else — visit more than one of its meetings. Even within the same program, individual groups tend to have different personalities. Finally, if you are not a group person but one of the program's approaches appeals to you, there's no reason you can't use its materials on your own. (See the appendix for more details.)

ery. The clinical psychologist Marc Kern has learned that high-functioning problem drinkers often find one-on-one counseling more appealing than group approaches. He also says that people tend to want private therapy when they have feelings of shame or concerns about anonymity.

One problem with this approach is that unless you have medical insurance with good coverage for mental health therapy, your insurance may not pay for extended counseling or for the particular counselor you want to see. You could wind up paying out of pocket, going to sessions less frequently, and/or following up with the support of a recovery group. (For more about how to find a therapist/counselor, see pages 268–72.)

Alcoholics Anonymous (AA)

How Heath F. found his way

"I've had a lifelong experience with alcohol," Heath F. told me, recalling a photo of himself as a baby in which both he and his father are holding bottles of beer. Heath vowed he wouldn't follow in his father's footsteps and develop a drinking problem. But by his thirties, he was drinking a case of beer a day — though "I was always crafty enough to keep myself well employed and functioning in society very nicely," he says (he even ran six marathons during his heavy drinking days). Eventually alcohol took its toll, both "emotionally and spiritually. For a long time, it worked every time; alcohol was the perfect escape. But then it stopped working."

Heath's resolve to quit drinking came at the age of thirty-six, when, he says, "I was sitting with a gun in my hands, ready to blow my brains out. I finally connected it to alcohol. I was faced with two options: to live or to die." Heath chose to go to AA. When he was twenty-one, he had been ordered to go to AA after being arrested for public intoxication. Fifteen years later, when he finally was ready, he says, "I knew what I had to do and where I had to go."

It wasn't easy in the beginning. The first year sober, Heath found he had to deal with a lot of the physical consequences of relinquishing alcohol, including insomnia and a period of sexual dysfunction. But AA gave him the support he needed. "One of the great things that AA provides is the fellowship. Most AAs will make themselves available to others on an anytime, anyplace basis. There's a listening ear whenever you need one," Heath says. In fact, he attributes much of his success to "the AA process," which he defines as "getting comfortable discussing your problems with other people."

AA also helped Heath have faith in a number of ways. He explains, "I finally had faith that if I did things a certain way — that is, by following the twelve steps — things would be okay, and I would be okay. The steps provide a unique blueprint for living. By practicing them, I do things that do not seem instinctual but provide positive and immediate results." Although he still struggles with the concept of a "higher power" in the form of God, Heath maintains that AA helped him "recognize a spiritual realm." He describes one of the first spiritual experiences of his sobriety: "I was sitting in my back yard, and it was warm — cicadas chirping, with a few puffy clouds overhead. I was swept over by this feeling that just told me, 'You're free and can go.' Prior to that, I felt like a dog on a short tether." He adds, "When you accept that you can't control everything and turn your life over to some higher power, you have a peacefulness — a state of calm that comes after turmoil."

In AA's tradition of reaching out to others who are still suffering with alcohol problems, Heath gets fulfillment from his many hours of work helping newcomers in AA. Now sober for nineteen years, he continues to go to AA meetings once or twice a week.

History, background, and program overview

The mutual, therapeutic understanding of people with the same problem was the initial inspiration for AA, which was founded in 1935, when a newly abstinent New York stockbroker, Bill Wilson ("Bill W.") connected with a surgeon, Robert Smith ("Dr. Bob"), who was still struggling with a serious drinking problem. The two met through the Oxford Group, a nondenominational evangelical Christian fellowship whose practices were among those used in establishing AA. Bill W. not only shared with Dr. Bob his own battles with the bottle but also emphasized his view of "alcoholism" as a spiritual, physical, and mental malady — a unique approach in the 1930s, which remains AA's stance today. The two men continued to get to know each other, and weeks later Dr. Bob took his last drink, marking the beginning of AA. The founders started working with problem drinkers at a local hospital. By 1939, three successful groups had emerged, and AA had one hundred members. That same year this core fellowship published its basic textbook, *Alcoholics Anonymous,* which is also known as the "Big Book."

The cornerstone of AA is its twelve steps (see page 110), suggested guides to progress and principles describing the experience of AA's earliest members. The foundation of the AA recovery process entails admitting complete defeat: that you are powerless over alcohol and that your life has become unmanageable. As such, recovery in AA requires abstinence; "alcoholism" is viewed as a progressive illness that can be arrested but not cured. Although newcomers are encouraged to start with the first step and then work through the remaining steps at their own pace, members do not have to follow or accept all twelve steps.

The steps embody a spiritual approach to recovery, with seven out of twelve referring to God, a "higher power," or a "spiritual awakening." As N. Peter Johnson, Ph.D., coordinator of alcohol and drug studies at the University of South Carolina School of Medicine, points out in his *Dictionary of Street Alcohol and Drug Terms,* "higher power" has to do with "assistance from outside of self." Therefore, for someone who is not religious, a higher power might be the power of a recovery group or therapists, not a deity. (For one master, the "higher power" was his dog!)

According to Barbara McCrady, Ph.D., a Rutgers University researcher who has studied and written extensively about AA,

"AA sees the alcoholic's major problem as one of selfishness and obsession with self — a condition that can only be remedied by turning outside of oneself." Heath F. comments, "Practicing alcoholics live with the singular focus of appeasing their own alcohol cravings at any cost. So qualities like integrity and honesty become compromised in order to get the alcohol." As such, the steps are intended to instill humility and honesty as well as to minimize self-centeredness.

Though the twelve steps serve as a framework for individual change, AA's twelve traditions lay the organizational groundwork by which groups usually operate. The traditions detail that the only requirement for membership in AA is a desire to stop drinking, that each group's primary purpose is to carry its message to the still-suffering "alcoholic," and that "there is but one ultimate authority — a loving God as He may express Himself in our group conscience." The traditions also stress the importance of anonymity and the autonomy of each AA group, which is free to manage its affairs as it pleases. Thus AA groups vary quite a bit from one to another.

AA encourages regular meeting attendance. (It's not uncommon to hear newcomers be advised, "Go to ninety meetings in ninety days.") Hallmarks of AA meetings are what are sometimes called "drunkalogs" (members' stories of their drinking past), celebration of sobriety anniversary dates (which most people start counting all over again if they have a slip with alcohol), and round-the-room self-introductions using first names followed by ". . . and I'm an alcoholic." (Note, however, that not all meetings include drunkalogs, and there is no requirement to call yourself an "alcoholic.")

Another of AA's cornerstones is sponsorship, which occurs when an experienced AA member — one who is further along in recovery — works with a newer member of the group. The sponsor, who is supposed to be the same gender as the person he or she sponsors, is available for contact at any time. Heath F. explains

The Twelve Steps of Alcoholics Anonymous

1. We admitted we were powerless over alcohol — that our lives had become unmanageable.
2. Came to believe that a Power greater than ourselves could restore us to sanity.
3. Made a decision to turn our will and our lives over to the care of God *as we understood Him.*
4. Made a searching and fearless moral inventory of ourselves.
5. Admitted to God, to ourselves, and to another human being the exact nature of our wrongs.
6. Were entirely ready to have God remove all these defects of character.
7. Humbly asked Him to remove our shortcomings.
8. Made a list of all persons we had harmed, and became willing to make amends to them all.
9. Made direct amends to such people wherever possible, except when to do so would injure them or others.
10. Continued to take personal inventory and when we were wrong promptly admitted it.
11. Sought through prayer and meditation to improve our conscious contact with God *as we understood Him,* praying only for knowledge of His will for us and the power to carry that out.
12. Having had a spiritual awakening as a result of these steps, we tried to carry this message to alcoholics and to practice these principles in all our affairs.

that sponsorship works two ways: "As with many things in life, we must assist our fellow humans not only for their sake but for ours as well. When you get out of yourself by truly helping someone else, you realize a spiritual satisfaction that is about as easy to describe as God is. One of AA's precepts is 'The only way you get to keep the program is to give it away.'" (For more details about AA, see pages 272–75.)

Is AA for you?

Who is best suited to AA? While there are no hard-and-fast guidelines, according to Dr. McCrady, studies suggest that people who are likely to affiliate themselves with AA tend to have

more severe drinking problems than others
more anxiety about and obsessive involvement with their
    drinking
less support from their spouses
a history of turning to others for support for their drink-
    ing problems
experiences of loss of control of their drinking
a greater commitment to abstinence
a greater desire to find meaning in their lives.

If you're looking for an all-encompassing, spiritual approach to recovery and to life in general, AA may be appealing. In the words of Dr. Kern, a supporter and leader of non–twelve-step groups, "None of the alternatives to AA has come close to the comprehensiveness of AA in terms of its number of tools, which include cognitive-behavioral approaches and catchy slogans, the sponsor system, a grand unifying theory, the written text, and a full-blown program of evolutionary steps. All of these components are not personally appealing to everyone, but the alternative approaches seem to lack a depth of richness that AA has captured." Also, AA is the only major recovery group that uses the one-on-one sponsor system, which can be more comfortable for those who would rather share with an individual than with an entire group.

According to the journal *Alcohol, Health & Research World*, there is limited evidence that AA involvement may be less beneficial for women than it is for men. Some studies suggest that women tend to prefer one-on-one approaches to groups. In addition to their alcohol abuse, women are more likely than men to have problems such as depression, which may not be adequately addressed at AA meetings. (Many AA members do receive additional help, such as counseling or alcohol treatment.) Note too that far more men than women belong to AA; its most recent membership survey revealed that 66 percent were men and 34 percent were women. (AA meetings for women only exist in some areas.)

In their own words: the masters speak out on some pros and cons of AA

The pros

The ways in which *Sober for Good* AA members have benefited from the program are diverse. There's Sue H. (nineteen years), who says, "With God in one hand and AA in the other, no obstacle is large enough that we can't handle it together — just for today." And there's Roxi V. (six years), who faithfully attends both AA and SOS meetings and offers a practical approach: "I shelve the things I have a hard time with at AA and take the good I see in the program."

Here are some more examples of the masters' positive experiences with AA:

◆ Borden S. has been in and out of AA since 1961, having had many relapses. But he never gave up and now has been continuously sober for more than seven years. Currently he goes to AA meetings about seven times a week, combining this experience with what he refers to as his "own rationale, based on Christian existentialism." He says of AA, "If I miss a week, I can't wait to go back." Borden benefits from the "oneness" he finds at AA meetings. He elaborates: "AA is geared to keeping a semblance of 'we are all alike' — it demands that you accept your illness and that you have the same illness as the person next to you. I go for the support and the intellectual reminder that the most important thing is that I don't drink."

◆ Sheri L. (twenty years), who was once "thrown out of a Hell's Angels party for being too crazy," showed up at her first AA meeting standing six foot one, weighing 320 pounds, and wearing tight blue jeans, a Western shirt, cowboy boots, a Stetson hat, and a .45 pistol on her hip. She says she was told, "Keep coming back, don't drink between meetings, bring the body, and the mind will follow. Put the plug in the jug, take the cotton out of one ear, put it in your mouth, leave the cotton in the other ear so what you hear won't whistle through that empty cavity. Be willing to put as much energy into your sobriety as you put into drinking. You have a disease called alcoholism, and the medicine for alcoholism is AA. Take a dose at least once a day." Now Sheri goes to AA meetings only about once a month, but she still credits the program with her equanimity, stating, "I have found that I can face death, divorce, remarriages, and illness. Today I am able to accept responsibility for others and myself. I am an employable, adaptable, and teachable person — thanks to the program of AA and my God. This program is teaching me to live life on life's terms and to enjoy it — to accept the good and the bad and to be grateful for both."

◆ Jordan L. (twelve years), who describes himself as agnostic and gay, says that when he first went to AA meetings, he "knew" it would not help him. He adds, "But I continued to go to lots of meetings until I found certain ones at which I felt somewhat comfortable and where there were people with whom I could identify. Several of these were nontraditional AA meetings." (He also attended a small number of SOS and RR meetings and read some of their literature, but he "primarily found the focus to be anti-AA rather than recovery from alcoholism.") He still attends AA meetings one to four times a week and finds that although many of the people in AA are religious, the program is not. Jordan admits that he attended AA meetings for about five years before he finally felt that the program would work in his life, but he now finds it to be "a design for living, a way of life, as AA literature says."

When AA falls short . . .

When asked if any approaches they had tried were ineffective, many masters responded that AA did not work for them. The top two reasons, evenly divided, related to difficulty accepting the "higher power"/spiritual concept and dislike for AA's focus on the past and the idea that you're in recovery for life. A number of masters objected to what they see as AA's rigidity and dogmatism, and quite a few did not like the emphasis on powerlessness. There was also a group of masters who initially found success with AA but who left the program because they became disillusioned with it.

Here are comments about what some masters see as the drawbacks of AA:

◆ "AA falls down because it has no professional counselors, doesn't focus on medical/health needs, and doesn't appeal to nonreligious folks, including atheists and agnostics. Also, mixing winos, beggars, homeless people, court-mandated felon and misdemeanor attendees, and hookers with well-dressed executives or suburban mothers who drink too much makes no sense." — Ed Shaw, who prefers to use his full real name (ten years, became a moderate drinker without AA, after trying AA)

◆ "While I credit AA with being the only program that teaches us 'alkies' how to live without alcohol and teaching me how to grow up and deal with life on life's terms, I feel AA is so strongly male-oriented that women are often left out and don't get what we need. Also, for me, sitting around the AA table is deadly — old (and new) war stories about drinking are very difficult for me to hear, and I feel AA dwells too much on the past." — Sunny B. (nine years, recovered with AA but left the program)

◆ "Although I've attended just about every kind of AA meeting, simply because it more often helped than not, I firmly believe that many of us need more affirmation and empowerment than AA alone provides." — Denise T. (fourteen years, recovered with AA but also attended other types of recovery groups and had therapy for depression). Later in her sobriety, Denise attended a sixteen-step empowerment group based on Charlotte Kasl's book *Many Roads, One Journey,* of which she notes, "I find that this philosophy's emphasis on strengths helps empower me to build on those, whereas AA's emphasis on 'character defects' makes them seem overwhelming." Nevertheless, Denise still attends AA meetings when she feels her attitude becoming negative. She explains, "The context of the fellowship and discussion of the available tools help me refocus on recovery and solutions instead of my problems."

Women for Sobriety (WFS)
How Rosa L. found her way

"I was drinking every day; I *had* to drink; and I couldn't stop drinking once I started." At the age of twenty-three, Rosa L. realized she had a serious alcohol problem. She also saw the connection between her alcohol abuse and some serious personality changes that led to horrible fights with the man to whom she was then married. Finally, one night while under the influence, she confided her problem to a friend, and through a recovering friend of his, she soon wound up at her first AA meeting, "really drunk." Within a week or so, she decided to go into a women's outpatient treatment program, where she was first informed about WFS. She began attending some of its meetings.

While Rosa was in the latter phase of her treatment, she remembered with pain several rapes that she had suffered as a teenager and young woman while she was inebriated. She explains, "It was then that I really had to reach out to people: loved ones, friends from meetings, and professionals — doctors, counselors at a rape center, psychiatrists." She continued to attend WFS and found that "the women at the meetings were there for me — all the time, anytime."

She also went to some AA meetings. But her attendance was sporadic and lasted only about a year. She vowed she would never attend again after one meeting at which men discussed their sex lives (or lack thereof), which offended her. She says, "Being in the middle of my awakening to my sexual abuse, I felt frightened, enraged, scared, and small." She adds, "Many women feel uncomfortable at AA meetings but don't know of other opportunities and just continue drinking in isolation for years and years, until they maybe find WFS. They often tell us this when they first arrive." Rosa also had problems with what she felt to be religious pressure at AA and "its insistence that everyone must have a 'higher power.'"

So Rosa chose WFS as her support group, because "it recognizes the importance of emotional and spiritual growth, but there is a respect for every kind of spirituality. There is no rule that you have to have a 'higher power.' In WFS we seem to first find the power within ourselves before reaching out elsewhere. We take control of our disease rather than admitting ourselves to be powerless. In my past, I was used to apologizing to everyone, to excusing my behavior, even my existence. I needed to go to a place where I was affirmed, where I could finally learn to say, 'I am a powerful woman, and I belong here!' Admitting that I was powerless over alcohol was not the way to do it. Instead, I turned it around and took control of my disease and of my recovery. Finding my long-lost power, with the help of WFS, allowed for my continued emotional and spiritual growth. I cannot tell you how many times I've said the WFS words, 'I am capable and competent,' in my head over the past ten years."

Rosa found that one of the most helpful aspects of WFS was its "emphasis on the present without ignoring the past." She explains, "I have been to many AA meetings where each person took their turn and told their horrible drinking story from beginning to end, but there was no talk about getting out of that pain and those memories. What really helped me at WFS was that it was always okay for me or anyone to cry about past pain. However, I would always walk out with new ideas about dealing with my pain in the present and with a feeling of being ready to tackle the world again."

For almost nine years Rosa attended the same weekly WFS meeting that she started with. (She no longer attends but still has close contact with many of the women from the group.) She also has had many years of psychological counseling and psychiatric treatment for depression. Aside from a few rocky weeks when she first finished treatment, Rosa has been sober for ten years and, like most masters, chooses to be totally abstinent.

History, background, and program overview

Women for Sobriety was founded in the mid-1970s by Jean Kirkpatrick, Ph.D., the accomplished only child of a prominent Pennsylvania family. When she was a young adult, her own alcohol abuse led her to AA, where she got sober while working on her doctoral degree in sociology at an Ivy League school. Three years later, however, her insecurities got the best of her and she turned to the bottle, initiating a drinking bout that lasted more than a decade. She eventually returned to AA but found that the group's philosophies didn't speak to her anymore. So she began curbing her alcohol consumption herself, discovering that by changing her thoughts when she was lonely or depressed, she could avoid drinking for short periods of time, which gradually became longer. According to WFS literature, "Her sobriety was achieved by realizing that she was a capable woman and that all of her problems were a creation of her own mind."

Dr. Kirkpatrick's self-prescribed method proved successful, and in the 1970s, now sober, she decided to reach out to other women. Changing the way she thought about and reacted to problems became a hallmark of her recovery plan, initially dubbed the New Life Program. In 1976 the program, renamed Women for Sobriety, garnered national attention as a result of a United Press International story picked up by newspapers around the country.

Dr. Kirkpatrick founded WFS because she felt that women with drinking problems require different recovery programs from men. In contrast to AA's twelve steps, which are intended to instill humility and limit self-centeredness, WFS is designed to bolster members' sense of self-value. According to WFS, women begin drinking abusively to cope with stress, loneliness, frustration, emotional deprivation, and other feelings. Therefore, as Rosa's story suggests, WFS members learn to manage these issues by sharing them with other women and encouraging one another, and these actions play a key role in achieving sobriety. The program emphasizes substituting positive, self-affirming thoughts for negative, self-destructive ones.

In addition to helping women get sober, WFS tries to boost their confidence that they can improve their lives. As such, it endorses the idea the individuals should be self-reliant and solve their problems through willpower and rational analysis. But, Rosa notes, "It does not deny the power or wonder of emotions." She adds, "At WFS, we do not wallow in our past, although we continue to learn from it in order to live a better life today and to plan for what we want tomorrow." WFS encourages members to attend to their physical health via diet, relaxation, meditation, and physical exercise, but Rosa has not found any pressure regarding these issues.

The cornerstone of WFS is its New Life Program, based on thirteen statements or affirmations (see page 119). These statements encourage members to take responsibility for their thoughts and actions. Although spiritual growth is listed as a goal, the WFS program does not focus on this nearly as heavily as AA does. Rosa says, "At WFS, all spiritual beliefs are accepted and encouraged. The longer I was sober, the more I became aware of my spirituality. The simultaneous acceptance and lack of pres-

The Thirteen Statements of the New Life F

1. I have a life-threatening problem that once had me.
2. Negative thoughts destroy only myself.
3. Happiness is a habit I will develop.
4. Problems bother me only to the degree I permit them to.
5. I am what I think.
6. Life can be ordinary or it can be great.
7. Love can change the course of my world.
8. The fundamental object of life is emotional and spiritual growth.
9. The past is gone forever.
10. All love given returns.
11. Enthusiasm is my daily exercise.
12. I am a competent woman and have much to give life.
13. I am responsible for myself and for my actions.

Copyright © Women for Sobriety

sure from WFS women really helped me grow, both spiritually and emotionally."

Of her meetings, Rosa says, "Most weeks, we would discuss one of the statements, but if anyone had an emergency, this would be dealt with. Or if a lot of new people came one night, we'd get down to the basics again, starting with the first WFS statement. Despite this wonderful flexibility, each meeting opened the same way, with the WFS motto: 'We are capable and competent, caring and compassionate, always willing to help another, bonded together in overcoming our addictions.' For almost nine years, I heard the same introduction from our moderator and the same statements read by the women in the circle. It was so soothing, like music to my soul."

WFS does not use the sponsor system, yet many members share phone numbers and call each other between meetings for support. Like AA, WFS views "alcoholism" as both a psychological and a physical disease. However, WFS takes the position that abusive drinking begins as a means of overcoming emotional issues and then evolves into addiction. As such, the only way to recover is to abstain completely. Also like AA, membership in WFS requires "a desire to stop drinking" as well as "a sincere desire for a new life." According to WFS, "Your illness of alcoholism will always be in your life, but you need never be ill again." As you accept your drinking problem, WFS believes, "you are already beginning to control it and your life."

Although WFS is not affiliated with AA in any way, some masters belong to both WFS and AA, a relationship that is not discouraged by WFS. (For more details about WFS, see pages 275–77.)

Is WFS for you?

To determine whether WFS is for you, consider what WFS members have said they like about the program. According to a 1992 survey of about six hundred WFS members conducted by the researcher Lee Ann Kaskutas, D.P.H., and published in the *Journal of Substance Abuse Treatment,* the foremost reason for attending WFS meetings was their provision of a nurturing, supportive atmosphere. Other common responses concerned the importance of female role models, sharing of women's issues, and preference for an all-women group, as well as philosophical aspects of WFS such as its focus on self-esteem, self-reliance, and positive approach to life. Some women liked WFS's less structured format and the fact that they were not pressured to call themselves "alcoholic." (According to WFS headquarters, a new survey is in the works.)

About one third of the WFS survey respondents made positive comments about the meeting environment, noting that it provides a safe forum in which to discuss basic women's concerns. In addition, a women-only program can be more comfortable for a newly recovered woman who feels vulnerable and does not welcome advances from men, which may occur in mixed-sex meetings.

What an honor to have such wives.

Some evidence suggests that compared with men, women who abuse alcohol are more likely to suffer from depression, low self-esteem, alcohol-related physical problems, marital and family instability, a history of sexual or physical abuse, and a pattern of drinking in response to life crises. Also, women may be more inclined to drink when they feel powerless or inadequate. WFS seems to provide a comfortable place for addressing all of these concerns.

While little research has been conducted on the effectiveness of specialized approaches for women, one study compared women in a program designed with a focus on women's problems with women involved in a traditional, mixed female-and-male approach. It revealed that those in the special program remained in treatment longer, were more likely to complete the program, and were better off psychologically, socially, and physically than those in the mixed-sex program. (WFS does have literature for a Men for Sobriety program, but at this writing there are only two men's groups in Canada and none in the United States.)

On the negative side, some people find some of WFS's affirmations, such as "Happiness is a habit I will develop," a bit simplistic and patronizing. One woman described certain WFS ideas as "Pollyanna-ish," a point acknowledged by Dr. Kirkpatrick herself. Of the WFS statement "Enthusiasm is my daily exercise," Rosa says in good humor, "Somehow this turned into a ritual joke, because no one wanted to read it because we all hated being enthusiastic. To get over that, we would sing or scream the words, sometimes even jumping up to say them in a very enthusiastic manner!"

SMART (Self Management and Recovery Training) Recovery
How Rick N. found his way

Rick N. came from what he describes as a family "no more dysfunctional than any average American family of the days of *Leave*

Began in highschool [illegible] / Bolton [illegible] / accepted day / cry child

It to Beaver." When he was faced with adolescent turmoil, however, alcohol offered a way out. Under the influence of alcohol, he found, "All those problems melted away. I wasn't self-conscious and shy anymore but felt outgoing and witty. Within a few weeks I was going steady with one of the school cheerleaders. People began asking *me* where the party was every weekend! I felt popular. I had an identity. I was happy again. I mistakenly attributed all of these new developments to alcohol."

Rick concludes, "The next fifteen years were a phantasmagoric blur of alcohol and drugs — by age twenty-nine, I was depressed and nearly suicidal. After several serious, but failed, attempts at moderate drinking, I quit on my own." After he had been sober for several months, Rick went to a counselor, who told him that without traditional treatment or AA, he was doomed to fail at trying to stay sober. So he admitted himself to the Hazelden treatment program and continued to go to AA meetings afterward. "What followed was a six-year downward spiral of moral inventories, self-condemnation, shame, atonement, and bowing to external authority in twelve-step meetings," Rick laments. "For me, the promises of happiness and serenity never materialized."

By this time Rick had become a counselor in a traditional substance abuse program. But "an incredible sense of incongruity grew in me. I no longer believed in what I was doing." He reread *A Guide to Rational Living,* a book about cognitive-behavioral approaches to problems by the renowned psychologist Albert Ellis, Ph.D. (see Books Recommended by the Masters, page 299).

Around this same time, Rick became depressed over the ending of a relationship and wound up being referred by his boss to a psychiatric hospital. "They insisted that I was depressed because I wasn't working the twelve steps correctly and that I must accept a higher power," he says. Against advice, he left the hospital, and not long after that he lost his job. Months later, still plagued by feelings of "guilt, shame, and personal worthlessness," Rick remembered the book by Dr. Ellis. "Unemployed and out of money, I managed to find my way to his New York office, and Dr. Ellis consented to see me. In just two thirty-minute sessions, he helped me realize that even if I was the pathetic wreck that I had been taught to believe I was, I still had me! He then demonstrated how cognitive-behavioral principles could help me develop an effective philosophy by which to live. Vindicated, validated, and empowered, I was finally back in the driver's seat."

Now sober for twenty-one years, Rick, who recently completed his master's degree in social work, is currently a coordinator for three Self Management and Recovery Training (SMART Recovery) groups, which use the approaches of Dr. Ellis. In retrospect, he says, "For the decade following my experience with Dr. Ellis, I wondered, 'Why isn't there a program that utilizes techniques like Dr. Ellis's as the foundation for recovery? Why can't people be encouraged and motivated to seek their own solutions creatively instead of looking for answers outside themselves? Being told that quitting on my own volition was impossible, that I had a disease that made me powerless, and that the power to quit had to come from outside me was most unhelpful. SMART Recovery would have made things easier by supporting my belief in my own competence."

Although the SMART Recovery program wasn't around when Rick became sober, he says that the approach he used was entirely consistent with what SMART Recovery teaches. "One of the things that Dr. Ellis taught me was to accept myself without conditions — and that I could be just as responsible for my emotions as I had learned to be with the decision not to drink. This is one of the main goals of SMART Recovery — teaching people how to handle emotions and problems in new ways, without turning to alcohol or drugs." Rick adds, "Consistent with SMART Recovery's focus on lifestyle balance, I have tried to keep myself on track emotionally by constantly asking, 'What do I really want? What are my goals and values? What are my priorities?'" He sums up by saying, "Nobody stays recovered unless the life they have created is more rewarding and satisfying than the one they left behind. I consider myself *recovered* because I have no interest in reinventing my former addictions."

History, background, and program overview

A relative newcomer to the recovery program scene, SMART Recovery was launched by a group of professionals who were originally affiliated with Rational Recovery (RR; see pages 128–29). But SMART Recovery established itself as a separate group in 1994, when RR altered its direction. The cornerstone of SMART Recovery's program is cognitive-behavioral modification, which helps members recognize both environmental and emotional triggers for drinking and respond to them in new ways. SMART Recovery participants learn that it's not necessarily the situation that determines how they feel and act but what they say to themselves about the situation. They learn how to challenge irrational, self-destructive thoughts — thoughts that often lead to problem drinking — and replace them with more rational ones so they remain sober. (For more on cognitive approaches, see chapter 9.)

As master Murray K. (six years) explains, "Some kinds of thoughts are a voice from the past that can lead you to drink. In SMART Recovery, you learn to respond to such thoughts with other thoughts that contradict and disprove them. For instance, you might have been yelled at by your boss at work, and as you're driving home you find yourself passing the liquor store, thinking, 'I had a bad day, so I deserve a drink.' *Appropriate* self-talk is telling yourself positive, sensible things that lead to a more appropriate response than drinking. So in this case, you might say to yourself, 'The fact that I had a bad day has nothing to do with deserving a drink; it won't solve my problems at work.' By the time you've thought the whole thing through, you've already passed the liquor store and you'll be stronger the next time you're in a similar situation."

A basic tenet of SMART Recovery is that although addictive

behavior may have some biological underpinnings, it is essentially a bad habit rather than a disease. The program's standpoint is that drinking serves a purpose: it serves as a coping mechanism for facing life's problems and upsets — which, of course, is counterproductive. Recall how Rick mistakenly attributed his relief from his adolescent insecurities to alcohol and how this attribution made his early experiences with alcohol "powerfully reinforcing." He *learned* to cope by drinking; cognitive-behavioral approaches taught him how to undo this.

Unlike most other recovery programs, SMART Recovery does not use any particular slogans or steps. But it does use a "4-Point Program," which teaches participants how to do the following things:

Enhance and maintain the motivation to abstain, through such activities as taking stock (described in chapter 4). Rick N. states, "Without realizing it, I engaged in what SMART calls 'cost-benefit analysis' and decided that the benefits of drinking and drugging were not worth the costs."

Cope with urges to drink and refuse to act on them. "Once I quit," Rick recalls, "I had confidence that I could, as Dr. Ellis says, 'stubbornly refuse' to give in to temptation. This is consistent with what SMART Recovery teaches in a technique we call 'DISARM.'"

Manage thoughts, feelings, and behavior — essentially, to deal with life's problems in a sensible way, without turning to alcohol.

Develop a positive, balanced, and healthy lifestyle. Rick explains, "I wanted something out of life — as SMART Recovery says, something much more 'meaningful and enduring' than the momentary pleasure of drinking. So even more motivating than the painful consequences of using was the vision of what life could be if I changed my ways."

With its emphasis on self-reliance rather than reliance on a "higher power," SMART Recovery makes no recommendations about spiritual beliefs. The group does not oppose belief in a "higher power," however, and people with and without religious or spiritual orientations are welcome. Some SMART Recovery members attend AA meetings as well, but the vast majority do not. A sponsor system is not part of SMART Recovery.

Both SMART Recovery and AA are based on abstinence. However, people who are unsure about pursuing long-term abstinence are welcome to attend SMART Recovery meetings. Likewise, those whose ultimate goal is moderate drinking are welcome at SMART Recovery groups, because many of the strategies used to promote abstinence can also help facilitate successful moderation. Specific tools to teach people how to cut back on their drinking and to drink moderately, however, are not used at SMART Recovery meetings. Individuals who want to learn these strategies would probably be better off at a Moderation Management or DrinkWise group (see pages 283–84). There are no specific requirements for SMART Recovery membership — the groups are open to people with any kind of addiction as well as to those who just want to learn the skills SMART Recovery teaches for living a more productive life. (For more details about SMART Recovery, see pages 277–80.)

Is SMART Recovery for you?

If you favor rational, logical approaches to life and its problems, SMART Recovery is likely to appeal. Its basic tenets are based on research and on well-accepted psychological strategies used for behavior problems of all sorts. As SMART Recovery's president, Tom Horvath, a clinical psychologist, states, "SMART Recovery is good for people who take lots of responsibility for their lives —

those who feel they're in control of events rather than the other way around."

Because SMART Recovery encourages members to come up with their own ways of thinking and viewing behavior, it is also apt to be of interest to anyone who doesn't like slogans and pat answers. Its approach may also appeal to a nonreligious person or to someone who is religious but doesn't care for AA's style of spirituality. With its emphasis on learning how to solve problems more effectively and on "learning to trade off momentary for enduring satisfactions," SMART Recovery offers a comprehensive approach to people interested in developing a more balanced and healthy lifestyle.

SMART Recovery has a more didactic meeting format than the other recovery groups, with the coordinator taking a more active role in facilitating meetings. A number of SMART Recovery's group leaders are trained professionals. If you like leadership and something specific to work on each week, SMART Recovery may be the way to go. Its approach to addiction is rather intellectual, which attracts people who want a matter-of-fact approach to recovery.

SMART Recovery also holds promise for those who don't want to dwell on the past but instead want to move on with life. Murray K. states, "I attended meetings for a year, ran a group for two years, and decided I'd given enough back. I had my problem resolved, and there was no further need to attend meetings." However, people who feel a need to talk about or make up for their past might find AA more to their liking than SMART Recovery.

SMART Recovery encourages members not to depend on the group and to leave when they've achieved comfortable sobriety. According to Dr. Marc Kern, who coordinates a SMART Recovery group, "The concepts of the program are not easy to master and are rather abstract. People tend to think they get it right away, and they leave SMART Recovery too soon. In fact, it takes

Rational Recovery

"Rational Recovery is not about going to meetings to sit around and cry over how much you drank and what an ass you were and how sometimes you just would like to have a drink. RR is about going on with your life and leaving the alcohol-filled hell behind. Life without alcohol is my choice and that is a natural choice. There is nothing about using alcohol that is natural, not even talking about it. When I completed twenty-eight days of RR, nothing was tough. I made a commitment to myself that I would never drink alcohol for the rest of my life, and I will not! Period! This is very natural and easy for me." — Richard D.

Jack Trimpey's *The Small Book* presented the original Rational Recovery guidelines and principles, which put forth two broad approaches for resolving alcohol problems: cognitive-behavioral techniques and a "thinking skill" that Trimpey, a social worker, based on the experience of self-recovered people, which he calls Addictive Voice Recognition Technique (AVRT).

When RR and SMART Recovery parted ways, RR had been holding self-help meetings across the country. (It was up to each group to decide which affiliation to maintain. Accordingly, some masters who initially recovered using RR switched to SMART Recovery.) One of the factors that led to the split between RR and SMART Recovery was Trimpey's decision to shift the focus of RR away from cognitive-behavioral approaches and toward AVRT. RR now offers an approach for self-recovery that one can learn about through RR materials and its Web site (from which cognitive-behavioral approaches have been eliminated) rather than through a program with support groups. When I recruited the masters, some leftover groups still called themselves RR groups, but Trimpey no longer endorses recovery groups and discourages people from trying to locate RR groups. Also, there is no longer a twenty-eight-day residential option.

RR, Trimpey says, is "an educational approach to planned, permanent abstinence" — not to be "confused with or seen as an alternative to other recovery group organizations and addiction treatment methods." AVRT involves recognizing your thoughts and feelings that support continued drinking, then personifying them as your "Addictive Voice" or "it." Trimpey posits that these thoughts come from a primitive part of the brain, the midbrain, which he also refers to as "the beast brain." Trimpey theorizes that another part of the brain can override the appetite for alcohol (and other drugs). According to RR, "In order to defeat your addiction, you must *compete* with your midbrain for control of language . . . 'It,' the Addictive Voice, is simply any thinking, imagery, or feeling that supports any use of alcohol — ever."

The user of AVRT is taught to recognize, override, and take control of this voice. For instance, when Maost R. has thoughts that tempt him to drink, he says, "I just tell them to go away, shut up, or whatever, and they comply." A critical part of AVRT is making a "Big Plan" to quit forever. No one-day-at-a-time philosophy here; the message is a lifetime commitment to abstinence for anyone experiencing problems related to drinking.

RR's approach can be useful for some people who don't need or want support in recovery. It is important to realize, however, that RR opposes recovery groups of any kind. For instance, its Web site states, "Rational Recovery is the antithesis and irreconcilable arch-rival of Alcoholics Anonymous. RR is *right;* AA is *wrong.*" It also advises, "Recovery groups of all kinds are bad company."

You can learn more about RR's approach at its Web site, by reading Trimpey's book *Rational Recovery: The New Cure for Substance Addiction,* by watching its videotapes, and by subscribing to the RR journal.

For more information about Rational Recovery Systems, contact:

Rational Recovery Systems, Inc.
P.O. Box 800
Lotus, CA 95651
Phone: 530-621-2667
Web address: http://www.rational.org
e-mail: rr@rational.org

time to master the strategies." If you're looking for a long-term support group that has the same faces for years on end, you might want to combine SMART Recovery with another approach.

Because the program is quite new, you are less likely to find role models with long-term sobriety than in other programs, although I heard from some long-sober masters, like Rick N., who have become SMART Recovery members.

Secular Organizations for Sobriety, also known as Save Our Selves (SOS)
How Louise L. found her way

"I probably had a problem from the first time I took a drink at the age of eighteen," Louise recalls. "Every time I drank, I got drunk. I could never have a drink like my buddies. I didn't know how to have fun without alcohol." But she was always able to hold responsible positions, which, she says, gave her enough money to feed her habit. After a confrontation with a coworker who suggested she get psychological help, Louise went to a psychiatrist, who treated her for depression with "loads of psychotropic drugs," which Louise says made it *easier* to keep drinking.

Eventually she went to her family physician and talked to her honestly about the amount she drank. They considered the possibility of AA, but the physician didn't think Louise would connect with the group. Nevertheless, she did periodically attend a women's AA group for about three years. She explains, "Some of it was pure nonsense to me, with the 'Big Book' thumping, but AA is still the biggest ship in port, so it was nice to have the option of an all-women's meeting."

However, as a "nontheist," Louise really connected with SOS, which she found out about through a newspaper ad after she tried to get sober for a few months. Not only did she like the secularity of the group, but she received great benefit from its main tenet: that you have to make sobriety a priority, separate from everything else in your life and contingent on nothing in your life. The psychiatrist Louise had seen was correct in saying that she was depressed, both before and after she got sober. But before she could deal with that, she says, she needed to separate her drinking from her personal problems. "The 'sobriety priority' worked for me," she explains, "because I began to view my other issues as what they were — other issues. Making a distinction between my not drinking and everything else freed me to work on staying sober, while other things became ancillary or secondary."

Once Louise decided she could remain sober *despite* her problems, she was free to deal with the depression, which entailed resolving issues from the past. "If there's no payoff in staying sober, why not drink? I had to find a reason to live in order to quit for good," she says. So in addition to remaining active in SOS, Louise began to see a new therapist, who led her through "the worst torment" of her life. She explains, "I had a lot of stuff to get rid of — like remembering my drunken father breaking two of my older sister's bones when she was a child, then recalling that same sister's drowning years later, when she was drunk. If I was going to stay sober, I needed someone to help me through the pain that I had been anesthetizing all those years." While helping her sort through the pain, the therapist helped Louise see also that she had a reason to live.

Now sober for ten years, Louise spent much of her spare time the first six years running groups for SOS. Because of her leadership role, she had a powerful motivation for remaining sober. But she moved recently and is much less involved with SOS, which poses no problem for her. She told me, "I now have the tools to stay sober. I keep a clear picture in my mind of the last time I took a drink — the guilt, the shame. Drinking is not an option anymore. I cannot think of a single situation that drinking would not make worse."

History, background, and program overview

Louise L. was attracted to SOS because of the very things that led James Christopher, a former problem drinker, to found the organization in the mid-1980s. He had tried AA but felt uncomfortable with the notion of turning his life over to a "higher power." Finding that focusing on self-reliance and personal responsibility was far more effective in dealing with his alcohol problem, Christopher left AA early in his recovery and remained sober on his own. In 1985, when a national magazine published an article about his recovery approach, "Sobriety Without Superstition," Christopher got responses from all over the world. The interest in this article led him to hold SOS's first meeting a year later in North Hollywood, California.

Unlike most other recovery groups, SOS has no structured program. But it does have "Suggested Guidelines for Sobriety" (see page 133). The centerpiece of the SOS approach is the "sobriety priority." The idea is that when you are still addicted to alcohol, it assumes top priority in your life. To change, you have to make *not drinking* your top priority. (For more on this idea, see page 79.) Making sobriety a priority entails not drinking despite life's ups and downs. Louise says, "It's easy to stay sober when things are going well. But having been through a wrenching couple of years recently, with the dissolution of my marriage and grinding loneliness, it has been really important for me to separate my feelings from my not drinking. Life goes on, and sobriety must be the priority." In short, the message of SOS is that *you don't drink, no matter what.*

SOS suggests establishing a "cycle of sobriety" consisting of daily acknowledgment of your addiction to alcohol, daily acceptance of the addiction, and daily prioritization of sobriety. How you do this is up to you; "SOS is not a cookie-cutter program," according to Christopher, "but rather a self-empowerment approach." SOS does encourage members to use "daily do's" — strategies or helpful sayings that members come up with that strengthen their resolve to stay sober. Each morning, for example, Louise reminds herself that there is no situation that a drink would not make worse. Another of her "daily do's" is to try to

SOS Suggested Guidelines for Sobriety

To break the cycle of denial and achieve sobriety, we first acknowledge that we are alcoholics or addicts.

We reaffirm this truth daily and accept without reservation the fact that as clean and sober individuals, we can not and do not drink or use, no matter what.

Since drinking or using is not an option for us, we take whatever steps are necessary to continue our Sobriety Priority lifelong.

A quality of life, "the good life," can be achieved. However, life is also filled with uncertainties. Therefore, we do not drink or use regardless of feelings, circumstances, or conflicts.

We share in confidence with each other our thoughts and feelings as sober, clean individuals.

Sobriety is our Priority, and we are each responsible for our lives and sobriety.

From *How to Stay Sober,* by Jim Christopher, 1988

notice the "small happinesses" that each day holds — for instance, enjoyment of her cats, the friendly wave of a neighbor, the fun of driving her 1970 VW bug.

While AA maintains that sobriety can be achieved only by turning to a "higher power," SOS advocates taking responsibility for problem drinking and handling it as a separate issue, distinct from any religious or spiritual beliefs. Accordingly, the SOS approach can allow atheists and religious people to work on sobriety together.

SOS recognizes both biological and learned factors as the roots of alcohol problems but leaves it up to the individual to decide whether "alcoholism" is a disease. People can recover in SOS, but they are not cured; addiction to alcohol is seen as permanent, but the addiction can be arrested, according to Christopher. Like AA and most other recovery groups, SOS equates sobriety with complete abstinence from alcohol.

Christopher notes that relapses are often part of the recovery process and SOS takes them seriously, considering them life-threatening. People who slip are still welcome in the group and are given extra support. (For more details about SOS, see pages 280–82.)

Is SOS for you?

SOS is apt to appeal to agnostics, atheists, and others who are not comfortable with the "higher power" aspect of AA. Although some religious people may feel awkward around the greater number of nonreligious people that SOS meetings attract, Jim Christopher has found that the program has been well received by those who want "separation of church and recovery." (Although SOS considers itself "the proven alternative to twelve-step programs," some masters belong to both SOS and AA.)

SOS is more for those who are self-directed, less for people who want to be told what to do and who want a specific program for staying sober. In fact, Christopher stresses, "SOS is not just a group program; it's also an individual program. Many people find SOS materials helpful for quitting on their own." He adds that people who don't like SOS's suggested tools are encouraged to craft their own approach to recovery.

Louise points out that "SOS may require a little more self-discipline and a little more motivation; since we don't have a program or sponsors, it is up to the individual to do the work. The group will support you but will not tell you what you need or what you should do."

Finally, while SOS certainly welcomes those who are trying to figure out whether they have a serious drinking problem, Christopher's insistence on abstinence makes this option less appealing than a program like SMART Recovery for someone who is not sure about committing to abstinence.

LifeRing Secular Recovery

As this book headed to press, I was told that a number of SOS groups and the unofficial SOS publishing house, LifeRing Press, had changed their names and affiliated with LifeRing Secular Recovery (LSR). LSR is the name taken in 1999 by former SOS groups in northern California because of a name conflict with another organization. Although its philosophy is currently the same as SOS's, LSR has established itself as a separate group because of differences of opinion about how the organization should be structured. Accordingly, some masters who recovered with SOS are now involved with LSR. LSR's Web site contains useful information as well as specifics about how to locate both LSR and SOS groups in the United States, Canada, and abroad (see pages 281–82 in the appendix).

Formal Treatment
How Elise C. found her way

At the height of Elise C.'s alcohol problem, she was traveling a lot on business and drinking in her hotel room, on planes, at lunch, at night — anytime. The turning point came when her boss caught her drinking on the job during a business trip. The next day, after flying home first class (that is, with free drinks), she bumped into a friend at the airport and saw the concern in the friend's eyes. Elise was so shaken that she went directly to an airport phone, called the psychiatrist she had been seeing for depression, and made an appointment for that afternoon. "He told me that he had already decided he couldn't see me anymore because I was unwilling to deal with my drinking. He said we weren't going to make any progress if I continued to 'anesthetize myself to the pain rather than face it.'" Elise broke down and asked him for help.

The options the psychiatrist laid out for her were AA, outpatient treatment, or inpatient treatment. She chose the inpatient route. The next day Elise went to see her boss. She notes, "I was fortunate, because she was very supportive and my insurance paid most of my costs." Within a week Elise had checked into a twenty-eight-day program. (This took place about eleven years ago, when she was thirty-one years old.)

After completing the paperwork, she was escorted to a shared room in the medically supervised detox area, which felt very much like a hospital. "They searched all my belongings and took away mouthwash, Tylenol, perfume, vitamins — any substance I might take myself. I retreated as fast as I could to the smoking lounge to hide behind my *New York Times* but rapidly discovered that it was a social lounge, not a library. That was where I met my first fellow patient — a nine-time rehab veteran on heroin. I came face to face with the harsh addict reality and wanted to run."

Elise was out of detox in less than forty-eight hours, having had insomnia as her only physical problem. After that, she moved to a room with two regular beds and desks — "nothing fancy but less hospital-like" — where she was alone for several days. To break her isolation, she supposes, the staff insisted that she move in with another woman, who remained her roommate throughout treatment.

Elise describes a typical day as follows: "We'd have an early breakfast, classes — behavior modification, lectures from the medical staff — group therapy with a dedicated counselor, lunch, activities (including outdoor walks, free time, afternoon classes), then dinner and an AA meeting." On weekends the participants were allowed to leave the facility for a few hours.

Of her fellow patients, she says, "We had a mix of drug addicts and alcoholics, young and old. Many were back after relapses. My best friend became the fellow I met in detox, who turned out to be an incredibly bright twenty-something guy, now a lawyer. Several were there on court orders. Quite a few older ones were there because their families had intervened. Most were amazed that I had checked myself in."

In summarizing her treatment experience, Elise recalls, "We spent a lot of time formally and informally talking about family. We also explored our triggers for drinking, and the counselors encouraged us to make any changes we could before returning home. For instance, my family went to my house and threw out what little alcohol was left, wineglasses, and corkscrews. They also washed my windows so I could see the sun shining, planted flowers, and bought me an orange juicer. These acts were both symbolic and practical and meant a great deal to me."

Elise credits her treatment at the program for turning her around and "creating that determination never to go back, to succeed and move on." She adds, "It was a highly charged and positive experience, due in large part to having a great counselor and to my fellow addicts, who had a profound effect on me."

The treatment center had an aftercare program, but Elise never went. She explains, "Once I'd left, I was ready to move on. I did go to AA meetings occasionally for about six months, and even had a sponsor briefly. I was determined never to slip. I never have."

Elise says she formed her own support system by going public about resolving her alcohol problem with close friends and colleagues. She "clung" to Antabuse (see page 92) when she first got out, convinced that it was her "lifeline." About two months later, when she had to stop taking the drug because of side effects, she was terrified. "I kept a bottle of it around for at least a year, thinking I'd take a pill if I got tempted, but I never did. I just moved on." Today she has "a strong marriage, a beautiful little boy, a successful career, a nice home, and security for the future." She concludes, "I don't want to screw that up by drinking again."

Inpatient treatment versus outpatient treatment

According to the National Institute on Alcohol Abuse and Alcoholism, "On any given day, more than 700,000 people in the United States receive alcoholism treatment in either inpatient or outpatient settings." Inpatient programs, like the one Elise attended, can be run by private hospitals, publicly funded facilities such as VA hospitals, or private residential facilities for substance abuse treatment, such as the Betty Ford Center and the Hazelden Foundation.

Insurance companies are much less inclined to pay for inpatient treatment than they were a decade ago, when Elise recovered. To be covered today, you would probably have to show that such treatment is a medical necessity — for instance, that you are at risk for severe withdrawal symptoms, have a liver disorder, or have serious psychological problems. In the past, inpatient treatment typically lasted twenty-eight days, but many insurance companies today will not cover treatment lasting that long. In 1999 the average length of inpatient treatment in the United States was eleven to fifteen days, depending on the state and the insurance company, according to A. Thomas McClellan, Ph.D., director of the Treatment Research Institute at the University of Pennsylvania.

Currently, *outpatient* treatment programs, which have been shown to be more cost-effective, are far more common than residential stays: in the United States, more than 90 percent of all addiction treatment is outpatient. Like inpatient programs, outpatient programs can be found in privately and publicly funded hospitals or private organizations; they offer group counseling, individual counseling, or both. In outpatient treatment, you sleep at home and visit the treatment facility for your care. Not only is this come-and-go kind of treatment less expensive, but you can hold down your job or go to school while participating, which allows you to work through the ups and downs of everyday living while you adjust to life without alcohol. (A number of programs now offer both inpatient and outpatient services, which provides patients with a transition after the residential phase of treatment ends.)

The more intensive outpatient programs (sometimes called

"day treatment") often begin with full- or half-day sessions five or more times per week. As recovery progresses, the sessions may get shorter — say, one to two hours twice a week. Other programs involve less than ten hours a week spread over the course of several days, or you may find an evening program. Some places offer individual appointments with a chemical dependency counselor, whom you see regularly. (See "What's a CD counselor?" pages 288–90 in the appendix.)

What goes on in treatment?

Inpatient and outpatient facilities do not vary much in programming, according to Dr. McClellan, whose nonprofit institute researches addiction treatment methods and programs across the United States. Generally speaking, both forms of treatment involve primarily group counseling but also some individual counseling to help build motivation, build skills to resist alcohol use, find new activities to replace drinking, improve problem-solving abilities, and facilitate better relationships.

The treatment approach that became the standard for the vast majority of inpatient and outpatient treatment programs in the United States is known as the Minnesota model. (It had its origins in the 1950s in work carried out at several facilities in Minnesota, including the Hazelden Foundation.) As in the program Elise C. attended, this model blends AA's twelve-step recovery approach with professional concepts and practices. Based on the disease theory of "alcoholism," it employs both recovered people and professionals such as physicians, social workers, psychologists, and nurses. (As mentioned in chapter 2, more than 90 percent of treatment centers in the United States are based on the twelve-step approach; 83 percent hold twelve-step meetings on-site.)

In this traditional model of treatment, after patients attend detoxification, they receive education about "alcoholism" and addiction as well as a mix of individual and group therapy. Elise says the people who were in her program heard talks from the medical staff on the physical effects of drugs, alcohol, and nico-tine. "I was put off at first by having to sit through a lengthy ses-sion including testimonials on heroin addiction," she says, "but I came to see how easy it was to slip from one addiction to another and let go of the false belief that I was somehow better than the person who did heroin." Indeed, an essential part of the tradi-tional approach is "milieu treatment" — that is, living with oth-ers who have had similar experiences and difficulties and who can offer insight and advice on the recovery process.

Elise had individual therapy with someone who she thinks was a social worker who had recovered from a drug or alcohol problem. "My counselor worked hard to help me let go of anger about childhood and realize that I couldn't change what had hap-pened but I certainly could change how I treated myself now and in the future. We also worked on expressing feelings that I'd long been taught were inappropriate." Toward the end of treatment, Elise was required to have some counseling with family members, a practice common to many programs.

Another activity that might go on during treatment is writing an autobiography or a journal about your history of alcohol use and its consequences. Elise says, "We had to complete our life story and share it with the group. It was hard to do, and the coun-selors meant it to be a challenge — an exposé, not a résumé." Yet another common activity in treatment programs is learning re-lapse prevention strategies (see chapter 9).

Confrontational approaches have also been part of tradi-tional treatment but are no longer common. Elise says that once a week her group would have a challenge session, in which a few patients sat at the front of the room and listened to others' obser-vations about them, with no chance to respond. She recalls, "I got challenged about my coolness and detachment. I was chided about carrying my Day-Timer and my *Wall Street Journal* like some kind of shield. That hit close to home." She adds, "Some people kept telling me I'd be back because I wasn't fully buying into the twelve-step program."

A major aim of the traditional treatment process is for patients to participate in frequent AA meetings and to begin "working the steps" as they go through the program. Both inpatient and outpatient treatment are usually followed by aftercare, which might consist of time in a halfway house, participation in AA, monthly group sessions (which act as booster shots to reinforce commitment to sobriety), and alumni reunions at the treatment center.

Elise says, "I initially grabbed on to the AA concept of powerlessness, but I've found over time that it doesn't completely fit for me. It smacks too much of victimhood, and I am a big believer in accountability for my own actions. At my program, they basically said you'd fail if you tried to go your own way. So far, I've proved them wrong."

Is formal alcohol treatment for you?

"Because I was in such pain, I felt I needed to make a dramatic move to change my behavior," says Elise. If, like Elise, you feel a need for an intensive first attempt at sobriety, formal alcohol treatment can be the way to go. It can also be appropriate for people who have tried and failed at less intensive approaches, such as quitting independently or with recovery groups.

You will certainly have to consider whether your health insurance covers formal alcohol treatment. If not, can you afford it? If your insurance company will foot the bill, it might require you to go to a specific treatment program, so check this out ahead of time. Also, you should consider whether treatment will become part of your permanent medical and health insurance records. It might be wise to find out how this information could be used against you — say, in the case of divorce proceedings.

Whatever the case, you may decide (as many celebrities seem to do) that you want to get away from it all at an inpatient program — to go someplace where you're removed from your regular life and someone takes care of you. Inpatient treatment can be a good choice for someone who is in an extremely disruptive, abusive home situation. Certainly if help with family issues is in order, formal treatment is more likely than a recovery group to address this. For example, a treatment program might involve family members in a structured way and shield you from demanding or vengeful behavior on the part of those close to you.

Another advantage of formal treatment is that you can be assured of professional supervision; for instance, you may feel more comfortable in a group situation if you know that a professional is in the room. Or maybe you're someone who, at least in the beginning, would like the accountability imposed by a treatment program, such as knowing that you have to see a counselor regularly and do the weekly homework assignments or tasks he or she gives you. Anyone who suffers from medical disorders or serious psychological problems such as depression or anxiety is likely to benefit from the involvement of professionals in treatment programs.

Although most treatment programs in the United States are twelve-step–based, the National Treatment Center study suggests that newer programs are somewhat less likely to be so than older ones. Out of curiosity, I contacted a spokesperson for a large university-affiliated medical center with a number of different treatment programs, who told me that working through AA's steps had been a focus of treatment in the past but that the programs now devote a larger percentage of time than in the past to other approaches, such as supportive and cognitive-behavioral counseling. However, these programs do continue to "strongly encourage AA" and include lectures about the twelve steps, visits from AA members, and advice to attend AA meetings. Now they also include information about other groups, such as WFS, and are willing to work with people who do not want to go to AA, but only if requested. All in all, if you're not predisposed to a twelve-step approach, it may take some doing to find a different treatment program. (See "Shopping for a treatment program," pages 286–88.)

Alternative Treatments for Alcohol Problems

From nutritional remedies to acupuncture, some novel approaches to resolving alcohol problems have appeared over the years. Only a small minority of masters mentioned these. Just twelve people, for example, said anything about using a special, alternative diet or nutritional supplements. (For more on nutrition during recovery, see chapter 12.) One person said she benefited from acupuncture, but the counseling relationship she had with her acupuncturist appeared to be more important to her recovery than any physical procedure she underwent.

I asked William Miller, of the University of New Mexico's Center on Alcoholism, Substance Abuse, and Addictions, what studies show about the following approaches. Dr. Miller keeps track of scientific studies on treatment and recovery methods for alcohol problems.

Acupuncture — The jury is out. As of 1998, Dr. Miller and his colleagues had found only two studies suggesting a positive effect and one indicating no benefit when acupuncture was added to other treatments.

Nutritional supplements (such as vitamins) — Dr. Miller knows of no properly controlled scientific studies showing a benefit. He states, "Nutritional supplements are notorious for unsubstantiated claims. 'Very high abstinence rates' reported in uncontrolled studies are not persuasive."

Herbal remedies — To Dr. Miller's knowledge, there have not been any well-designed scientific studies showing a benefit.

Hypnosis — Based on four studies showing no benefit and only one reporting a positive effect, it appears that hypnosis is of very limited, if any, use for treating alcohol problems.

When I asked Dr. Miller if it would be wise to conclude that there is no harm in trying any of these approaches — along with recognized forms of treatment — he said, "It's a bit like asking whether there is any harm in trying the legion of unsubstantiated remedies for cancer. There is usually cost involved and risks of charlatanism. Time, effort, and resources devoted to unsupported methods may diffuse commitment away from approaches that are truly likely to help."

The Progressive Approach

You don't have to pick any one of the foregoing approaches as *your* approach. What you might try is a progressive strategy — known in the medical world as a "stepped care" approach — to deal with a drinking problem. With this method, you start out with less intensive options and gradually work up to more stringent approaches if the less aggressive remedies don't work. (It's like first treating high blood pressure with diet and exercise, then taking increasingly powerful medications if diet and exercise modifications aren't effective.)

Some masters, like sixty-two-year-old Jessica C., unknowingly used this progressive strategy. Jessica first realized she had a drinking problem when she was in her mid-thirties. Over the course of the next ten years or so, she tried various approaches, beginning with trying to manage her alcohol problem on her own and ending with going into alcohol treatment. After trying to cut back by herself, she went to a psychologist, who recommended that she stop drinking. This led to three years of abstinence, followed by four years of reasonably successful controlled drinking. With time, however, Jessica's drinking crept up until she was drinking "alcoholically" and her life was a shambles. At this point, she says, "I realized that just not drinking or controlled drinking did not work for me, because I had given it all I had. So I went to a new therapist, and with her prodding and my checking out various recovery groups, I finally got tired and gave up and asked to go into treatment." After attending a traditional twelve-step–based inpatient treatment program, she got help from both AA and Women for Sobriety. In essence, Jessica dealt with her drinking problem by using a stepped care approach, and she has now been abstinent for more than fifteen years.

In contrast, as *the first course of action* for their drinking problems, a number of masters were advised or forced to do more or less the opposite of what Jessica did: they went directly into formal treatment and then into regular, long-term AA attendance. For some masters, this aggressive approach worked. For others, it backfired. And for others still, it may have been unnecessary.

Take the case of Janet C., who drank three to five drinks a night at the most. Even though she had decided to quit drinking before her therapist suggested it, the therapist proceeded to recommend a one-month outpatient alcohol treatment program for Janet and her husband. The program in turn suggested that Janet go to three AA meetings a week for a year, which she dutifully did. After that, she stopped going to AA, and without any further contact with recovery groups, she has remained abstinent for well over a decade. Questions are now being raised about whether it makes sense to encourage or coerce problem drinkers like this to use stringent resolution methods as their first course of action when a less aggressive, less costly strategy might do.

For a severe drinking problem, a formal treatment program might indeed be the best first approach. (Even then, it's not always necessary, as the masters demonstrate.) But since most alcohol problems are not severe, using a stepped care approach — perhaps starting out by trying to solve your problem on your own, with the help of a book, or with brief intervention from a professional — can make sense. If these approaches aren't adequate, the next step might be to move on to counseling and/or a recovery group and then possibly to formal treatment, if necessary. (Actually, many masters tried moderate drinking as their first option; because of its controversy and complexity, the approach warrants a separate chapter, chapter 8.)

However you choose to get sober — be it through obtaining formal treatment, going to recovery group meetings, seeking professional counseling, or quitting drinking on your own — the message from the masters is that you have to do it your way.

7

You *Can* Help

The Masters' Advice to Family and Friends

Can family and friends help a loved one with an alcohol problem? What do the masters have to say about this? Contrary to the prevalent notion that there's little or nothing others can do to change the behavior of a serious problem drinker, their responses — along with some research — suggest that there *are* things family and friends can do that could make a difference. The masters' experiences provide insights and strategies worth trying (ideally, under a professional's guidance) with a problem drinker who is not ready to get sober or who has had repeated encounters with traditional treatment approaches, only to relapse.

Elena G.'s Story

Elena G. comes from a family riddled with alcohol problems; when she was eight, her father died while under the influence in a drunk driving accident, and just recently her mother died from alcohol-related health problems. That's why Elena swore she would never drink, a vow she stuck to through adolescence but that fell to the wayside when she started dating her husband-to-be, Brett, in her early twenties. On one of their first dates Elena told Brett that she didn't like the taste of alcohol, so he ordered her a sweet-tasting sloe gin fizz. Within months she was ordering two drinks to his every one.

Brett told me, "Elena's alcohol problem was apparent within the first year of our marriage. But I didn't see it as serious, because she had just started drinking." He began to recognize the depth of her alcohol involvement seven years later, when she became pregnant with their son yet continued to drink excessively on occasion. "One time, I recall her getting drunk and throwing up blood," he said. "That's when it really hit me that she had an alcohol problem. I thought, 'If you still do this when you're carrying a baby . . .'"

The happy ending of the story is that after years of stashing liquor bottles in secret places, downing daily quarts of hard liquor, and experiencing regular blackouts, constant marital fighting over her drinking, and drunken nights that sometimes left her lying in her own urine and vomit, Elena got sober and has remained that way for twelve years. She and Brett are still together, and their son, Glen, has grown into a delightful young man who is pursuing a graduate degree. I talked with the whole family about what they think helped, didn't help, and might have helped Elena come to terms with her drinking problem.

"My dad made me a liquor cop"

According to all three of them, what didn't work was nagging, humiliation, and trying to control Elena's drinking. Brett says, "I would try to hide her bottles, take it from her. But she doesn't like anyone controlling her. I also tried embarrassing her. That didn't work either. I did it all wrong." Eventually, he says, "I learned that there is no way you can make someone stop drinking." Similarly, Glen says, "I hid my mom's liquor and dumped it down the drain. My dad made me a liquor cop because I was supposed to keep an eye on her. This was very stressful for a little kid."

Elena's drinking was indeed hurting her son. He notes, "No one knew about her alcohol problem — people were shocked when they eventually found out about it. As a child, it was very embarrassing and difficult to carry the secret." Glen's biggest fear was that his parents would get divorced. He explains, "There was lots of fighting going on — as an only child, I felt it was my job to save the family and take care of everything. Life was unpredictable. One time, after a soccer practice, no one came to pick me up. My mom was in a bar, drinking with a friend. It all left me with a fear of being abandoned."

Glen agrees with his father that trying to control the drinking and nagging were to no avail, adding, "I don't think anything would have really helped until *she* was ready." Elena tried to quit drinking a number of times before finally succeeding, but her efforts would last only a few days. Of these attempts, she says, "The thought of never drinking again *terrorized* me." Starting in the late afternoon and continuing into the "wee hours of the morning," she drank. During the day, she downed milkshakes, fast food, and whatever else helped her nurse her hangovers — all of which packed on a lot of excess weight.

Of her husband's and son's efforts to get her to abandon alcohol, Elena says, "Most of the time they just made me angry. The nagging, fighting, threatening, and reminding me the next day of all the horrible things I'd done the night before just made me want to drink even more. Eventually," she recalls, "Brett knew he wouldn't get me to stop, so he tried to be more understanding. He would fix me my drinks, trying to make them weaker. What he didn't know was that I was sneaking to my hiding places for booze and drinking more afterward."

"Dear Mom, I love you so much. I'm afraid you're going to kill yourself"

Finally, Elena's love and concern for her child — and, in turn, his love and concern for her — won out. Normally Glen would protect her, hide her problem, not bring friends home, and clean up after her accidents. But when he was about nine, he started to become disrespectful. For instance, if Elena offered to help him with his homework, he would say something like "Dad will help me; I don't need a drunk's help." His feelings didn't really hit home with Elena until one night when she showed up at one of his Little League games — which she rarely did, because it "cut into her drinking time" — obviously under the influence. After the game, Glen went over to her and quietly and angrily said, "Mom, don't ever come to one of my games again." His words compelled her to go home and drink some more, but it was the beginning of the end of her drinking.

The final straw occurred several months later, when, after passing out from an evening of drinking, Elena awakened at four A.M. to find a note from her son tucked inside her shirt. The note read, "Dear Mom, I love you so much. I wish you would stop doing this because I'm afraid you're going to kill yourself." As Elena explains, "Almost all of the other attempts to get me to stop drinking, especially from my husband, were done in an angry and arrogant way," but this note got through to her. She had had it with her drinking — she was "sick of being sick." But the greatest motivation was her desire to stop hurting her son: "I felt so sad in seeing his sadness."

"I didn't want to disappoint them"

When her husband and son awakened the next morning, they were both dubious about Elena's tearful vow to end her drinking days and seek help. Glen remembers, "I felt guilty, but I was skeptical. I didn't know how long it would last and kept waiting for the other shoe to drop. But it didn't."

That very night Elena went to an AA meeting. She says of her initial experience, "I wanted to get the hell out of there because I wasn't as bad as them." She didn't go back for nearly a week because of what she describes as a deathly flulike sickness, which she now recognizes as withdrawal from alcohol (and for which she should have sought medical help). "After I got through it, my

family was ecstatic that I hadn't drunk for three or four days."
She went back to AA but was still uncomfortable, until a woman
whom she never saw again gently squeezed her arm and whis-
pered, "I know this doesn't make sense now, but stay — it will."
She felt the woman's compassion and continued to go to meetings
frequently for several months. Before the first year's end, she
stopped going to meetings because she "outgrew them" and the
"mud, blood, and beer stories" depressed her. Since then, Elena
has stayed sober on her own.

Looking back on it all, Elena says, "If you had asked me
twenty years ago why I drank, I'd have said, 'I don't know — I
have a beautiful home, a wonderful husband, and a great kid.'"
Now, however, she feels that from the time she was a child, there
was a "black hole" inside her. She explains, "I grew up in housing
projects with an alcoholic mother on welfare, and I never completed high school. I felt like a loser inside." Because these feelings
remained when she got sober, Elena says the first two years of sobriety were particularly difficult. "Many times I was angry at myself for telling my husband and son that I had quit drinking. I
wanted to go back, and drinking was constantly on my mind. But
I didn't want to disappoint them. That kept me sober."

"There was a beautiful woman inside me"

Elena also found it helpful that her husband offered to give up alcohol too, which he did for the first several years of her sobriety.
She notes, "He was tremendously supportive. He started telling
me I looked nice, even though I was up to 260 pounds. And my
son kept telling me how proud he was of me."

Still, sobriety was something Elena fought for tooth and nail
until she unexpectedly found something more to stay sober for.
About two years after she quit drinking, she had lost thirty
pounds, and a woman stopped her in a store to comment on how
handsome she was and invite her to attend a model search that
evening. Elena decided to check it out and found herself chosen

out of three hundred women to be one of a small handful of potential models. This launched her into her current successful career as a plus-size, "mature" model, and she proceeded to lose another forty pounds. "I had never worn makeup or taken care of my appearance. My newfound vanity gave me new motivation to stay sober. There was a beautiful woman inside me who had been dying for so many years."

Today, Elena's family has no regret about sticking with her through it all. Brett says, "I'm very proud of her. I'm glad I married her, and I'm glad I stayed with her." She went public with her past when the local paper wanted to do a story on her career as a model and the tale of her drinking days tearfully came out. She has since shared her story in numerous newspaper accounts and on national television shows, including *Oprah*.

Elena is now also involved with motivational speaking, sharing her drinking story with audiences ranging from young people to prisoners to women's groups. "I've read that millions of women drink in their homes, in secret," she says. "More need to hear that it's never too late to turn it around. Who better than me to let other women know that there is life not only after booze but after fifty, after gray hair, after two packs of cigarettes a day, and after weighing more than two hundred pounds!"

Misconceptions About Helping the Problem Drinker

Estimates suggest that for every problem drinker, there are five other people who suffer as a result. Many of these "other people" — like Brett and Glen — feel helpless. The idea that you can't do much to change a loved one with a drinking problem is in part perpetuated by Al-Anon, the widely available support program which espouses the idea that people affected by a problem drinker cannot change or control anyone but themselves. The group suggests in its literature that the only way to motivate the problem drinker is to allow the drinking (and its consequences) to become "so painful in itself that the alcoholic will seek escape from the intolerable pain caused by drinking."

To be sure, quite a few masters responded to my question about how others can help with comments suggesting powerlessness. Ralph C. states, "Unless a person really does want to quit for himself, nothing a friend or family member says or does will make a difference." Although it's certainly true that alcohol abusers have to make the decision to quit for themselves, that doesn't mean you can't do anything to move the process along.

Indeed, the bulk of the masters' responses to this question suggests that there are many things you can try, which might make it easier for you to deal with the situation and live more peacefully. Research studies too suggest that family members can play a major role in getting unmotivated loved ones to seek help.

Support Doesn't Have to Come from Those Who Have Been There

Five of the masters' ten most frequent responses to the question "When you were finally successful at taking hold of your drinking problem, what approaches did you use?" had to do with the importance of support. *But rather than agreeing with the popular idea that support has to come from others who are "in recovery," the masters indicate that it can come in different ways* — from friends and family, a counselor, *or* other sober people.

Not surprisingly, those who got sober with formal help were more likely to stress the importance of support from recovery groups and other recovered people than loners who didn't use ongoing formal help were. Comments about the importance of having a relationship with another person who has recovered were more likely to come from masters who achieved sobriety through twelve-step programs than from people who did so in nontraditional ways — again, not a surprise, given AA's emphasis on sponsorship. Loners were more likely to emphasize that support from family and friends was important to their recovery than were those who got sober through AA.

What the Masters Have to Say to Family and Friends

Overall, the masters repeatedly mentioned the importance of putting the responsibility for dealing with the alcohol problem squarely on the person in question while continuing to love him or her. Their advice suggests that what works depends on the individual. As such, they offer many different — and sometimes conflicting — strategies. Doing the "right" thing can depend on how severe the alcohol problem is and on how in touch with it the person in question seems to be. What works for someone who is highly functional in daily life and who knows that alcohol is causing trouble, for instance, may not be the solution for someone who denies that there is a problem.

What the masters say in this context is not necessarily what worked for them when they were still drinking; their comments largely reflect their opinions in retrospect. Some of them offer ideas about approaches that they think *might* have helped at the time. Also, their advice may reflect some of their more recent experiences working with still-struggling drinkers.

Certainly no one expects you to become an expert, and getting professional help is advised (see pages 268–72). But about the worst thing you can do is nothing. When asked what didn't help, Herbert Z.'s wife responded, "Inertia. Not doing anything will not help, nor will the problem go away." As the alcohol expert Dr. Marc Schuckit says in *Educating Yourself About Alcohol and Drugs,* the goal is not to "rescue" a loved one with a drinking problem. "If you care," he writes, "your job is to do everything possible to maximize the chances that he or she will seek help and stop substance use."

Here are the most common suggestions drawn from the masters' responses to my request to "list three things you think friends and family members can do to help a loved one who is still struggling and/or is not ready to deal with a serious drinking problem":

Suggestion #1: Don't make it easy
for the drinker to keep on drinking

The masters' most frequent comments about helping a loved one had to do with discontinuing "enabling," along with putting the onus for the drinker's behavior and its consequences on the drinker. Betty B. captures the gist of these responses: "Do *not* cover up for them. Let them be responsible for their actions." Here's how Herb N. puts it: "Accept your responsibility, if any, for enabling, and then transfer 100 percent of the responsibility back to the alcoholic once you have talked it over. He or she is then unable to use you as an excuse."

"Enabling" includes protecting the problem drinker from the negative consequences of alcohol use. After all, if someone makes excuses when you miss appointments because of drinking too much, reheats dinner because you've missed it after stopping at the bar on the way home from work, readily has sex with you even if you're drunk, or lends you money every time you lose your job, what incentive is there to quit? That's why Jordan L. admonishes, "Stop bailing them out of trouble."

In Elena G.'s case, her young son, Glen, unwittingly did the wrong thing by cleaning up after her when she vomited from drinking too much. In contrast, her husband, Brett, probably did the right thing when he made her clean up or refused to call in to work saying she was sick when she was hung over. Heather F.'s husband caught on to the fact that he was encouraging her drunkenness when he comforted her during sobbing bouts, which regularly occurred while she was under the influence. "At first he felt sorry for me because I would drink and let out all my feelings of sadness," she explains. "But when he figured out what was going on, he said, 'I'm not doing this anymore.'"

Ralph C. acknowledges, "Although it's hard not to want to bail someone out of a tough spot, it's the best way for that person to regain confidence and self-respect." He shares a story from his own experience. When he was just out of treatment, he needed transportation. He finally scraped together two hundred dollars to buy "an old rust-bucket," which ate up a fair amount of money in repair bills. He found out later that his dad and brother had "debated long and hard" about whether to help him out financially. "Fortunately for all concerned," Ralph says in retrospect, "they let me deal with it by myself. It gave me a goal and sense of accomplishment once I was able to afford a more reliable used car."

The bottom line is that it's critical to stop all behavior that supports — or could support — drinking.

Suggestion #2: Don't stop loving them

A powerful theme in the masters' advice for families and friends is continuing to love the problem drinker unconditionally — being supportive, offering encouragement, and not abandoning him or her. Calvin A. advises, "Work with them to recognize that you care for them but that their behavior is harmful to themselves and others." Zoe A. offers, "Reassure them that you love them unconditionally — that you will be there for them, but that does not include picking up the pieces for them." A somewhat different but important message from Jean A. is to "be supportive and nonjudgmental — as much as you can without compromising yourself." Clay R. sums up: "Love from family can be crucial to the alcoholic's recovery. It does not necessarily include acceptance of the alcoholic's drinking. Make it clear that it is the drinking and not the person that you do not accept."

One way to show your love and support is to provide positive reinforcement for sober behavior. Master Maost R. suggests,

"Find opportunities for pleasant relating when the person is sober. Express a desire for unencumbered relating, as in 'I can enjoy you more when you are sober.'" He adds, "But this is very unlikely to have any effect when the person is under the influence."

Suggestion #3: Don't nag, criticize, preach, or complain

Many masters agree with Elena and her family that nagging, begging, confiscating liquor, and sorrowfully reminding the person of the night before are to little or no avail. Thomas V. attests, "The more I was urged to cut back or quit, the more I denied I had a problem. My advice is, 'Don't push.'" Herbert Z.'s wife offered insights about why this approach doesn't work. She told me, "Nagging makes you feel bad, and addicts use it as another reason to use [the substance] and criticize you at the same time. It's a bad cycle to get into. Herb saw nagging as my attempt to control him, and it gave him another reason to believe that I was the problem and not him."

Betty B. says, "Long before I walked through the doors of AA, suggestions had been offered to me about my drinking. But the help was always from people who presented themselves as superior and who looked down at me as though I was a bad person. The overtone of parental disapproval was always present." AA appealed to her because instead of hearing "This is what you should do," she heard, "This is what I did."

In working with families of problem drinkers, Robert J. Meyers, M.S., director and developer of the Community Reinforcement and Family Training (CRAFT) family intervention program for problem drinkers at the University of New Mexico, finds that it is far more constructive to identify specific problem behaviors when the person is sober than to nag and complain about drinking. Master Clare J. says, "Let him or her know when a specific drinking incident has created a problem — but be objective and neutral, and don't nag." For instance, you might say, "Last night when you drove home after the card party, I was really worried that you might get stopped by the police or have an accident." Meyers adds, "Rather than continue to complain about how tired you are of the drinking, it's better to put it in terms of how the drinking affects you." You could say something like "I miss the way we used to go for walks every night when we first got married."

Heather F. gives several examples of how loved ones pointed out specific problems caused by her drinking and how it affected them. "It had a big impact when, after a night of drinking and socializing with my sister and her husband, my sister reminded me of a heated argument he and I had. I asked her, 'What argument?' I had no recollection of it. A little later, the depth of my alcohol abuse really hit me when my sister lovingly said, 'I'm not being judgmental, but I'm really alarmed because you seemed completely normal, not drunk, last night. That shows that your tolerance for alcohol is really high, and I'm just worried about you.'" Heather didn't stop drinking right away, but she maintains that her sister's comments planted some seeds that stayed with her until she was ready to quit.

Another incident had an even greater impact, right after Heather gave birth to her first child. "During an evening spent with my best friend and her husband, it was obvious that I was right back to my pre-pregnancy drinking habits. The next morning my friend called me and kind of jokingly but matter-of-factly said, 'The old Heather was back last night — I really liked you better when you weren't drinking during your pregnancy.'" That same day Heather made her first call to get help.

Dr. Marc Schuckit, who has worked with problem drinkers and their families for decades, suggests in his book that when you do address a drinker, you should do so when the person is not under the influence, irritable, or hung over. He notes, "The best times are actually when the individual is feeling fairly good and/or experiencing some remorse about how his or her life is going."

Suggestion #4: Address the drinking problem directly

Over and over, the masters shared comments like these:

◆ "Let them know that you are aware of their drinking problem. I thought I had everyone fooled, and they never told me otherwise." — Jackie D.

◆ "Hold a mirror up to the person, showing his or her behavior clearly and honestly." — Anne H.

◆ "Be open to discussing the behavior — it makes the loved one uncomfortable, but it needs doing." — Sarah N.

◆ "Explain that you think they have a problem and which of their actions gives you that idea. Offer to help." — Simon T.

Although nagging and complaining are certainly ineffective, so is the contrary tack of ignoring a drinking problem. Both Herbert Z. and his wife agree that avoiding the problem is counterproductive. She told me, "In our family, Herb's drinking was hidden from the public and other family members. I was constantly mediating between Herb and the children and Herb and the world. I was exhausted from keeping things looking okay. Herb didn't have to acknowledge or deny anything. There was tremendous relief when I first named the problem — initially to Herb, then to friends and family. I said to him, 'Herb, from what I know about it, it looks like you are an alcoholic.' Saying and hearing the words in a loving conversation made it real for both of us. We could each decide on our own how we would respond. It was no longer unspoken and hidden — kind of like unveiling the two-ton elephant sitting in the middle of the room."

Herbert says, "When my wife asked me to consider whether I might be an alcoholic, I rejected the idea, but I took enough warning from the question to modify my drinking in the direction of less hard liquor and more beer and wine instead. This softened my drinking behavior somewhat."

Although Elena G. says that her husband was forever on her back, not once during her drinking years did an employer address her alcohol problem — despite the fact that she held more than thirty jobs in twenty years. "None of them lasted for long," she remembers. "I would come into work hung over or return from a lunch break high from drinking. Often I would get sent home, or they would fire me. I never connected it to my drinking." Because the employers never told her that her alcohol use was the reason for termination, Elena thought she was fired for incompetence, which only made her drinking worse.

Similarly, Herbert Z., a lawyer who was able to practice despite his heavy abuse of alcohol, often to the point of unconsciousness, does not recall anyone other than his wife intervening about his drinking. He notes, "People just accepted me the way I was and made adjustments. I don't remember running into any direct challenge to my drinking from school authorities when I regularly got drunk in college, nor from employers or doctors later in life." Looking back, he says, "It might have helped if someone somewhere along the line had said, 'Stop or you have to go.'"

A number of masters said they wish they had been confronted. As Kathryn N. puts it, "I don't know if I would have listened, but I've always wished that someone in my family or friendship circle had expressed concern about my drinking, and then I would have stopped sooner." Amy P. laments, "When I called my sister two nights in a row telling her the exact same thing, I wish she had confronted me. She knew I was drunk but didn't mention it. Several other people spent lots of time on the phone with me and knew I was drunk but never confronted me. I believe it would have brought reality to me sooner if these people refused to talk with me and said something like 'Call me back when you haven't been drinking — I am not going to speak with you until you are sober.'"

Martin E. offers some sound advice if the person seems resistant to facing his or her alcohol abuse: "Don't avoid opportunities to relate the drinking problem to other problems." Robert Meyers agrees, noting that "you don't have to put the alcohol problem up front. Another way to go about it is to point out some other problem the person is having related to his drinking." In Elena's case, someone might have helped her look at the fact that she couldn't hold down a job — and led her to see the connection with alcohol.

The masters disagree about just how confrontational family and friends should be when addressing the alcohol problem. Many stress that the approach should be nonthreatening and loving but honest. A good number of others think that family and friends should consider serious confrontation, such as giving an ultimatum with consequences or arranging a formal intervention. (See page 164, "Three Approaches for Helping Family and Friends.")

Whether you use a confrontational or a gentler approach may have to do with what else you've already tried. Timothy O'Farrell, Ph.D., chief of the Harvard Families and Addiction Program, offers some logical advice: "I would not start with confrontation. But if direct, softer approaches don't get the person's attention, then I'd consider more confrontational strategies."

Suggestion #5: Seek help

I must confess that when I interviewed Elena G. and her family, I was dumbfounded to learn that they never sought help of any kind in the twenty years of her severe alcohol abuse. Elena says, "If my husband had sought help, he would have been admitting how serious my problem was. It was a big family secret." But other masters emphasized the importance of *not* going it alone when someone you care about has a drinking problem. Zoe A.'s comment captures the essence of many of their suggestions: "Join a support group to keep your own life buoyant and prosperous and to analyze your own negative coping strategies."

Not surprisingly, many of the masters who took traditional twelve-step recovery routes suggested going to Al-Anon, also a twelve-step–based program. Also, a number of masters made a general comment that family and friends should seek counseling for their own benefit. Herbert Z.'s wife did both. "About a year after talking to Herb about his problem, I started going to Al-Anon meetings. One of the things I learned there was that I was ready to do something for myself in order to find some relief from my husband's drinking problem. So I also started seeing a therapist, who helped me decide what to do in and out of the marriage. Going to both Al-Anon and counseling not only helped me but also provided Herb with another reality check about his drinking."

A number of studies suggest that marriage and family counseling can motivate a problem drinker to make a commitment to change. If physical violence or abuse is involved, professional help should definitely be sought.

Suggestion #6: Detach, separate, walk away

Somewhat at odds with the message of continuing love and compassion is the more "tough-love" message that came from many of the masters — some of whom gave both suggestions. A more compassionate approach may be in order in the beginning, but a time may come, particularly after you've tried to help repeatedly and failed, when you need to walk away from the situation. Kerry G. suggests, "If it's adversely affecting you, don't put up with it. It's hard to do, but sometimes losing the people you love is what it takes for the message to sink in."

Billy R. advises, "Decide how much you are willing to put up with. Let the person know what will happen if he doesn't stop. And whatever you decide, stick to it. Don't make idle threats." Regretting that her limits were "pretty blurred" when Herbert Z. was drinking, his wife suggests that you need to "set limits for yourself and be prepared to act on them. This will help you survive *and* communicate that there is a serious problem in the house."

It's essential, as Clay R. emphasizes, for loved ones to "firmly withdraw from the alcoholic if he threatens the family's or any family member's security or well-being." Likewise, Robert Meyers stresses the need to separate from a drinker who is physically abusive.

Suggestion #7: Set a good example

From her own experience, Elena G. thinks it's important for family and friends not to drink in front of people they'd like to stop drinking. Indeed, one of the common themes in the masters' advice to loved ones is to be good role models, setting an example by taking steps like avoiding drinking around them and not bringing alcohol into the house. Elena adds, "Don't let your good times revolve around drinking." She recalls how many of the things she and her husband did together used to involve alcohol: "Every event I perceived as a good time revolved around booze. And Brett just went along with me. We would go to his softball games and out for beer afterward. And if we went to parties or summer picnics, alcohol was always involved."

In short, if a major focus of your relationship with a problem drinker has been alcohol — say, you go to a lot of parties with friends who drink, or you're in the habit of having nightly cocktails together — it's wise to reexamine how you spend time together and then try to find sober alternatives, such as going for walks in the evening or attending cultural events more often.

Elena G. maintains that her husband *did* try to get her to do something other than drink at night, like go to the movies. She says she would refuse because the activity cut into her drinking time. As Robert Meyers points out, the mistake in this case was that the husband made the choices — it's important for the decisions to be left to the person with the alcohol problem.

Suggestion #8: Take care of yourself

"Live a full life of your own."

"Make sure you live a life of your own that does not depend on the undependable person."

"Carry on with your life after you've let the alcoholic know you aren't babysitting anymore."

"Let them go, and focus on your own health and peace of mind."

These comments from masters underline the importance of taking care of yourself despite the problems with the drinker. Often, however, in an attempt to hide a family member's alcohol abuse from others, spouses withdraw and isolate themselves from friends and other family members. Taking care of yourself might mean signing up for a class in the evenings, getting together with buddies from the past, or going away by yourself for a weekend.

Suggestion #9: Be there for them when they're ready

Most of the comments on this subject went like this: "Be available when the alcoholic reaches out." "When they hold out their hand for help, grab it." "Help as many times as you are asked. Be there."

When I asked Elena why she thinks her husband stayed with her through her drinking days, she responded, "His parents taught him that if you care about someone, you never give up on them. I think he always thought I'd come out of it. He just didn't know it would take twenty years!" She feels that one of the most important messages for friends and family is to "encourage the problem drinker to try again and again." Calvin A. adds, "Be loving but firm, and understand that they may need a number of tries to get and stay sober."

A number of masters recommended encouraging *any* positive change in the drinker. Thomas V. advises, "Encourage efforts to quit even when they don't seem to be working. Relapses are learning experiences." Although Elena's husband and son were skeptical of her vow to quit because of her many short-lived attempts, their praise made it all the more difficult for her to go back.

If the person seems somewhat ready to change, you might also help him or her explore recovery alternatives. Herbert Z. goes so far as to suggest, "Put scientific literature about alcoholism (not religious or moral tracts) in their way where they just might glance at it or pick it up. Make sure that they are aware there are alternatives." Jean A. says, "Do the research to see what kind of help is available in your area, so that when the person is ready, you will have that information for them." You might even attend some recovery groups yourself to have a better understanding of the options. SMART Recovery and SOS, for instance, welcome friends and family members at their meetings.

Three Approaches for Helping Family and Friends

Chances are, if you call around trying to find help for dealing with someone with an alcohol problem, you'll be referred to the self-help group Al-Anon. Or you may be advised to arrange a family intervention to persuade the drinker to enter treatment. Another option is to seek out one of the family programs that have recently appeared on the scene, which offer behavioral approaches designed to engage the problem drinker *and* to better the lives of family and friends. The results of a well-designed research study recently published in the prestigious *Journal of Consulting and Clinical Psychology* suggest that the family approach is far more effective than others in getting an unmotivated problem drinker to get help.

Al-Anon

Al-Anon Family Groups provide support to people affected by someone else's drinking — whether or not the person is still drinking. Alateen is part of Al-Anon and is designed for younger relatives and friends (through age nineteen) of problem drinkers. Although Al-Anon is separate from AA, it is based on the twelve steps and twelve traditions of AA, which members are encouraged to practice and apply to their lives. The program holds that "alcoholism" is a family illness and that changed attitudes can facilitate recovery. However, one of its main tenets is that others cannot change the problem drinker; only the problem drinker can change himself or herself.

Al-Anon advocates detaching yourself from the drinker's problems while continuing to love him or her. The group encourages its members to reach their own potential and build satisfying lives regardless of what happens at home. Al-Anon is not designed to get the problem drinker into treatment; rather, its intent is to provide support for the drinker's loved ones.

Some research suggests that Al-Anon does indeed achieve its goal of helping family members cope better. As such, its main benefit appears to be improved functioning for the family member who attends Al-Anon, not for the problem drinker.

For more information, contact:

Al-Anon Family Group Headquarters, Inc.
1600 Corporate Landing Parkway
Virginia Beach, VA 23454

Phone: 757-563-1600, or 888-4AL-ANON for meeting
  information
Web address: http://www.al-anon.alateen.org

Formal intervention

In contrast to Al-Anon, the goal of intervention *is* to get a problem drinker to agree to enter treatment as a first step toward sobriety. Typically, a formal intervention is a confrontational meeting organized by the drinker's family to lay out the negative impact of the alcohol abuse over the years and the consequences family members are prepared to carry out if the drinker refuses to accept treatment. According to the National Council on Alcoholism and Drug Dependence (NCADD), "The most successful interventions take place when the team members — family, friends, and coworkers — have been well prepared by an intervention professional." This organization suggests that an intervention should be done in a caring, loving manner with the intent of providing factual information about the effect the person's drinking has on those who care about him or her.

As common as interventions are in U.S. treatment centers, there is little research support for their effectiveness. In fact, in a recent examination of studies on ways to get unmotivated problem drinkers to seek help, Timothy O'Farrell, Ph.D., of Harvard Medical School, and William Fals-Stewart, Ph.D., of Old Dominion University, conclude that formal intervention "apparently does not work very well to promote treatment entry, despite its adherents' claims." One problem seems to be that families who begin the process of a formal intervention more often than not do not go through with the family confrontation meeting; when they do complete that meeting, their loved ones *are* more likely to enter treatment.

Interestingly, when I asked the masters for advice for family and friends, not many suggested formal intervention. Nor did many get sober as a result of such confrontation; just 7 out of the 222 masters stated that a formal intervention was the turning point in their recovery.

To find local individuals who are trained in conducting formal interventions, contact the National Council on Alcoholism and Drug Dependence by calling 800-654-HOPE or 800-NCA-CALL.

Behavorial family programs

Less common than Al-Anon and formal interventions are research-based behavioral programs involving spouses or other family members. According to Robert Meyers, programs like CRAFT are designed to help loved ones get unmotivated problem drinkers to seek help. These programs typically work from a premise opposite to the "powerlessness" approach of Al-Anon, teaching family members that they can learn specific skills that will have a substantial effect on the drinker's alcohol use and increase the odds that the drinker will seek help. Family members are taught how to communicate more effectively with the problem drinker, how to reinforce nondrinking behavior, and how to plan enjoyable activities that can replace drinking. A main focus for participants is learning how to interact with the drinker in a positive way when he or she is not drinking.

According to a recent study in the *Journal of Consulting and Clinical Psychology,* initially unmotivated problem drinkers whose loved ones (primarily spouses and parents) had been trained in the CRAFT approach were more than three times as likely to seek treatment by the end of one year as those of family members who received a counseling approach based on Al-Anon.* (Although the focus of Al-Anon is not to get the drinker into treatment, family members looking for help are commonly referred to the group.) Compared with formal intervention, the CRAFT program led to nearly double the percentage of problem drinkers seeking help.

Unfortunately, if you try to locate a behavioral program for families in the United States, your options are few. Aside from the CRAFT program, I am aware only of the Counseling for Alcoholics' Marriages (CALM) project, affiliated with the Veterans Administration Hospital in Brockton, Massachusetts. The CRAFT program has been conducting training sessions for professionals across the country and may be able to connect you with someone in your area. To locate a private therapist for help in this area, seek out a behaviorally oriented addiction specialist who is knowledgeable and has experience with non–twelve-step family approaches.

---

* Participants in the study worked through Al-Anon's initial steps and became familiar with the program's philosophy while working with experienced counselors. Participants were also encouraged to attend Al-Anon meetings, which most of them did.

For more information, contact the CRAFT program:

Phone: 505-768-0109
e-mail address: bmeyers@unm.edu
Web address: http://unm.edu/~craft

Contact the CALM project by calling 508-583-4500, extension 3493.

For Family and Friends of the Newly Sober Person

Once the drinker decides to get sober, how can you increase the odds that he or she will *stay* sober? Elena G. says, "I don't know how easy it would have been if my husband had not quit drinking for the first several years or if we had had liquor in the house." After the first two or three years of her sobriety, Brett asked if she minded his having an occasional drink, and she said it was okay with her. Because her six brothers and two sisters "all have alcohol problems to varying degrees," Elena also found it easier to avoid them the first few years after she quit drinking.

One of the biggest surprises for Elena and Brett in early sobriety was the fact that life did not immediately become terrific. Brett says, "The financial problems were still there, we still had fights (but less frequently), and she still had bad mood swings." For Elena, "Life still sucked. Throughout the first several years of sobriety, I can't tell you how much anger and hostility I felt. I despised anyone who could drink socially and despised the fact that I couldn't."

After she had been sober for a year, Elena noticed that her son had a low opinion of himself and suggested that they all go into family counseling, which they attended for about a year, finding it helpful. Research suggests that family and marriage counseling increases the odds of staying sober and also helps with family adjustment.

But Elena continued to feel lonely, sad, resentful, and very moody. Recently, however, her life has taken a huge turn for the better, since she started seeing a psychiatrist who diagnosed her as having bipolar disorder, formerly known as manic depression. Since she has been on medication, she feels like a new person. Glen told me he is happy that his mother did not turn back to the bottle to self-medicate her depression. All in all, he says, "I'm completely proud of her — I'm more than that, I'm *immensely* proud!"

8

One Drink Does Not a Drunk Make

How the Masters Determined Whether They Could Ever Drink Again

One drink for a recovered "alcoholic" and she'll pick up drinking right where she left off — isn't that a fact? While it is true that the vast majority of the masters feel they cannot have any alcohol, a handful have found that they are able to drink moderately. Another dozen or so have a small amount of alcohol on rare occasions without getting into any trouble. I am not suggesting that moderate or even occasional drinking is a workable goal for most people with serious drinking problems. But this select group of masters is living proof that at least for some people, one drink does not necessarily a drunk make.

Quite honestly, I was hesitant even to bring up the subject of "drinking again" — in part because it's controversial and risky, but also because so many of the masters have made a firm commitment to abstinence. In fact, one after another told me that he or she had tried for years to control drinking with no success. Most would say that it's simply easier not to drink at all.

However, the small number of masters who *are* moderate and occasional drinkers, along with studies showing that moderate drinking is possible for some former problem drinkers, convinced me that it would be a gross oversight not to address the issue when presenting the many approaches for dealing with alcohol problems. Indeed, although research shows that people with very serious drinking problems recover predominantly through abstinence, a sizable body of evidence also indicates that those with less serious problems resolve them more often than is commonly believed by learning to cut back and control their drinking.

Nolan H.'s Story

Always the kind of guy who liked to walk on the wild side, Nolan H. was addicted to both alcohol and cocaine by the time he was in his mid-twenties. Now a churchgoing forty-six-year-old father and responsible married man, he still rides a motorcycle and jet-skis at speeds of more than sixty miles per hour — new highs that have taken the place of drugs and alcohol in his life. His alcohol problem has been resolved for twelve years now, but not in the stereotypical way. He's one of the small number of masters who have been able to return to nonproblematic drinking.

More than a decade ago, after the birth of his second child, Nolan knew he was in trouble when he stayed out partying with the boys until the morning's wee hours. "At two A.M., high on cocaine and beer, I was pacing in my living room, with my heart racing — still going one hundred miles an hour. I realized that what I was doing wasn't normal," he says. Not prone to expressing his emotions openly, Nolan slipped his wife a note that morning announcing that he was going to go into treatment and making it clear that he didn't want to back out. After taking about a month to get his business affairs in order (and having a few final flings with drugs and alcohol), he checked in for a one-month stay at a residential treatment center. Aside from attending AA meetings for the first six months after treatment, he has maintained sobriety on his own since then.

At first it wasn't easy to stay away from his drug-using friends and from bars, but the six-foot-one-inch Nolan soon discovered the joy of running. "When I quit drinking, my weight was up to 237. So I started running, lost weight, and began to feel good." He adds, "The up side of not drinking began far to outweigh the down side. The down side was giving up a couple of hours of pleasure, if that. The up side was that I would get up in the morning and feel so good about myself, my body, and my family. I felt good about abstaining." And abstain he did — for eight years.

"I don't let situations control whether I have a drink"

Then, four years ago, Nolan started wondering whether he could have a glass of wine or a beer now and then and proceeded to try it. Since that time he has been able to drink moderately, but does so only in social situations, never at home. He might have two to three beers twice in one week, then go several weeks with no alcoholic beverages at all. Nolan has no desire to drink unless he's in a restaurant or out with the guys, such as after a sporting event. He admits that he has gotten intoxicated — which for him means having a blood alcohol level above the legal limit for driving — but rarely, maybe once in an entire summer. He adds, "If I know I'm getting a little looped, I usually quit. I just don't want to get drunk."

How does he keep himself from going overboard? Nolan explains, "I've been labeled an alcoholic, and all the men on my father's side were alcoholics. So I always keep an awareness in the back of my mind. If enough people tell you you have a tail, sooner or later you'd better turn around and take a look. I don't take it lightly. I'll say to myself, 'Gee, buddy, you've had some drinks twice this week — that's pushing it.' He adds, "Sometimes when I have an urge to drink, I think of my wife and kids and ask myself, 'Is this the right thing to do?'" Nolan also mentioned that he never allows a circumstance, like being angry, attending a party, or having someone push a drink on him, dictate whether he drinks. "I don't use excuses for having a drink — if I want one, I have it. But I don't let situations control whether I have a drink," he explains.

For those who might doubt that a former alcohol abuser can return to moderate drinking, I spoke to Nolan's wife (with his permission) to confirm that he is now able to manage his alcohol intake. She is not usually with him when he drinks, but her estimation of how much alcohol he consumes is consistent with his description. Although it worries her that he drinks at all because of his history, his current drinking habits have had no negative consequences and no impact on their family.

When I asked Nolan how he is able to exert control over his drinking, he replied, "I never want to go back to feeling that way again — that terrible feeling of regularly coming home drunk and high on drugs, the way I felt the next morning, the guilt." He added, "Tell me I can't do something, and I'll show you that I can. If you want success in life, you don't want alcohol and drugs to control you."

The Masters Who Drink Moderately — or Occasionally

Nolan's story leads to what is probably the hottest controversy in the area of alcohol recovery: the issue of whether serious problem drinkers can ever drink again without putting their sobriety at risk — that is, in moderate amounts, without having problems because of it. The traditional school of thinking is that the only solution for an alcohol problem is never to pick up the first drink, because one drink inevitably leads to another — and another. The trick, people say at AA, is to avoid the single drink that starts the cycle.

So how do we explain the twenty masters who *do* let alcohol cross their lips, at least on occasion? Six of them consider themselves moderate drinkers, consuming alcohol more than once a week, while another four are occasional drinkers who have alcohol no more than once a week. The remaining ten are near-abstinent, meaning that on rare occasions they might have a sip or a small amount to drink. Fifteen of these twenty sometime drinkers or sippers have at least ten years of sobriety. (About half of them gave no information about how long they've been having some alcohol. Of those who did, a few indicated that they've been doing so for many years, and more have been doing so for just a few years.)

We could argue that these people were not "alcoholics" to begin with. But some of them once consumed vast amounts of alcohol, and most had serious problems because of their drinking. At his worst, Nolan H. could easily put away ten to twelve drinks in an evening. However, he does not consider himself to be an "alcoholic" and feels that his main problem was cocaine addiction.

Briefly, here are the stories of some other masters who have resumed drinking in a nonproblematic way:

◆ Murray K. resolved his alcohol problem six years ago, using principles of SMART Recovery and Rational Recovery. Before this, he says, "I drank anything I could get my hands on, any way I could get my hands on it — if I had to steal money or sell things for fast cash to get enough money for a quart of beer, I did it." For the first three years of sobriety, Murray says, he was completely abstinent. "But for the past three years, I have been able to go out and have a few drinks occasionally, every few months. When I do that, I do not drink to excess." He adds, "It is very rare that I get a fleeting thought to drink."

◆ Chico W. got sober ten years ago with the help of AA, and he still attends meetings anywhere from one to five times a week. For the first forty years of his drinking days, he says, he drank with "few adverse problems." But after that, when troubles developed at work and at home, his drinking became heavy for six years. At his worst, he drank at least half a gallon of vodka a day for four months. During his period of heavy drinking, he says, "I tried many potential solutions — religion, counseling, faith healing — so I could drink 'normally.'" Eventually he recovered by going into treatment, then to AA. He was totally abstinent for many years but now takes a drink on very rare occasions. He explains, "For instance, with very close nonalcoholic friends, I may drink a glass of wine at a special event."

◆ Pat A. has been on top of her drinking problem for nearly a decade, having attended AA for the first seven years. At her worst, she says, she drank "a bottle of wine, sometimes more," a day. Two drunk driving arrests led her to AA, about which she says, "At the time, I wanted the safety and guarantees of a close association with that organization." But after seven years of not drinking, Pat started attending Moderation Management meetings (see pages 283–84), and she now allows herself to drink five days a week, anywhere from one to three drinks at a time. "For me, alcohol is an elixir that I wish to fit into my life," she says, noting that her MM meetings make her accountable.

In the near-abstinent category of masters, there's Rebecca M., who quit drinking on her own and now attends AA — she sometimes has one to two swallows of something alcoholic, on rare occasions. Forty-three-year AA member Omen H. occasionally has a sip or a tiny amount of alcohol on a holiday or at a special dinner. Sandy V., who once hid bottles of booze around her house so no one would know she had a drinking problem, finds that now, twenty years into sobriety, she can have two small drinks on special occasions. Then there's Clare J., who will have something to drink at "dinners where the presentation of drinks or wine is excessively important to the hosts."

Certainly having a sip of alcohol or a single drink every once in a while is not the same as drinking on a regular or semi-regular basis. However, being able to have even small amounts of alcohol periodically runs against the widespread notion that any alcohol whatsoever is taboo for a "recovered (or recovering) alcoholic."

Who Can Drink Moderately After Having a Drinking Problem?

Experts are virtually unanimous in agreeing that moderate or controlled drinking is not apt to work for the vast majority of people with very serious drinking problems. So what kind of person is most likely to succeed with being able to drink moderately? Studies involving both people who have quit drinking on their own and those who have been through treatment indicate that most alcohol abusers who are able to return to controlled drinking have relatively less serious drinking problems or are people (like college binge drinkers) who "mature out" of heavy alcohol abuse as they become responsible adults. In general, research suggests that successful controlled drinkers tend to be women and people under forty. Also, they typically have alcohol problems of shorter duration (fewer than ten years).

Finally, individuals who are successful with moderate drinking tend to have the following characteristics:

Are psychologically stable
Are well educated
Are steadily employed
Don't regard themselves as "alcoholic" or "problem drinkers"
Don't subscribe to the disease concept of alcohol problems
Believe controlled drinking is possible
Develop alternatives to drinking as a means of coping with stress

Interestingly, several masters who have some alcohol on occasion were among those who affirmed that moderate drinking did not work for them. Former AA member Rose M. avows, "I tried controlled drinking, and it made matters worse." Today, she states, "I may have a sip of champagne on exceptionally festive occasions like graduations and weddings." Lucy L., who quit drinking after reading a book with "a graphic description of the physical consequences of alcoholism," says that trying to drink less didn't work for her. After three years of abstinence, however, she found she could "sometimes buy a regular-size bottle of wine (*not* a half-gallon)" and drink it over the course of a weekend. She notes, "My body seems to turn itself off after the first or second glass. Sometimes I will buy a bottle and forget it is in the refrigerator." She has been vacillating between moderate drinking and near-abstinence for the past several years.

What Exactly Is "Successful Drinking"?

When experts talk about a person who has successfully resumed drinking, they usually mean someone who can drink moderately without causing problems to health, behavior, or relationships. But how much alcohol is involved? Is it Pat A.'s several drinks five times a week, or is it more like Nolan H.'s two to three beers twice a week, then no alcohol at all for a while? Or maybe it's closer to Chico W.'s glass of wine on rare occasions? Then again, it could be the moderate drinking guidelines established by health officials as acceptable for health — no more than one drink a day for women and two for men.

One of the problems, of course, is that there is really no precise definition of successful drinking. Programs for people who want to drink moderately offer specific guidelines for limiting alcohol and avoiding intoxication. Moderation Management, for example, recommends no more than nine drinks per week for women, with a maximum of three drinks on any one day; no more than fourteen drinks per week is the guideline for men, with no more than four drinks in one day.

In addition to the amounts of alcohol consumed, you have to consider the extent to which alcohol controls your life. How much time and mental energy go into making an effort to control drinking? During the first few years after he resumed drinking, Nolan H. had to put quite a bit of thought into limiting his alcohol intake. At that time, he says, "I was always watching it and asking myself, 'Should I be doing this?' It was always on my mind."

The psychologist R. Lorraine Collins, Ph.D., of Buffalo, New York's Research Institute on Addictions, calls such people "restrained drinkers." She explains, "Restrained drinkers have to put a fair amount of effort into controlling their drinking and/or fighting the urge to drink. In contrast, a true *social* drinker is someone for whom alcohol presents little or no issue — he or she doesn't spend much time thinking about alcohol and is more inclined to be able to take it or leave it." Dr. Collins adds, "Certain former problem drinkers who choose to drink again achieve a peace with alcohol, and they don't have to worry about it anymore."

[handwritten: I am a restrained drinker]

Today, four years into his return to drinking, Nolan says, "I don't think about it as much as I did in the beginning. And when I do drink, I have more confidence now. There is no doubt in my mind that I'm a social drinker." Dr. Collins notes that like Nolan, some people who first have to make an effort to manage their drinking can become social drinkers. "Others go back and forth between restrained and social drinking. For someone who seems to be having a great deal of trouble with managing drinking, maybe it's time to reconsider abstinence."

In addition to considering the time and emotional energy you might have to invest, you should examine any problems alcohol is causing for you and those around you to help determine whether you can drink successfully. Nolan seems to meet the test of nonproblematic drinking, as affirmed by his wife.

Those Who Try to Drink Again Face Long Odds

The masters who are able to drink again are not alone, for studies of people who resolved drinking problems on their own suggest that as many as one fifth of them drink moderately — a number based on findings from three different countries. Some additional insights are offered by a large study by the National Institute on Alcohol Abuse and Alcoholism involving more than 4,500 people from the general population who were once classified as dependent on alcohol. At the time of the study, about half of the group had had one or more drinks in the past year, but they no longer met the criteria for serious problem drinking.

Bear in mind, however, that one year does not represent a lifetime. Alcohol-dependent people may be able to return to "safe" drinking for periods of time, but moderate, unproblematic drinking for an extended time appears to be unusual. This is supported by the work of Harvard University's George Vaillant, who has been studying two groups of men with alcohol problems over the course of their adult lives. By sixty years of age, only 11 percent of these men were controlled drinkers, defined as those who have more than one drink per month for at least two years with no reported problems. Dr. Vaillant concludes, "Long-term return to controlled drinking was a rare and unstable outcome."

A successful return to drinking for one in ten former problem drinkers is nonetheless notable, and suggests better odds than are commonly forecast. It does appear, however, that the majority of people who successfully resolve drinking problems choose not to drink at all, which most experts and masters alike would agree is the safest route.

When Moderate Drinking Fails

Since there is no test to determine whether you'll be successful with moderate drinking or you are someone for whom moderate drinking could end in tragedy, some argue that *all* problem drinkers are better off choosing abstinence. One AA member says, "Moderate drinking is like sleeping with a dragon. As long as the monster is asleep, you are okay. It's when it wakes up that you're in trouble."

Indeed, most people with serious drinking problems are not

satisfied with the amounts of alcohol deemed acceptable in moderate drinking programs, as the following comments from some of the masters who failed to control alcohol attest:

◆ "Moderation Management was completely ineffective for me. I might have one or two drinks for a few days, but *very* soon I was back to heavy drinking." — Amy D. (quit drinking with the help of both counseling and SOS six years ago)

◆ "Moderation in any form never worked." — Evan J. (quit drinking ten years ago by crafting his own program with the "basic tenet 'Don't drink'")

◆ "I tried social drinking for three years. I could control it for a while but *always* would come to a time when I would drink more than I intended and get into trouble. When I finally quit, I had to remind myself that others could drink, but for me it was poison. I visualized a skull and crossbones on any alcohol I saw." — Karen M. (got sober by praying and going to AA, which she still attends fourteen years later)

◆ "Moderation didn't work — I quit my 'diet' quickly." — Barney K. (has been sober through AA for fourteen years)

◆ "I tried every way to control my drinking. Nothing worked. After I had been abstinent for six years, I drank moderately once and got drunk once. After that, I knew total abstinence was my only choice. Once I feel the effect of alcohol, I don't want to stop drinking it." — Echo T. (has been sober with the help of AA for eight years)

◆ "Controlled drinking was not effective for me — I could not possibly control a disease. I also tried drinking wine only — I still got drunk." — Marguerite E. (quit drinking with AA's help nine years ago)

◆ "After three years of abstinence, I had a glass of wine at a wedding anniversary celebration, which led to a slow progression — from one drink every month or so to one drink a week when eating out. My controlled drinking got to be more and more drinking, and I eventually brought alcohol back into my home. For the two years before I went into a treatment center, I was back to drinking alcoholically — as much as twenty ounces of vodka a day." — Jessica C. (has been abstinent again for fifteen years and is active in Women for Sobriety)

◆ "Rationing didn't work because I always could justify, 'Just this once, a little more.'" — Thomas V. (has maintained sobriety for six years with the help of both AA and SOS)

Most masters would agree with Randall N., who says, "God bless those who can drink moderately or occasionally. I think they're playing with fire."

A few masters told of being lured back into drinking by reading about those who could drink moderately. Jessica C., whose single glass of wine was the beginning of a long slide, says that one reason she attempted to drink again after three years of abstinence was that she had been impressed by a study done about that time in which "a sample of men who were heavy drinkers used a controlled drinking plan and seemed to be successful."

Similarly, Heather F. had had more than five years during which "drinking just wasn't an option" and sober life was going well. Then, after reading about former problem drinkers who were able to drink again, she decided to give it a try. "I decided to see if I could just stick with having a few drinks on weekend nights. It started out fine, but by the end of a month, I was right back where I left off with martinis. The truth is, I don't want to

Moderate Drinking: Dangerous Lure or Realistic Alternative?

As I was writing this book, a highly publicized incident catapulted the issue of moderate drinking into a national debate. In March 2000, Audrey Kishline, the founder of Moderation Management, a support program for people who have experienced mild to moderate levels of alcohol-related problems and who want to cut back or quit drinking, drove in the wrong direction on an interstate highway and caused a head-on collision that took the lives of a man and his twelve-year-old daughter. According to news accounts, Kishline was found unconscious inside her crashed pickup truck with a half-empty bottle of vodka on the seat beside her. Two hours later, her blood alcohol level was reportedly found to be 0.26 — more than three times the legal limit in the state of Washington, where the accident occurred. Kishline pleaded guilty to two counts of vehicular homicide, and on August 11, 2000, she was sentenced to four and a half years in prison.

Some advocates of abstinence held up Kishline's accident as an example of

drink moderately. If I can't have more than one or two, it's not worth it." After a few weeks, Heather recognized that it was best for her to quit drinking completely once again, and she did.

The Problem with Abstinence for All

Pressuring all people with drinking problems to abstain ignores the fact that drinking problems exist on a continuum, from mild to life-threatening. Consider the case of Enrico J., a three-time drunk driving offender who was required to take part in a several-month abstinence-oriented treatment program, followed by weekly AA attendance for a year, when he was a young adult. When he protested that he was not an "alcoholic" but instead was part of a carousing crowd that abused alcohol, he was told he the failure of moderate drinking approaches for problem drinkers. At the time of the accident, however, Kishline was no longer a member of MM. Several months earlier she had announced that because she was unable to stick to the group's drinking guidelines, she had changed her "recovery goal to one of abstinence rather than moderation," in accordance with MM's advice that members should abstain if they are not moderating successfully. She went on to announce that she was attending AA meetings and also was planning to go to other abstinence-based programs. However, according to the *New York Times,* Kishline stated that when she failed at both moderation and abstinence, she was too ashamed to seek help and "gave up."

In fact, no program should be blamed for the Kishline tragedy. "Relapse is common, whichever approach the drinker adopts" is the way a prominent group of experts put it in a joint statement released in the midst of the widespread media coverage of the accident. In other words, even after people attend abstinence-based programs, it is common for them to relapse, but no program — whether it advocates abstinence or moderate drinking — can be held responsible for an individual's mistake.

was in denial. He says, "I wasn't ready to quit drinking, and didn't really need to — I needed to learn to be more responsible with my drinking." Now, ten years later, he can take or leave alcohol. He occasionally has a beer or two, but he enjoys it as a beverage rather than using it to get high. In fact, according to the alcohol expert and attorney Stanton Peele, "Most drunk driving offenders are not 'alcoholics,' yet they represent one of the largest groups of people coerced into abstinence-based programs in the United States."

Indeed, a number of experts at the forefront of alcohol research believe that more people would do something about their alcohol problem at an earlier point if at the outset they were offered a choice between abstinence and a moderate drinking approach. Heather F. admits that although she knew that she would probably be better off electing abstinence, she was not ready to make a permanent commitment to it when she first tackled her drinking problem. "If the therapists who allowed me to try drinking moderately had required abstinence from the start, I would have walked right out the door. Because I was able to experiment and make my own decision, I eventually came to see that abstinence is the best option for me."

Dr. Alan Marlatt points out that Canada, Australia, and some European countries routinely offer formal controlled drinking programs, which are likely to attract problem drinkers uninterested in abstinence. As a *U.S. News & World Report* feature stated, "By calling abstinence the only cure, we ensure that the nation's $100 billion alcohol problem won't be solved." If someone elects moderate drinking and it doesn't work out, then he or she can step up to an abstinence-based approach.

Some studies suggest that people who are offered controlled drinking approaches at the outset may actually fare better than those who are offered abstinence-oriented approaches. Perhaps the most famous of these studies was conducted by the psychologists Mark and Linda Sobell in the 1970s. It involved chronic male "alcoholics" who were randomly assigned to either controlled drinking treatment or a traditional abstinence-oriented program. According to Dr. Mark Sobell, "Three years after treatment, it was found that those who received the moderation approach did much better all around. Surprisingly, they even had more abstinent days than those who had been told to be abstinent."

Moderate drinking can also be part of a plan for recovery that starts out with a period of abstinence, goes on to a moderation trial, and involves a return to abstinence if moderate drinking doesn't work. Heather F. recalls, "My first chemical dependency counselor had me start out with three months of abstinence, followed by a trial of moderate drinking. When my drinking crept back up again, I realized that someday I would probably have to give up alcohol completely."

If people *are* allowed to choose whether they want to try moderate drinking or abstinence, won't they all flock to the option that still allows them to drink? Interestingly, studies suggest that even when they are trained in controlled drinking, many alcohol-dependent people wind up choosing abstinence. The psychologist Marc Kern says that a number of participants in the Moderation Management group he directs do just that after following a recommended thirty-day break from alcohol. "Some people find that after a month of no alcohol, it's just easier that way, and they stay with abstinence," he notes.

Dr. Sobell concurs: "Most people whose problems are serious will say, 'I want to stop drinking altogether,' because they just don't want to risk further consequences." He adds, "Occasionally someone will opt for a goal that is clearly not in his best interest, but the frequency of this occurring is far less than one would expect." Dr. Kern's and Dr. Sobell's remarks are echoed by other experts who conclude that when given a choice, people tend to elect goals that are right for their situations.

How the Masters of Moderate Drinking Set Limits

The masters who choose to drink from time to time use various strategies to make sure their drinking doesn't get out of hand. Their experiences support the observation of experts that former problem drinkers who achieve stable moderation not only drink less but make changes in their drinking practices. For instance, they switch to an alcoholic beverage that is not their favorite, they no longer hang around with a drinking crowd, and they drink in different locations or under different circumstances. Nolan H. changed his circle of friends and leisure activities so he was less influenced by the bar and drug culture. He also keeps careful mental track of how often he drinks within a given time period. Bill L., who in the past "abused alcohol in private," states, "Now I drink only in public, where I am very careful about my appearance and behavior. But my most important strategy is planning ahead. Being older and more aware, I now actively plan on not drinking much or at all. I set limits both on time spent drinking and the number and type of drinks I have. I also visualize how I appear to others when I am drinking."

Ed Shaw, a moderate drinker and master who is the cohost and producer of the worldwide radio program *The Ruth and Ed Shaw Show*, has a number of set conditions for drinking. He explains, "I plan when I will drink; it's conscious, not accidental. I normally don't drink any more than once a week, and I never have beer, because for me, 'just one' is bullshit. Also, I try to avoid big drunks who need company, as well as stay away from St. Patrick's Day parties where all they do is drink."

Not only do the masters who drink moderately rely on certain strategies to limit the amount of alcohol they consume, but they also take care of their emotional well-being in order to prevent themselves from going back to their old ways. For instance, Nolan H. has vowed not to drink because of "circumstances" such as being angry. He has found new ways of feeling good through exercising, coaching his sons' athletic teams, enjoying leisure activities, and pursuing his career. More than a decade into sobriety, four years of which he has spent drinking moderately, Nolan still takes stock of the pluses and minuses of drinking. He explains, "Just recently I passed up a day out with the guys because I knew it would be a whole day of drinking. I really didn't want to feel bad the next morning. The joy of drinking in a situation like this just doesn't outweigh the down side for me anymore."

Moderate drinker Pat A. not only attends Moderation Management meetings and keeps alcohol out of her home, but she's involved in professional counseling to resolve problems that initially led her to drink too much. She tries to deal with anger by exercising rather than drinking and has learned to speak up for herself. "I don't let a drink take care of something that does not sit well with me," she declares.

Finally, it's quite clear that even though they are not abstinent, these masters *have* made a long-term commitment to changing their relationship with alcohol — just as other masters have made a commitment to abstinence. Fifteen years into resolving his drinking problem, Jack B., who now has a beer or glass of wine each day, revisited the bar culture with its "various characters," which he sorely missed in the beginning of sobriety. He says, "After I returned to bars in a much more limited way, I came to see the people I had once viewed as fascinating as damaged, broken, beaten-down persons — a painful revelation, yet one that reinforced my commitment *not* to go down that road again."

Getting Help with Moderate Drinking

"The problem," Dr. Marlatt points out, "is that most people who try moderate drinking attempt it on their own, without any tools. If they were offered some professional guidance and had safeguards in place for monitoring their progress, then moderate drinking wouldn't have to end in disaster." Indeed, few masters indicated that they had had any formal help when they tried to drink moderately. That kind of help may be difficult to find in the United States. A study in the mid-1990s found that more than three quarters of two hundred randomly selected treatment programs saw controlled drinking as an unacceptable goal. Outpatient programs were less likely to object to this option than residential programs, according to the same study, but still, about half of them found controlled drinking unacceptable. In describing this study, the U.S. government publication *Alcohol and Health* says, "In general, program respondents indicated an unwillingness to negotiate treatment goals with their clients."

If you want to try moderate drinking, you would be advised to do so as part of a recognized program like Moderation Management or another one mentioned in the appendix, DrinkWise, and/or under the guidance of a professional who has experience in assessing the severity of alcohol problems as well as in moderation approaches. That way, you can get some sense of whether you are a candidate for moderate drinking, have access to helpful tools, and receive guidance if moderate drinking fails. For detailed information on these programs as well as books on the subject of moderate drinking, see the appendix, pages 283-85. For guidelines for finding mental health professionals, see pages 268–72.

Another Perspective: John A.'s Story

Let me close by saying that there's a big difference between trying moderate drinking as an early course of action for dealing with an alcohol problem and returning to drinking after a successful period of abstinence. True, some masters *are* able to drink again after having been abstinent. (One could argue that their long years without alcohol gave them enough "sober time" to get their act together in other areas of life, so that they can now handle unproblematic drinking.) *Nevertheless, it's risky to try moderate drinking if you've been contentedly abstinent for an extended period of time.*

John A., who is now a professional working in the recovery field, is a case in point. Like Nolan, John tried "experimenting" with alcohol — in his case, after eighteen years of continuous abstinence — but he arrived at a different conclusion. Over the course of six months, he says, "my experiments included things like having a glass of wine with dinner, having two to six drinks on social occasions, and even purposely drinking for the experience of intoxication." He points out that "on all occasions I was able to decide the conditions and circumstances for such use, and I never used more than a predetermined quantity. I never lost control or experienced negative consequences, other than a hangover."

As a result of his experiments, John decided the following:

How the Masters Handle Traces of Alcohol

When it came to deciding whether and when they could ever drink again, the masters had to consider whether they would consume foods containing alcohol as an ingredient. They also had to make up their minds about drinking substitutes for alcoholic beverages, such as nonalcoholic beer and wine, which sometimes contain trace amounts of alcohol. As with most aspects of recovery, the message from the masters about using these items is that you have to find what works for you.

It is interesting to note, however, that quite a few totally abstinent masters are not so rigid that they will forgo foods containing alcohol or forbid themselves nonalcoholic substitutes for beer and wine, which once again challenges the notion that alcohol must be avoided at all costs to maintain sobriety.

Here is a summary of how the masters handle such foods and beverages:

Foods containing alcohol. When questioned specifically about whether they'll eat desserts, casseroles, and other foods made with alcoholic beverages, close to three out of ten said yes, while just as many said that they will not. More commonly, the masters said it depends, citing such factors as the concentration of alcohol and whether the food has been cooked so that the alcohol has evaporated. Of those who are totally abstinent, about a quarter indicated that they will consume foods containing alcohol; another 40 percent eat such foods if they're cooked or if the alcohol concentration is minimal. "Yes" responses typically came from masters who recovered using nontraditional methods; about half as many AA members said yes.

Thus, some masters will not consume any alcohol whatsoever, while others do not feel that tiny amounts will lead them back to the bottle. Liz P., who refuses foods containing alcohol, worries that "the taste of a familiar alcoholic beverage might trigger a craving. I would question my own commitment to sobriety if I knowingly ate such a food. Plus I'm not sure if all of the alcohol really burns off." In contrast, Arnold C. says he does eat foods

How the Masters Handle Traces of Alcohol, continued

prepared with alcohol because the amounts are usually small and often cook off. (The truth is that the alcohol content of cooked foods varies, depending on the amount of alcohol added, the kind of beverage, and the cooking time. Wine tends to cook off more readily than hard liquor, and foods heated the longest tend to retain the least alcohol.) Arnold adds, "The 'one drink, one drunk' mythology prevents some people from seeing the obvious and from using common sense." Indeed, many of the masters do simply use common sense, like Phil Q., who states, "I try not to be obsessive. If a food tastes like booze, I won't take seconds."

Lilith V., who initially consumed nothing containing alcohol because she didn't want the "itch" to start, adapts a reasonable approach to cough and cold remedies containing alcohol. She occasionally takes "a medicine or tincture" containing alcohol, noting, "I monitor my motivations, my emotional responses, and the instructions — a teaspoon is *not* a tablespoon; if one is good, two is *not* necessarily better!"

Nonalcoholic beers and wines. Two thirds of the masters indicated that they do not consume nonalcoholic beers and wines, while the other third does. Of those who are totally abstinent, about three out of ten consume these beverages. Loners who maintain sobriety on their own are somewhat more likely to drink nonalcoholic beers and wines than are those who have or had outside support for their recoveries — which might reflect a trend at recovery groups.

The masters' reasons for not consuming nonalcoholic beverages vary. Some simply don't like the way they taste. Others think they can feel the effects of the trace amounts of alcohol these drinks contain. For instance, Leslie T. states, "I've had them, but I experienced startling symptoms — euphoria, facial flushing — that made me fear that nonalcoholic beverages might lead to alcoholic ones. So I ceased, and I now drink water, soda, whatever." Amy P. says she stays away from nonalcoholic beers and wines because she doesn't want to be reminded of the taste. For George M., "Nonalcoholic beverages are the most asinine beverages around — it's like having sex without orgasm, smoking without nicotine, bulimia: eating without eating."

In contrast, the availability of nonalcoholic beverages actually helps some masters maintain sobriety. When Rosa L. has an urge to drink, she sometimes relaxes with a nonalcoholic beer or a glass of nonalcoholic wine. Paul V., who indicates that he will drink "near beer" — say, at a business meal involving alcohol — makes the point that "many 'normal' people do the same."

Wine at church communion. Although the subject rarely came up (and I didn't specifically ask about it), a few masters mentioned how they handle wine when it's served during church communion. SMART Recovery coordinator Arnold C. says, "Sometimes I attend a Sunday mass for old times' sake. At communion I take a sip of consecrated wine — no effects, no 'loss of control.'" Former AA member Judy K. (eighteen years) says, "I drink a tiny cupful of wine when receiving communion every Sunday. At first I was very, very self-conscious about this. It wasn't that I felt that I would want more. It was because it was my deep desire never to consume alcohol again. And even this tiny amount, no matter how tiny, *was* alcohol. After a while this feeling left me. Now I don't even think about it as being alcohol but only what it truly is: the blood of Christ." (AA has no official policy about wine in church communion; instead, it leaves the decision up to the individual.)

After fourteen years of sobriety, Phil Q. recently told his twelve-year-old daughter that he had had a drink one Sunday. He explains, "I went to a reunion of a boys' choir I had been in forty-five years ago — it was the first Catholic mass I had attended in a very long time — and I decided to partake in communion with wine, in memory of the choirmaster whom we were honoring." When he told his daughter about this, she looked worried and asked, "What's that mean — what is going to happen?" Phil responded, "Well, I don't think anything's actually going to happen. But I'm not going to be able to say I've not had a drink in fourteen years." His daughter's reaction was to state decisively, "That absolutely shouldn't count." "Okay, I'm with you," Phil assured her. "It doesn't count."

1. I am not "powerless" over alcohol, in spite of the fact that I was once alcohol-dependent. I need not fear relapse.
2. The magic is gone. While I did experience a measure of euphoria on a couple of occasions, I mostly just felt intoxicated or impaired. It also concerned me that by the end of this time, my tolerance was increasing, and I felt practically nothing after two drinks.
3. It would be silly and pointless to return to the regular use of alcohol. The once-imagined rewards just aren't there.
4. At least for me, abstinence makes the most sense because it is
   a. Easier — considerable effort is still necessary to control alcohol.
   b. Safer — the only guarantee of no negative consequences is never to use.
5. Last, but by no means least, clear-headedness and self-efficacy are their own reward.

For several years since his experiments, John has again been abstinent, aside from occasionally using a medication containing alcohol or having a sip of champagne at a wedding reception. He notes, "I simply do not think regular use of alcohol would be a good idea for me. Besides, I have much more pleasurable and rewarding things to do with my time and energy."

John has tools and resources that might not be available to others who are experimenting with drinking again, and not everyone would have such insight or self-control. For many people — particularly those who once had severe drinking problems — if the door to drinking is opened after many years of abstinence, it can prove difficult to close again.

9

It's Not Enough Just to Stop Drinking

How the Masters Deal with Life's Ups and Downs Without Alcohol

At AA it's often said, "Just keep coming to meetings, and don't pick up the first drink." A main tenet of SOS is "Don't drink, no matter what." According to RR's philosophy, once you accept that you can never drink again, your other problems may fade and disappear. But is it so simple? Will you stay sober if all you do is make a commitment not to drink?

The masters reveal that resolving a serious alcohol problem entails much more than "just" giving up problem drinking. Long-term sobriety involves being able to cope with whatever life dishes up — both the good and the bad — without a glass of wine, beer, or liquor in your hand.

What the masters miss most about their drinking days is the way alcohol enabled them to escape, hide, or get momentary relief from painful situations, troubles, and feelings, so it should come as no surprise that their number-one difficulty in early sobriety — far ahead of all others — was dealing with emotions, personal issues, and problems in the absence of alcohol.

Over and over, however, the masters explained how they learned to manage the roller coaster of living without turning to the bottle. In addition, the testimonies of some masters prove that a short-term slip with alcohol does not have to become a full-blown relapse — nor do you need to start counting sober time all over again.

Leslie T.'s Story

From her early twenties to her early thirties, Leslie T. went from being a homecoming queen and a graduate of a prestigious university to being a solitary quart-a-day vodka drinker living in an apartment with nothing but a mattress on the floor and a calendar on the wall. It is difficult to reconcile this scenario with the well-spoken Leslie of today, a successful fifty-three-year-old woman with twenty years of sobriety under her belt who enjoys a rich personal and professional life.

As part of a wealthy, churchgoing southern family, Leslie was troubled at an early age by inconsistencies in her life, which gradually bred an internal despair that she eventually smothered with alcohol. When she went away to college, it didn't take her long to figure out that alcohol could afford her release and escape from all sorts of problems, emotions, and insecurities. Leslie had begun to associate drinking with feeling at ease socially, having great sex, and medicating both physical and psychological woes.

"My drinking fed existential despair, which fed my creative energy"

By the end of college, Leslie, who was then drinking almost daily, became engaged to an older fellow student, whom she married. "The marriage was fraught with conflict, and I used booze to forget the fights. I also drank to soothe hurt feelings when he refused my emotional and physical advances," she says. When she got a job with a civil rights organization, she continues, "I worked with a crowd of writers who drank at lunch, sometimes continued into the afternoon, and went out at night and drank some more. I drank right along with them. I used alcohol for all the 'normal' reasons — after a hard day at work or as part of the fun in a day at the beach. I also drank to boost myself up before ordeals at work and dosed myself to feel more comfortable before social events. I drank against my home town, I drank against the Vietnam War, I drank against social injustice and racism — man's inhumanity to man. My drinking was wed to my creative writing abilities — alcohol fed existential despair, which in turn fed creative energy."

After Leslie had an affair with a coworker, her marriage fell apart, jobs came and went, and she had numerous risky sexual encounters. She also endangered herself and others because of drunk driving. Toward the end, she was living on temporary financial support from her ex-husband, working in a clothing store, and spending everything she had on vodka, cigarettes, and just enough food for survival. Eventually she stopped showing up for work. All she had left was the mattress on which she lay for two weeks with her vodka and cigarettes before she went to see a lawyer about filing for bankruptcy. He suggested that she go to alcohol treatment, which she agreed to do as a ploy to get her creditors off her back. She lasted just four days at an inpatient treatment center before she checked herself out, against advice, but she did agree to go to an outpatient AA-based counseling group for women. That too was short-lived.

"I saw that they had a sense of serenity I didn't have"

Yet somewhere in this experience, Leslie began her recovery journey. The connections she had formed with alcohol would take years to break, but going through detox and spending a short time in treatment awakened her to the fact that probably she was an "alcoholic" and that most of her problems were caused by her drinking. By using "raw willpower," she then made a commitment not to drink.

She began taking steps to rebuild her life and facilitate sobriety. First, since she could no longer afford to pay rent, she accepted an offer to sleep during the summer on the porch of a man who had sprayed her old apartment for termites. She also went to several weekly AA meetings, which did not appeal to her intellectually but at the same time attracted her. "I saw that AA members had a sense of serenity — a comfort in their sobriety that I didn't have. AA also helped me to feel less isolated — I saw that I was not alone in many of the shameful behaviors of my past."

The intellectual side of Leslie kept leading her back to the library, where she read anything she could find about the nature of alcohol problems. She explains, "Learning that there was a scientific explanation for my dependence on alcohol helped me accept my disease, feel less alone, and have hope that one day there might be a cure for alcoholism." She also read "anything and everything escapist," watched soap operas, and walked for hours in the warm coastal town in which she lived.

Sobriety became easier after about a year, when Leslie fell in love with Sam, a somewhat older man with three sons from a previous marriage. "He gave me a love and a way of life that was something to get well for," she says. Three months later they were married, and they remain so to this day.

A little more than a year after her initial treatment experience, while Leslie was on her honeymoon, her old ways of managing problems got the better of her. An argument with Sam triggered a relapse into heavy drinking, which lasted less than a week and ended by a return to AA.

"To manage conflict, I knew I had to act differently"

The relationship took a rocky turn, however, when one of Sam's three teenage sons came to live with them, toward the end of Leslie's second year of sobriety. She says, "My stepson was a handful, and we didn't always agree about how to handle him." Following an argument with Sam, Leslie had another relapse — this one too lasting less than a week, but serious enough to land her in an emergency room with a near-fatal blood alcohol level of .40. She chose to go back into formal treatment — this time in an outpatient setting, so she could be available at home for her stepson — followed by escalated AA attendance.

Leslie didn't drink for another year, then had one last flirtation with alcohol, this time as a protest against her husband's unwillingness to have a baby with her. But after taking one sip of wine, she stopped herself. "For the first time since childhood," she explains, "I fell to my knees before a power greater than the bottle and greater than myself. There had to be something bigger than the booze — my best self? Reason? God?"

She now clearly saw that she was going to have to learn how to manage other aspects of her life in a new way if she was to prevent future relapses. So she became an active problem-solver, rather than continuing to turn to the bottle for false solutions. "To manage conflict, I knew I had to act differently. For instance, I recall one argument in which Sam threw every dish out of the kitchen cabinets. Rather than drink, I cried and went to an AA meeting." Recognizing that she needed more than AA to resolve the conflict in her marriage and with her stepson, Leslie sought counsel from a therapist who specialized in what is now known as cognitive-behavioral therapy. She and her husband also went to couples counseling and drew up an agreement about how they would handle her stepson.

Leslie has remained abstinent since her near-relapse, which occurred seventeen years ago. She continued to go regularly to AA meetings for about seven years, but today, aside from taking an occasional newcomer to a meeting, she is no longer involved in AA. She saw two of her stepsons through their late high school years and was recently thanked for "bringing both boys the only order they had ever known." Leslie is now employed by the U.S. government, continues to have a good marriage with Sam, exercises regularly, enjoys the opera and theater, dotes on her new baby grandson, and is even toying with the idea of going to medical school.

Recognizing the "Drinking and . . ." Connections

To stay off alcohol for good, Leslie needed to learn how to cope with life's trials without turning to alcohol — a process that took years, because, as she says, "Alcohol was involved with every aspect of my life, and every aspect of my life was involved with alcohol." For Leslie, it had been drinking and . . .

having a good time
having confidence
feeling at ease with men
getting relief from physical pain
getting relief from emotional pain
managing social discomfort
feeling uninhibited sexually
coping after a hard day at work
dealing with angst about life in general
releasing her feelings
being able to write creatively
soothing hurt feelings
managing conflict and anger

Similarly, master Michele D. describes her connections with drinking as follows: "At any social event, at any time, when my husband and I needed to celebrate or when we were feeling down, we drank. We didn't know how to have fun without drinking."

For someone who wants to become sober, the process of managing the ups and downs of life more effectively begins by recognizing your own "drinking and . . ." connections. Ask yourself, "When did I start drinking, and why? What did alcohol do for me then, and what does it do for me now?"

Separating Alcohol from the "Stuff of Life"

The ultimate flaw in using alcohol to manage life's peaks and valleys is that it backfires. Dorothy C. explains: "I am very nearsighted and wore heavy glasses; I felt like an ugly duckling. When I first drank, alcohol made me feel I wasn't ugly. I was also a sad person; as a child, I was sexually abused by my stepfather, so I lived in fear, tears, and shame. When I drank, I forgot these things and felt great. However, when I started abusing alcohol, it *gave* me fear, tears — all the things I drank for in the first place. And because of my actions when drinking, I would have shame and remorse. To remove all that, I had to have another drink." Since alcohol acts as a depressant, a vicious cycle had been established. In short, George M. says, "When I drank, all my problems seemed to go away, but they returned with a vengeance."

It isn't just negative aspects of life that become connected with drinking — the good times also often go hand in hand with alcohol. "Celebrations were a problem at first, as was having fun," Michele D. says of her early sobriety. "All of that was done with alcohol for years. Learning to have fun without alcohol was tough, and I'm still working on that one." Nine years into sobriety, Marguerite E. finds that times of celebrating and feeling happy are still her most dangerous situations.

If someone stops drinking and doesn't fill at least some of the void left by alcohol's absence, the result is that he or she will likely start drinking again. As Michele D. puts it, "Just to stop using alcohol and not fill that big hole it leaves will not work."

To manage life's day-to-day trials and tribulations in the absence of alcohol, a number of the masters said they first learned to disentangle emotions, feelings, and problems from drinking. Becky H. says, "I learned how to separate the 'stuff of life' from drinking, so that when I felt an emotion other than happiness, I could say to myself, 'This has nothing to do with drinking.' Billy R. adds, "The hardest part when I first quit drinking was convincing myself that no matter how fearful, depressed, or angry I got, I was going to endure whatever life would throw at me without drinking. I would ask myself, 'What's the worst thing that can happen?' and then decide that it would be better to have that happen than to drink." In short, the masters have accepted, as Frank

L. did, that "drinking will not make any problem easier to solve nor any outcome any better than it is."

Here are some ideas from the masters for separating alcohol from the rest of life.

Identify feelings, emotions, and problems

Jackie D. says, "When I drank, I never knew that my feelings could be separated and identified, which meant I never did anything appropriate about them. The hardest part of early recovery was that I had to learn to recognize what I was feeling — to discern sadness from anger from discomfort from anxiety, and to allow myself to experience happiness." Enrico J. explains that he was out of touch with his emotions until he went through treatment. "They would ask me how I was feeling, and I would automatically say, 'Fine.' Then they'd say, 'How are you *really* feeling?' and give me a long list of words to label emotions. Finally something would hit me, like, 'Oh yeah, I *do* feel sad.'"

Figure out *why* you're feeling what you're feeling

Once you have identified feelings, it helps to determine what prompted that state of mind. Marjorie A., who at first had a hard time living "without anesthetic," says, "Now when I have an urge to drink, I look at why I have that urge, what feeling I want to cover up — fear, sadness, anger — and I know how to deal with that feeling in a healthier way."

Express yourself

Rather than keeping everything inside, try letting out feelings and talking about problems — to spouses, friends, or fellow recovery group members. Kerry G. says, "I share my feelings and get out anything that's on my mind, including old issues. Before, I always hid my feelings behind masks, and I drank to get away from all the emotional baggage. Now I make sure it doesn't pile up." Her advice to people who want to quit drinking is to "share and express everything you need to — scream, yell, cry, write in a journal. Do what you need to do to get the turmoil out, and don't worry about how crazy it sounds or what anyone else thinks."

Practice prevention

Karen M. says, "At AA there is an acronym called 'HALT,' and it means never letting yourself get too hungry, angry, lonely, or tired. I think those four things are great to remember as damage-control tactics, since allowing those to go unchecked often led to my drinking in the past."

Accept uncomfortable feelings as part of life

Kemp M. says, "Once I learned to live peacefully with my unsolved problems, I didn't need alcohol." Pat A. adds, "I'm slowly learning not to be concerned if I'm not in a good mood for a little while." Remind yourself too that uncomfortable feelings pass, as does Sarah N., who finds that "it helps to realize that just because I feel bad today, I might not feel depressed tomorrow. I go through the feelings instead of avoiding them with alcohol."

Finding Solutions That Work

After her last flirtation with alcohol, in order to remain sober, Leslie T. needed to learn how to handle the tensions with her husband and her stepson effectively. "From my counseling, I picked up skills for assertiveness, anger management, and honest communication," she explains. "For instance, I learned how to argue without sarcasm and how to listen to what Sam was trying to express. Then, when we fought, I stood a better chance of managing the conflict without drinking."

Leslie is one of many masters who went out of their way to say that in sobriety, they've learned to cope with problems in a better way. Jackie D. says that one of the most important steps she took to keep herself from drinking again was "to attack problems head-on and see progress." Now, she maintains, "I can articulate problems better, I don't let things drag, and I am determined not to let issues go unresolved. One of the secrets of sobriety is moving toward discomfort and solving the problems before they become insurmountable."

Although facing problems head-on was important for many masters, others found that getting out of harm's way was an effective way of managing difficulties, so they removed themselves from problematic situations that might put them at risk for drinking again. For instance, before Krista O. quit drinking, she says, "I was in a high-power, stressful job that was not suitable either for my personality or for getting into recovery." So she left that position and now has a "simple, stress-free" job, more suitable for her and more conducive to staying sober.

The masters have found solutions for a host of problems commonly associated with drinking.

Depression and moodiness

Whatever the cause of depression, it can become a way of life for problem drinkers and usually needs at least partial resolution when drinking ends. The masters' most common strategy for dealing with the down times is (as obvious as it sounds) doing something to make themselves feel better — for instance, talking with someone, undertaking physical activity, or turning to religion. Many masters have sought counseling for depression and other issues, and about twenty said they take an antidepressant medication; a few of these people take St. John's wort, an herbal remedy that is said to help with mild to moderate depression. Amy P. says, "I have a lifelong history of depression, even prior to my drinking problem, and have been on and off antidepressants all my adult life." Quite a few masters mentioned that they have fewer mood swings now that they're sober.

To handle depression, the masters say they have used these strategies:

◆ "I sleep, read, or talk to friends and know that it will pass."
— Rebecca M.

◆ "Because of meditation and exercise, I find my mood is very good and stable." — Charles G.

◆ "If I feel myself getting really down, I talk with my psychiatrist." — Amy P.

◆ "I have to remove myself physically from the presence of others, most often by going for a drive and letting the truth come through. Also writing my thoughts on paper helps immensely." — Lilith V.

◆ "I use antidepressants, exercise, contact with supportive people, proper diet, and exciting literature." — Dorothy W.

◆ "I exercise, spend time outdoors in the sun, and responsibly care for my lovable dog." — Zoe A.

Stress

Rather than turn to alcohol, many masters now do something that will really help alleviate stress. A number of them mentioned exercise as a stress reducer, while some said they used relaxation techniques or meditated. Others told me they prayed or turned to religion. Research suggests that it is not necessarily how much stress problem drinkers have in their lives but how well they handle it that determines whether or not they stay sober.

Here are some of the masters' personal ways to manage stress:

◆ "I decompress by sharing my concerns and heeding advice rather than just bitching. I get facials, manicures, massages, and go away with friends on trips." — Nancy B.

◆ "I do something physical — usually change the furniture arrangement." — Jordan L.

◆ "I offer a quick prayer for relief. Breathing is also good — a couple of deep breaths return some measure of serenity to my mind and release the tensions in my body. If all that fails, I grab a cup of chamomile tea and hide in a closet until it passes." — Lilith V.

◆ "I work and do tai chi." — Wayne W.

◆ "I get immersed in music and dance." — Rafael P.

Anger

The most frequent responses from the masters about how they now handle anger concerned dealing with the situation appropriately and directly — that is, expressing their anger or talking it out.

◆ "I punch pillows, take brisk walks, write, and say what's bothering me." — Denise T.

◆ "I try to handle anger before it builds up to large levels." — Sarah N.

◆ "I walk and climb stairs." — Camille G.

◆ "I get mad and LET IT GO." — Jeanne F.

◆ "I use progressive relaxation techniques." — Clarence C.

◆ "I write things down to sound off." — Amy P.

◆ "I express my anger (appropriately) to the right person." — Rod R.

◆ "I take deep breaths and go for a brisk walk outdoors. The walking cadence and fresh air dispel all bad feelings." — June R.

◆ "The last time I got really furious I went home and lay on the bed and let the waves of rage run up and down my body. After a while, I fell asleep, had a nice nap, and woke up refreshed." — Herbert Z.

◆ "Generally I call a friend or my sister to ventilate." — Nancy B.

◆ "I try to walk away or take a hot bath." — Vincent A.

Dealing well with the "stuff of life" is by no means an easy task or something that takes place overnight. Like Leslie T., many masters learned to manage these challenges more effectively with help from private therapists. Indeed, two thirds of the masters indicated that they had at some point had personal counseling, and many stressed that they had benefited from therapy *in addition to* recovery group support. A number stressed that counseling helped them deal with underlying issues that may have played a role in their drinking problems.

Over the course of her recovery, Leslie T. has had therapy to deal with her deeper issues of depression as well as with an eating disorder. She has found it helpful to explore with her psychiatrist the connection between a childhood weight problem and her adult problems of bingeing and purging with both food and alcohol.

Ben H. used alcohol to deal with the pain of his adoptive father's physical abuse during childhood, as well as issues related to having been adopted. Since quitting drinking, he has found that he still feels a great deal of pain. "But I deal with it without alcohol," he asserts, "by exercising, seeing a psychologist on and off, and taking antidepressant medication."

To this day, even though they're well into sobriety, a number of masters say that finding solutions entails *continuing* to seek support when their problems are beyond them. For example, after nine years of sobriety, Michele D., who went to AA sporadically in the past, realized that she was at risk for relapsing when the man she was in love with died. She resumed going to AA and began working with a sponsor.

Celebrating and feeling happy

The masters' most common responses to how they handle these positive experiences had to do with learning to enjoy them without drinking.

◆ "I go out for a meal or coffee, take a walk, or get close to nature." — Michele D.

◆ "I like to clean my house, try a new recipe, experiment with a new ethnic restaurant, do something for someone else, or buy flowers for the table." — Zoe A.

◆ "I remind myself that the quickest way to spoil the moment is to take a drink." — Clare J.

◆ "I go to AA meetings and talk about how happy I am." — Marguerite E.

◆ "I reward myself with a new book, massage, music, or maybe even a little chocolate." — Ann M.

◆ "I used to love champagne. Now I celebrate things with sparkling grape juice — it's festive and fizzles." — Amy P.

◆ "I jump around and sing." — Jay J.

Accepting That Life Goes On — with Turmoil

Just because the masters have learned to cope more effectively with the roller coaster of day-to-day living does not mean that turmoil ceases. Martha B. (five years) has found that in many ways, the past three years have been more stressful than any others in her life. During this time she moved to be with her husband and in so doing gave up a $54,000-a-year position for low hourly wage employment. She also left her friends of many years, as well as her family and support system. "Yet I deal with it and have chosen not to drink," she states. "A lot of it is sheer willpower, but I do ask God for help on a regular basis." In addition, she is in counseling and goes to AA three to four times a week.

Someone who has been abusing alcohol for a long time may have personal, physical, and material damage caused by drinking that will take time to repair. Chico W. found that when he first sobered up, it was difficult to regain the respect of his family, friends, and employer. "I thought, incorrectly, that everything would return to normal, but it took four years to restore my marriage, and I changed employers after fifteen months," he says. And as Becky E. says, after having one of the worst relationships in her life during sobriety, "It just goes to show that *not* drinking doesn't create instant nirvana or effect a personality transplant."

Some masters deal with wounds from the past in the midst of maintaining sobriety. During recovery, Denise T. got in touch with severe physical abuse she had experienced as a young child. Although she continues to make progress in dealing with her painful past — with the help of AA, other self-help programs, professional counseling, and antidepressants — her childhood wounds are not fully healed. Because of them, she felt she had to leave her job working with abusive parents and their children. She says, "I stay motivated to remain sober through my faith in a higher power and the satisfaction of learning to live fully *in spite of my past* rather than live in fear while trying to escape it."

Finally, Leslie T. makes the point that it's not always possible to fill every void when you give up alcohol. In her case, she has not been able to fully replace the relief from stress that alcohol afforded her, nor has she recaptured the uninhibited feelings in lovemaking that she had when drinking. Perhaps most difficult to accept, she feels that her creative writing abilities have never been as strong when she is sober as they were when she was under the influence. Nevertheless, she maintains that these "benefits" of drinking certainly were not worth the havoc alcohol wreaked in her life. She concludes, "I think it can be helpful to know that one need not resolve every issue in order to function well and enjoy life, as I do most of the time — without drinking."

Neil H. is a living testament to the fact that it's possible to remain sober without resolving problems. He maintains that he has no relationships with women and no sex life, which he says tends to make him "cranky," and he describes himself as "always angry." In response to questions about how he handles depression and feeling happy, he simply says, "Drinking is not an option." Neil has remained sober for well over a decade.

Getting Counseling While Still Drinking

Although many people believe that you can't get anywhere in therapy until you become abstinent, some masters did benefit from professional counseling while they were still drinking. (This is more likely to work if your alcohol problem is not a severe one.) Michele D., who showed up "somewhat drunk" for her first therapy session, saw a psychologist for four years before she finally quit drinking. He did tell her that he wouldn't help her if she continued to arrive under the influence, and he always asked her about how much she was drinking. (She says she was honest with him.) Michele and her therapist were able to work on her relationships with her father and her then husband (also a problem drinker), on helping her get in touch with her feelings, and on dealing with her anger and sense of abandonment. Thus, even while she continued to drink, Michele was able to do some of the work that would eventually help her become abstinent and remain abstinent for nine years.

In contrast, for three years Heather F. saw a psychologist who told her that once she resolved her depression, her drinking would subside. She protests, "It was the other way around: if I had quit drinking, not only would I have felt less depressed, I would have been able to deal with my underlying issues more directly and more readily." In other words, to make optimal progress, you will eventually have to come to terms with the drinking. If a person is abusing alcohol very heavily, abstinence may be essential for making *any* progress.

Using Positive Thinking

Quite a few masters commented about the importance of using positive thinking or changing their way of thinking in sobriety. Some, like Leslie T., were formally schooled — either through their recovery group or in therapy — in using a technique known as cognitive restructuring. With cognitive restructuring, a person learns how to catch him- or herself thinking negative trigger thoughts that might lead to drinking, then to examine them critically, and finally to challenge them and turn them into something positive or constructive, thereby preempting drinking.

Here's how some masters combated self-defeating scenarios.

Self-fulfilling prophecies — setting yourself up for something by telling yourself it will happen

Regina S., a SMART Recovery coordinator: "There was a war going on within me when I was trying to quit drinking. I would tell myself, 'I can't stop drinking; there's something wrong with me.' Treatment professionals would say I couldn't get sober without AA." Finally, with the help of cognitive strategies, she started telling herself, 'Of course I can do this. I can do many things. No one is putting that bottle in my hand. There is no line reaching out from that bar to hook me in for a drink.'"

Catastrophic thinking — believing that the worst possible events will come to pass

SOS participant Cheryl T.: "All my life I've been afraid of social situations. So I would think, 'I'll make a fool of myself — I need to drink to fit in.' Now I remind myself that I don't need to drink because my fears never come true — I always wind up having a good time and can do it without drinking."

Rationalization — making excuses to allow yourself to drink

Regina S.: "About a week after I had quit drinking for good, I thought, 'You really didn't do very well this year.' I'd had a few relapses. 'You may as well have a couple of drinks before getting really serious.' I challenged this with 'Just because you've always done this doesn't mean you have to keep doing it.' I was also able to remind myself that although I hadn't been 100 percent sober that year, I had made great progress."

"Should" statements — having regrets or beliefs about obligations that have little or no basis in fact

Cheryl T.: "I used to obsess about disagreements I'd have at work, going over and over in my mind, 'I should have said this' or 'I shouldn't have said that.' And I'd find myself drinking over such matters. Now I ask myself, 'How much will any of this matter ten years from now?' When I look at the big picture, I calm down and get things in perspective."

All-or-nothing thinking — being a perfectionist about unrealistic goals

Leslie T.: "When I was having trouble with my stepson, I would tell myself, 'I'm not cut out to be a mother.' My therapist helped me to be able to say to myself, 'I don't have to be able to handle everything perfectly or have all the solutions in order to be a competent stepmother.'"

Poor-me talk — feeling sorry for yourself

Bryce G., a SMART Recovery member: "After my first year and a half of abstinence, I found myself trying to make connections between my past and my present. In the process, I'd find myself feeling angry at my parents for being incompetent and abandoning me. I'd challenge these thoughts by asking myself, 'Where is it written in stone that I should have had Ozzie and Harriet for parents — or, for that matter, that many people have parents like that?'" This helped him stay sober, because in the past anger had led him to drink.

Master Marjorie A. shares a useful cognitive exercise she did in early sobriety: "Every time I had negative thoughts, I literally replaced them with affirmations that my therapist and I wrote together. I wrote the affirmations on tags and stuck them all over my apartment. Slowly, they became the things I thought of before the negative stuff occurred to me."

how to manage that conflict. As Jessica F. advises, "Look for the common thread in your relapses. Break that thread."

Renew your commitment; rather than wallow in feelings of hopelessness and remorse after a lapse, go back and take stock of the costs of drinking and the benefits of not drinking. Dorothy C. went through this process when, after twenty-three years of sobriety, her husband's death precipitated a full-blown relapse — one that she stopped after nine months. At first, she says, "I was lonely, hated God, and lost contact with other alcoholics — I wanted to escape from the hurt." But she got back on track by returning to AA and taking stock: "I had learned what it was like to live life sober, and after having been drunk for nine months, I made a decision — I did not want to live my life drunk or to die." (She counts her sober time as follows: "I like to say I have thirty-nine years less nine months.")

Make an immediate plan for recovery. When AA member Echo T. had a one-day return to drinking, she says, "I decided a one-day-at-a-time program could start just as well the next day as months later. I knew I didn't want to go back to hell on earth." According to Dr. Marlatt, "Time is of the essence — the more quickly you engage in an immediate plan of action, the greater your odds of not continuing to drink." A plan might entail getting rid of any alcohol around the house, avoiding social situations involving alcohol, and/or planning substitute activities for drinking (like going for a walk at drink time). This is also the time to enlist support; rather than be ashamed, return to a recovery group, talk to supportive relatives and friends about what happened, or see a mental health professional.

AA friends. Shortly after that I sought professional help for managing our family problems." In essence, Leslie followed the steps many experts suggest in managing a return to drinking: put the lapse in perspective, try to figure out what precipitated the drinking, do something about it quickly, and come up with ways to prevent such slips in the future.

For the masters who did have such an experience, it didn't

necessarily signify a need to begin counting the time spent in sobriety all over again. Like Leslie, some are able to look at the big picture. She notes, "After each of my slips, I remember asserting that I could not and would not go all the way back to beginning sobriety. Today I say that I've had twenty years of sobriety punctuated by two brief but serious relapses." Similarly, Rosa L. had a few rocky weekends after she got out of treatment, and over the course of her ten years of sobriety has had "one beer in Mexico, and another time some amaretto." She declares, "I count my sobriety date as the day I went into treatment, because despite my relapses, I see this as having been a process — one long attempt to get sober."

However, many people — alcohol treatment professionals included — view *any* return to drinking, even one drink, as a true relapse. AA member June R. says, "I remember that if I have one sip, I'll undo over eight years of sobriety and have to start over." Nearly half of the masters expressed this black-and-white view. (Such responses were evenly divided between people who used traditional and nontraditional recovery methods, but loners were much less likely to define a relapse in this way. This suggests that some of those who think that consuming any amount of alcohol counts as a relapse may get this idea at recovery programs.) Louise L., who was once highly dependent on alcohol, graphically expresses this perspective: "When I relapsed, my SOS group never called it a slip. As a group, we are not into euphemisms. Drunk is drunk, sober is sober, relapse is relapse, and dead is dead."

The problem with the notion that one slip will lead you right back to drinking at your worst is that it can become a self-fulfilling prophecy: if you believe this and you have one drink, you might keep right on drinking. According to Dr. Alan Marlatt, people who consider drinking any amount of alcohol to be a relapse and who then do have a slip are much more likely to have a *serious* relapse than those who have been taught to be prepared for slips and to manage them appropriately. Dr. Marlatt explains, "When a commitment to abstinence works, it really works. But when someone who is not totally committed slips and has not been adequately prepared, that person really falls."

Identifying Your Vulnerable Points

WFS member Marisa S. shares the sentiments of a number of masters when she emphasizes, "It's important to realize that relapse is a process and doesn't come out of the blue. It's very important to be aware of one's vulnerable points. We all have them — times when we need to be particularly careful with ourselves." For her, the vulnerable points that triggered relapses were "depression — not caring anymore, extreme work stress, or anger that I didn't feel I could face."

In this same vein, a number of masters define a relapse as a way of thinking and behaving that occurs *before* someone even resumes drinking. Jason T. notes, "A relapse is when you stop doing what you need to do to stay sober. Relapse comes before you pick up a drink." AA member Sue H. agrees: "The thought comes before the drink. Old attitudes, blaming, complacency, and stopping going to meetings. We call it 'stinkin' thinkin' . . . Hanging on to resentments and anger. All those feelings that we stuffed for years."

Ironically, Heather F. discovered that she's vulnerable when everything in life is going well for her. "My last relapse occurred when life couldn't have been going any better. I had said jokingly to a friend, 'Now watch me screw it up by drinking.' Shortly after that, I did." But she learned from this, which was her last relapse. "At first I was just aware of the connection between things going well and having a desire to drink, but I couldn't understand why. Then, shortly after that last relapse, I was having an argument with my father when he barked at me, 'What right do you think you have to be happy?' That's when it all came together: I saw that I turned to alcohol when everything was going great because my entire life I had been given the message that I didn't deserve to feel happy. I saw the connection between being taught to deny feelings of happiness with my need to sabotage the good times."

Awareness of your vulnerable points can prevent lapses and relapses. Heather F. says, "Now I can head off a relapse by telling myself that I have every right to be happy and not feel guilty when my life is going well. I no longer have to wreck the moment by having a drink."

After twenty years of sobriety, Leslie T. finds that she has few vulnerable points but will admit to "escaping with reading" after a hard day at work — something she has done since early sobriety. She adds, "More recently, music and exercise have joined the list of remedies for day-to-day problems, and I have on several occasions come home from work, cranked up the CD player, and curled up in a fetal position. At some level, angst remains, but with the knowledge that my life is rich in love and rewarding in work."

10

Recall the Past, Live in the Present

How the Masters Stay Motivated

It's one thing to quit drinking —
most problem drinkers have done it many times. But it's another
thing to "stay quit." So how do the masters *maintain* sobriety? In
the beginning they used all kinds of tricks to help them avoid
backsliding: they found multiple ways to limit exposure to alcoholic beverages and manage tempting situations. Many of them
still use these strategies — but how do they stay psyched?

You might imagine that the masters stay motivated by associ-
ating with others who have recovered, helping other problem
drinkers, turning to a "higher power," or faithfully continuing to
attend recovery group meetings. While these aspects of recovery
are important to many, other explanations of how the masters
keep themselves from relapsing were far more common.

The masters make it clear that it takes much more than the
obvious to stay sober. A deeper shift in thinking takes place. Over
and over, they told me that they remain motivated by *never allowing themselves to forget the past*. This is the most powerful, consistent theme in all the information from the masters, and it cut
across all recovery methods. Seven out of ten masters, whether
they recovered in traditional or nontraditional ways and whether
they are loners or joiners, said that they keep the memory of the
past fresh.

The masters counterbalance the negative memories of their drinking days with a keen awareness of the many rewards of sobriety. Although they remember the past, many of them have moved on and see themselves as recover*ed*, not recover*ing* — challenging the notion that an "alcoholic" who quits drinking is forever "in recovery."

Phil Q.'s Story

From his late teens through his mid-forties, Phil Q. drank to get drunk each night, all the while moving up in a career that wove through various positions at prestigious national magazines, finally landing a vice presidency at a major company. He seemed to get away with it, drinking what he wanted with few apparent consequences — the perfect picture of a high-functioning "alcoholic." Even his boss, who was also a close friend, was shocked when Phil was sent to an alcohol treatment center. Phil told me, "From age thirty-two or so until I was forty-four, I knew I was an alcoholic, knew that I could function reasonably well as one, and kept drinking."

But after two humiliating drunk driving arrests, Phil was sent to a treatment center. Once he had some time away from alcohol, he began to compare what his drinking did to him with how much better he felt when sober. Now abstinent for fourteen years, Phil lists the three most important things he does to keep himself from going back to the bottle:

1. I remember how unpleasant it was to start shaking and vomiting in the afternoon every day.
2. I remember how much better my life became once I stopped.
3. I remember that I was never satisfied with only one drink, or only four. I always had to drink myself drunk, and knowing that makes me realize that moderation can't be in the cards for me.

As Phil's career burgeoned and he continued to get drunk nightly, no one seemed to know he had a serious alcohol problem. His own first inkling came in the form of withdrawal symptoms — gagging, nausea, and shaking every day by five o'clock in the afternoon. "It was then that I realized my dependence on alcohol was physical as well as psychological," he says. "My body needed alcohol, and it was an incredible source of embarrassment to have these symptoms, which I was sure others noticed."

Phil downed a nightly pint of bourbon with orange juice and bitters, moved on to wine with dinner, and ended with a pint or so of Scotch, consumed over three to four hours before he fell asleep. By his mid-thirties, his drinking had begun spilling into the day-time. But if people noticed, no one seemed to care. His wife went to bed early while he stayed up drinking. "My moods were really high or really low. At its worst, my drinking was ruining my marriage and starting to hurt my job performance," he explains.

"If I was going to be cured, it would be because of what *I* did"

After his second drunk driving arrest, when the judge offered him the option of month-long treatment, Phil agreed to go so he wouldn't be sent to jail. After two miserable days in detox, he spent most of the remaining time at the treatment center "feeling like a child being put through all this dumb stuff." Even recalling his mother's suicide by jumping off a roof when he was seventeen didn't bring any revelations. One incident, however, was reveal-ing: when asked to talk about his feelings for his nine-year-old adopted son, Phil "wept copiously."

One night, after several weeks in treatment, Phil found him-self wondering, "'When are they going to make me better?' It was then I realized that if I was going to be fixed, cured, or made better, it would be because of what *I* did." He left treatment and did not attend AA beyond the six months required by the court. "I found the meetings joyless," he explains. "I was really glad I wasn't drinking anymore. But I am success-oriented and ambi-tious, and I didn't have a sad story to tell."

"I'm not a believer in signs, but incredibly good things were happening"

Phil began to recognize day-to-day changes that reinforced his desire to remain sober. "I noticed that the spoon in my hand wasn't shaking anymore. Sleeping, which used to terrify me and required quite a ritual from age seventeen on, suddenly came easily to me. But the best thing was not feeling so awful at the end of the day. I started liking myself more. Friends who hadn't known I had a drinking problem said I was much nicer to be around now that I was sober."

In the short run, there was also a down side to not drinking. "For the first six months," he explains, "I felt incredibly vulnerable and exposed, like I was under a microscope. I had to relearn everything — how to be a father, how to be a husband." The toughest part of quitting, however, was what it did to his self-image: "After six or seven drinks, I had thought of myself as fairly gregarious, funny, spontaneous, creative, slightly manic, engaging, and smart. When I became sober, I felt incredibly dull and boring. I missed who I wasn't anymore."

Soon, however, Phil had more motivation to stay sober. Six months after he got out of treatment, he and his wife initiated proceedings to adopt a Korean sister and brother, something Phil's wife had refused to do as long as he was drinking. While awaiting the children's arrival, Phil and his wife found themselves expecting a baby. Having been told that they could not have biological children, they were delighted. He says, "I'm not a believer in signs, but there were a lot of incredibly good things happening in my life."

Although he had feared that "everything would collapse" when he got sober, Phil instead found that "life only got better." He lists as the current pleasures in his life "being the best father I can be — nothing gets in the way of being with my kids. I enjoy being a fairly fit fifty-eight-year-old and being an uncommonly reliable and confident businessman — I'm good at what I do, and that feels terrific." But mostly, he says, his source of motivation is "my general state of well-being. I'm getting in my life that state of near-bliss that I sought with alcohol. Not often, but often enough. Now the pluses so far outweigh the minuses, there's no question I would ever go back."

Keeping the Memory Fresh

When I asked the masters, "How do you stay motivated? What keeps you from going back to problem drinking?" the number-one response — far exceeding all others — was the same as Phil's: they keep fresh the memory of what life was like when they were drinking.

◆ AA member Lilith V. recalls "the mornings after, the guilt and shame of waking up in some unfamiliar place, lying naked beside some stranger, the fear of retribution for misdeeds, real or imagined."

◆ SOS member Neil H. stays motivated by "recalling the incredible pain of withdrawal and the feeling of total despair — that you are losing your mind or have already done so, that you have soiled the memory of yourself with your loved ones."

◆ Charles S., who quit drinking fourteen years ago with the help of AA, stays motivated with "a vivid, almost cinematographic recollection of the bad way I felt when I drank and when I went through an incredibly long and painful withdrawal."

◆ Heather F., who recovered largely with counseling, cites a recommendation she once heard at an AA meeting to "think the drink all the way through." She adds, "I think past the first drink to what awaits me on the other side."

◆ Jane W., who quit on her own and then started going to WFS, says, "I remind myself that hangovers suck!"

For motivation, some masters who drink moderately keep alive the memory of when they drank too much so they don't go back to their old ways. Edgar J., who has a glass of "moonshine" or cognac about three times a year and an occasional drink when he goes out to dinner, states that he stays motivated not to go back to his daily half-gallon of hard liquor by recalling "the money and time I wasted while abusing alcohol." Other masters think about how drinking affected relatives with serious alcohol problems. Karen M. says, "I remind myself of my history, heredity. All of my sisters, my brother, my parents, and my grandparents had drinking problems in the past." Sara F., who, at her worst drank far less than most of the masters, thinks about the alcohol-related deaths of two of her aunts, one of whom "literally exploded, leaving dried blood everywhere" because of alcoholic cirrhosis of the liver. She says, "I realize that this could easily happen to me. I also reflect on the fact that my father still drinks, and I could easily be like him: violent, angry, bitter, and unloving. Everything I'm not!"

For some masters, recovery group meetings serve as a reminder of the consequences of drinking. Edgar J., who stopped abusing alcohol on his own fourteen years ago and who is not an AA member, declares, "Once a year I purposefully go to the seediest AA meeting around, just to keep my edge and look at where I could be . . . There but for the grace of God go I."

Celebrating Sobriety

Almost in the same breath as Phil Q. describes how he never forgets his history, he says, "I celebrate sobriety." He elaborates, "Reminding myself how full and rich my life has become is a form of positive reinforcement that I use frequently. I'm alive. My wife stayed with me. We have four terrific kids. I don't have physical withdrawal symptoms. I've become better at what I do. I'm healthier."

Indeed, the second most common theme that emerged from the masters' responses to the question of how they stay motivated is *appreciating how good nondrinking life is*. Other masters describe what they cherish about the sober life:

◆ "I felt older during my last years of drinking, when I was forty-seven, than I do now, at seventy-three. Sex is great. Life has all kinds of possibilities: people to meet and work with, books to read, places to see." — Emerson A.

◆ "I completed college with honors. I have a clear head and can make rational decisions. I am a good role model for my daughter and nieces and nephews. I feel I can accomplish whatever is important enough to pursue. I have the insight and confidence I never had while drinking. I am 'present,' not in another world — able to truly be there for my loved ones." — Karen M.

◆ "I *like* sobriety. I have self-respect, better reasoning, fuller enjoyment of pleasure, no guilt feelings, and the ability to appreciate myself and others." — Clay R.

Of his three new children in the first year of recovery, Phil Q. says, "They became my celebration." This reflects another common response to my question about motivation: quite a few masters emphasized the importance of relationships with family, children, and/or other loved ones.

Finally, a powerful motivator for staying sober is simply feeling better about yourself. Many masters said they have more self-esteem and are more confident, happier individuals than they were when drinking. A good number remarked on their improved health. And many simply stated that life is better, richer, fuller, and more peaceful. I received numerous comments about having more choices, more possibilities, and more control over their lives than ever before.

Recovered or Forever Recovering?

Although the majority of masters stay motivated by reflecting on painful images of the past, a number also suggested that they see themselves as having gotten over their alcohol problems, which runs counter to the prevailing view that problem drinkers should never consider themselves cured. Here's what some of them had to say:

◆ "I am recovered rather than recovering, as the alcoholism 'experts' insist. I don't even think about alcohol in personal terms and haven't for many years. Making a lifetime career of recovery is not necessary for all ex-alcoholics." — Rose S. (sixteen years, quit drinking on her own)

◆ "After twenty-one years of sobriety, I quite honestly never think about drinking under any circumstances and therefore consider myself recovered." — Violet F. (quit drinking with the help of AA, now involved in SOS)

◆ "Since I don't have a drinking problem, I don't need help. It's over." — Arnold C. (quit drinking fifteen years ago, at the age of sixty, by educating himself about various recovery approaches)

◆ "I used to have an alcohol problem, but now I do not have one." — Jackie A. (eleven years, quit on her own after trying several recovery programs)

◆ "I view my alcohol and drug abuse as a bad habit that I have overcome." — Cheryl T. (five years, quit with the help of group therapy, SOS, and exercise)

To be sure, some masters chided me for looking for people who had resolved serious drinking problems. Denise T. expressed popular thinking on the subject when she wrote, "Those who know about the field understand that an addict or alcoholic is *never* recover*ed*. Alcoholism does not get cured." Dorothy C. adds, "Speaking only for myself, I will always feel I am in recovery. It would be dangerous for me to think I am recovered."

Phil Q. seems to hold a position in the middle of the debate, noting, "I do not see myself as recovered *or* recovering, and I never use these words. They don't mean much to me — any more than the whole disease question about alcoholism means anything to me. It all sort of seems a diversion that doesn't have much significance. I just know that if I decided to drink someday, I wouldn't have just one." If Phil's twelve-year-old hears him say he's an "alcoholic," she corrects him sternly with "You *were* an alcoholic." He responds, "No, honey, I still am — I just don't drink anymore. Whatever it was that made me unable to be responsible about alcohol is still with me, and it always will be."

But I do frequently have just one.

Nevertheless, Phil is adamant that he does not want recovery to be the center point of his life. This is one reason that he rejected AA. He elaborates: "People in recovery groups often remain alcohol-centered. I realize that I am going to have to refrain from drinking for the rest of my life, but I don't want to think about it every day."

"More Meetings, More Sobriety"?

The masters' experiences also do not bear out the often-heard idea that you have to go to meetings for life in order to stay off alcohol. One slogan sometimes heard at AA meetings is "More meetings, more sobriety; fewer meetings, less sobriety; no meetings, no sobriety." Actually, of the 222 masters, only about half indicated that they go to meetings now. Not surprisingly, masters with traditional twelve-step recoveries are more likely to do so than those who recovered with the support of nontraditional groups. A number say they go infrequently, sporadically, or "as needed."

Many masters (forty-six) who once had formal support — mainly from recovery groups — indicated that they have stopped going to meetings. Sarah N. (seven years) served as a moderator for WFS meetings for years but got "burned out." She explains, "I now want to use the energy to fight other battles."

Of the ninety-seven who recovered with the help of AA, twenty-six have ceased going to meetings. However, fourteen of these people continue to follow AA tenets. The other twelve said they no longer attend because of dissatisfaction with AA or because they don't use its tenets. Tom C. (thirteen years), for instance, discontinued meetings about five years ago because he now feels "comfortable in recovery" without meetings. Anne H. (twenty years) says she no longer goes because she is "blessed not to be 'thirsty' anymore." She explains that "nondrinking has become as much my identity as drinking and partying used to be."

These masters' decisions are in accord with AA's book *Living Sober,* which encourages attending meetings "as long as we enjoy them, profit from them, and keep the rest of our lives in balance." John L., who described himself as "Mr. AA" during the first five to six years of his recovery, now says that he goes to AA meetings only about once every two months, noting, "AA is not as much a part of my life since I have filled my life with work and having a child."

Some of the masters who still attend recovery groups do so more to help others than to help themselves. One long-time AA member said, "Every time I'm about to quit AA, someone will come up to me and say, 'That's exactly what I needed to hear.' When I'm thrown these occasional carrots, it keeps me going."

Delivering Yourself from Temptation

By finding ways to limit exposure to alcoholic beverages and to manage difficult situations that might trigger an urge to drink, the masters have discovered that it's easier to stay motivated. These strategies were particularly helpful when their sobriety was new, but many of the masters still use them in their lives today.

For instance, Phil Q. says, "I stayed away from places where I usually drank. I also avoided certain situations — not because they were tempting, but because they made me feel uncomfortable. To this day, I stay away from circumstances where most of the participants are drinking too much, or I leave if I find myself in them."

One of the greatest challenges in early sobriety can be dealing with alcohol cravings, which are typically triggered by the sights, smells, people, places, feelings, and thoughts associated with drinking. As Louis S. puts it, "You have to change your playgrounds, playmates, and playthings." The masters share numerous examples of how they did this — or still do:

◆ For Louise L. (ten years), listening to music from her drinking days continues to trigger a desire to drink. "I simply had to stay away from clubs and not listen to the music that I listened to when drinking," she says. *I do not want to give up going to soltys or dancing!*

◆ Michele D. (nine years), who often drank after meeting stressful deadlines, says that in the beginning, driving home from work was a signal for drinking. She took different routes home to break the association.

◆ Karen N. (five years) says of her early sobriety, "I disposed of all alcohol in my house, and my drinking buddy moved out — I had to stop seeing him for a long time. I also avoided going out to restaurants and bars with friends for fear of being tempted." She still steers away from drinkers, and the only alcohol she keeps in her house is "stuff that's so vile" she has no desire to drink it.

The masters have developed creative strategies to deal with the tough times, especially in the beginning of their sobriety.

Dealing with the drinking hour and passing the time formerly spent drinking

Many masters — with both traditional and nontraditional recovery stories — indicated that one of their main methods of staying sober was (and in many cases still is) *finding substitute activities for drinking*. Leslie T. says, "I filled my days with silly diversions. For instance, I walked eight miles a day, including some walking at quite odd hours." To break his "cocktail time" ritual of many years, Heath M. says, "I ate a lot of carrot sticks and tried many diversionary tactics, like going to the library, gardening, finding afternoon AA meetings, and improving my cooking skills." June R. recalls, "I cleaned a lot of drawers and closets."

Like Heath M., other masters dealt with their difficult times of day in early sobriety by getting involved in recovery groups. To get through his former "start-drinking time" of six P.M., Herbert Z. went to his outpatient treatment program right after work and stayed there, "safe in the sobriety counseling sessions." By the time he got home, he says, "The most vulnerable moments were behind me. And I was so primed with sobriety thoughts, I could last the night." Karen M. says of her early sobriety, "I was newly divorced, with a three-year-old. I had no job. So I immersed myself in AA, getting very active in the program — chairing meetings, helping others, reading, and studying all the literature. I decided I had to stay away from bars and not date people who drank. I kept very busy in nondrinking activities."

Dealing with social functions involving alcohol

Both in early sobriety and today, many masters simply don't put themselves in circumstances that tempt them to drink. For Kerry G. (fifteen years), managing a social life was particularly hard at first, since she got sober in her early twenties, when she was in college, which meant that "I could no longer participate in normal twenty-one-year-old-type activities." She explains, "I had to give up college parties and distance myself from a lot of my friends. I felt like my life was over. I dealt with it by keeping a journal and sharing how I felt — the anger, the depression, the loneliness." She also went to AA meetings, kept busy, and had "lots of orange juice, chocolate, and coffee."

As simple as it sounds, the masters' number-one answer for how they now handle parties, weddings, business dinners, and traveling is to drink some sort of nonalcoholic beverage. If Phil Q. can't bow out of a cocktail party, for example, he'll have cranberry juice with soda water and lime. Duane L. says, "I get something nonalcoholic and keep it full. If all else fails, I tell people I'm driving." If necessary, Zoe A. will go to a corner market and buy her own soda or other nonalcoholic beverage. At parties and weddings, Katherine A. stays far away from the bar, toasts with water, and doesn't locate herself near wine that's already been poured, because she doesn't want to smell it.

Another helpful rule of thumb is to avoid situations where drinking is the primary activity — say, a cocktail party or wine tasting. Phil Q. states, "Unless my absence would be awkward, I skip cocktail parties."

Dealing with drinking buddies

About one in four masters went out of his or her way to stress the importance of getting rid of drinking friends and/or finding new friends who don't abuse alcohol. Some found that they just drifted apart from their old drinking buddies. Phil Q. states, "There are certainly friends who knew me only as a drinker and who know me almost not at all today." Military man Clarence C. adds, "When I stopped drinking, I found out I had no friends who were nondrinkers. I felt like a stranger at work and stayed at home with my family at night and on the weekends. Some of my drinking buddies would try to test my commitment, but my new conviction to sobriety was too strong, and they eventually faded from my life."

Likewise, during Annie B.'s drinking days, she made sure her friends were heavy drinkers, so her behavior was the norm. When she quit drinking, her most important steps included "dropping drinking friends." This was especially tough because her husband at the time was her drinking buddy. The relationship ultimately ended. Now she has friends from her WFS group, is close to her grandchildren, and says, "I enjoy and really get to know new people who enter my life."

Cal T.'s story illustrates what can happen if you stay with a carousing crowd. At one point earlier in his life, he quit drinking for about four years. But as a police officer, he found "there was a lot of drinking and raising hell after hours. There was also a sense of risk and being there for each other, and drinking was part of it." So for a while he "pretended" he was drinking. He eventually discovered that "it was easier to go back to drinking." Years later, when he quit for good, he says, "I abandoned a huge network of drinking friends." He admits that it was very difficult to leave that group, but as he separated from them, he became much closer to his wife, who gave up alcohol at about the same time. "I eliminated dysfunctional drinking relationships," he explains, "and enhanced those with my spouse, family, and fellow hobbyists."

Some masters discovered that their alcohol-based friendships were not what they thought they were. When Marjorie A. got sober, she found, "With the exception of one friend who also quit drinking, the rest of my friends dumped me. I spent many lonely nights with my journal and good music. I went to movies alone and would go for long walks." Slowly, new relationships came her way through her work. She began these new friendships with specific activities, never going to a club, restaurant, or party where drinking might be involved. Now sober for eleven years, she actually likes being alone, has just three or four close friends, and no longer feels uncomfortable in bars or restaurants.

Dealing with alcohol at home

When I asked the masters if they live with anyone who drinks, four out of ten answered yes, and almost half keep alcoholic beverages in their homes. (Some have it on hand for housemates or guests; others use it in cooking.) Phil Q. says, "My wife has a couple of drinks a day. It's not a problem for either of us." They keep some wine on hand for her as well as other alcoholic beverages for guests.

Some people find that it's not difficult to live with a social drinker, as long as that person is discreet about drinking. Explains Heather F., "I don't care if my husband has his nightly gin and tonic as long as he doesn't announce to me that he's making himself one. And I prefer not to know where he keeps the gin. When we have company, I ask that alcoholic beverages not be left on the counter." Since the smell of alcoholic beverages is a "big trigger" for Jack T., he has always had the following rules for housemates: "Drink, but rinse your glass out so I don't smell it after. Don't leave open bottles or cans around."

It's important to emphasize that since nearly all the masters have at least five years of sobriety, they may find it easier to handle alcohol in their homes now than they did early in recovery. Surely, when sobriety is new, it's easier for most people if their live-in companions don't drink, are willing to give up alcohol for a while, or drink only in the sober person's absence. And obviously, life is easier for someone who is trying to avoid alcohol if none is kept at home. To this day, Liz P. (sixteen years) keeps no alcohol around, stating, "If I did get the desire to drink, I would have to go out of my way to get alcohol. Hopefully, before I did get it, there would be enough time for me to change my mind. I don't think it's necessary to have it on hand for guests." In contrast, after twelve years of sobriety, Janet C. finds that she can have any kind of liquor around, with one exception: "I won't have martini ingredients in our home. Those might tempt me, but nothing else does."

Finally, it helps some people to get rid of any items they associate with drinking, like favorite "rocks" glasses or wineglasses. Phil Q. reflects, "I once had a Scotch glass that was big and thick and heavy. It held four shots easily — so I could say I had two

How the Masters Handle Business Situations

The temptation to drink can be extra high if you're in a job with peer pressure to drink — say, one that involves traveling or sales. Here are some of the masters' ways of handling business situations involving alcohol:

◆ Dorothy W. immediately turns her wineglass upside down and focuses on the people around her. When on business trips, she takes along phone numbers of support people, and she enjoys going to AA meetings in new places.

◆ Clarence C. excuses himself from meetings right after the business is done and before socializing might begin.

◆ Declining politely with "I have a medical problem" works nicely for Frank L.

◆ Marguerite E., who is in sales and marketing, sometimes says, "I'm not drinking tonight." Other times she "bows out gracefully from the situation." In hotels, she does not take the minibar key.

◆ When Alison D. first quit drinking, she made sure she didn't fly first-class because of the free drinks served, and she told colleagues and acquaintances she was on antibiotics and therefore couldn't drink. She no longer finds it necessary to take these measures.

drinks before dinner when in fact I had had eight. I loved that glass, but after I stopped drinking, I couldn't find anything to put in it that seemed right. So I ended up throwing the glass away. I felt very resolved and final in parting company with that dear friend."

Bear in mind that there is often a difference between then and now in the way the masters resist temptation. That is, they commonly did things in the beginning of sobriety that they no longer need to do. For instance, Rick N. used to rehearse before going to

How the Masters Handle Drink Pushers

Giving in to social pressure is one of the most common causes of relapse. Drink pushers range from people who think you don't really have an alcohol problem, to those who don't want to lose a drinking buddy, to people who are just plain insensitive. Here are some strategies the masters use to fend off the pushers:

Just say no. By far the most common response when someone foists drinks on the masters is a simple, polite, or assertive "No thanks." Zoe A. told me, "I flatly say no. End of matter." Dorothy W. explains, "I firmly say, '*No*, thank you' and realize the pressure is about them and not a shortcoming on my part."

Simply say, "I don't drink." Charles S. "firmly and gently" says, "I no longer drink." Emerson A. tells people, "Thanks, I don't drink." He feels he owes no explanations.

Explain that you have or had a drinking problem. A number of masters are blatantly honest about why they don't drink. Janet C. says, "if they get really pushy, I tell them I'm an alcoholic." According to Lance L., "If they don't know my history, they get a quick lesson." Fern J.'s words are "No, thanks. I'm a nonpracticing alcoholic." Elise C. will say, "I had my quota years ago."

Blame it on a health problem. Rebecca M. simply says that drinking makes her sick. Quite a few other masters tell people they are allergic to alcohol. Andrew A. says, "I have an allergy — drinking makes me break out in spots."

Leave the situation. Annie B. asserts, "If they push, I leave." Likewise, Marguerite E. will either leave or walk away from the situation.

Ask the person to stop pushing. Violet F. asks, "Why is it so important to you that I drink?" When someone asks Muffy G. why she doesn't drink, she stops them in their tracks with "Because when I drink, I tend to take off my clothes and dance on the tables, and my husband doesn't like it!"

weddings or parties so he could withstand the presence of alcohol. He no longer finds a need to do this. In the beginning, Annie B. kept no alcohol in her house and avoided parties. Within six months, she found she could keep anything around except wine, her drink of choice. Then, after about three years, she was able to have any type of alcohol on hand, and she is now able to attend parties.

The masters' stories show that for every rule in alcohol recovery, there is an exception, which brings us back to this: you have to find what works for you. George W. *purposely* chose not to change his whole lifestyle when he got sober. After he finished treatment, he just made up his mind "not to drink" and got strong support from his wife and family. His position on social events and drinking is as follows: "I'm not going to stay locked up in a room avoiding situations involving alcohol." When I last talked with George, he had just returned from a trip with "three buddies who drank like fish." He acted as the designated driver and says, "I kind of got off on it." This approach has worked for him for eleven years. *Nevertheless, it's easier for most people to stay motivated if they don't place themselves in situations that tempt them to drink.*

11

With or Without a "Higher Power"
How the Masters Handle Spirituality

Given the central role of spirituality in twelve-step programs, it comes as no surprise that another important element of many masters' recoveries is spirituality, be it traditional religious beliefs, turning their will over to a "higher power," or finding inner peace in a nonreligious sense. When I asked the masters if they had experienced any spiritual growth since resolving their drinking problems, nearly two out of three responded in the affirmative.

What caught me off-guard, given the centrality of a "higher power" to AA's program, was the dearth of people who used these words in describing their spirituality. Although spirituality is essential to many masters, it takes different forms for different people, and it is not necessarily the concept of a "higher power" that guides them. In fact, numerous masters have a kind of spirituality that in no way fits the traditional twelve-step view that to recover, you must turn your will and your life over to "God as you understand Him." Perhaps even more surprising, for some masters, spirituality has little or nothing to do with recovery.

Charles G.'s Story

Charles G. describes himself as "a Christian who doesn't go to church as often as he should." Nonetheless, his routine of prayer,

Bible reading, meditation, and exercise is now central to his recovery and his overall quality of life. Interestingly, until he resolved his drinking problem, religion had a low priority in his adult life. En route to becoming sober more than six years ago, Charles explored a number of different religions, including Zen Buddhism, before electing to go back to the Christianity of his boyhood. But as a SMART Recovery group coordinator, Charles does not use AA's "higher power" spirituality to stay sober; instead he bases much of his day-to-day recovery strategy on rational thinking.

Unlike the majority of masters, whose drinking escalated to serious proportions when they were teenagers or young adults, Charles says, "I did not develop an alcohol problem until I was in my forties. It grew into a bad habit over many, many years." Alcohol became very much part of his professional life; as an executive in a leading import business, he participated in the company tradition of unwinding at workday's end in the boardroom, which had its own bar. Charles recalls, "I'd drink like the rest of my colleagues: a few drinks at the office, then a few more when I got home, and maybe a few after dinner. It wasn't unusual to have six or seven drinks just about every night." But there was a gradual shift, not only in the amount he drank but also in his rationale for drinking. He notes, "I started drinking more to anesthetize myself, particularly when there were business problems." When the company he worked for went out of business, he says, "I became very depressed and drank around the clock."

"I decided to get fit, and through this change I got more energy"

Subsequently, for about a year Charles drank a bottle of Scotch a day. He describes this time in his life as follows: "I was depressed, lethargic, overweight, had trouble sleeping, and had high blood pressure. My relationships with my wife and my two children were poor. In the morning I needed a drink to 'calm my nerves' and to attempt to function. I did not like myself, and it was a never-ending nightmare." As for spirituality during his drinking days, Charles states, "We took our kids to the obligatory church services on holidays, but I just hadn't thought much about religion since I was a boy."

Finally, at his wife's urging, Charles started going to AA, which he drifted in and out of for three years, sometimes actively participating in the program and once staying sober for as long as a year. But when he became involved in a new business that involved a great deal of travel and exposure to alcohol, he returned several times to drinking. The final time led his wife to confront him: "Get cleaned up, or it's the end."

At this point Charles went to a month-long, twelve-step–based inpatient treatment program, where he received great benefits both from the one-on-one counseling with a therapist and the camaraderie with others in the same circumstance. "It was very relaxing — kind of like being at camp," he reminisces. While at the program, he started to exercise and began reading various books about recovery.

Not long after his treatment, Charles's wife heard about Rational Recovery, and the two of them set about finding a local group, which became a SMART Recovery group when the two organizations parted ways. Not only did Charles find he could open up better in these meetings than at AA, but the group's approaches appealed to him. Soon a positive cycle came into play, one that had begun in treatment. He explains, "I decided to get fit, and through this change of habit and ritual, I got more energy. This helped me to grow a new business and become successful."

"I use the practices of my rituals to put problems out of my mind"

Charles also found it therapeutic to go to his local bookstore and spend hours browsing and reading books about religion, addiction and recovery, meditation, and personal improvement. His travels in the Far East and the Middle East, as well as a friend who practiced Zen Buddhism, had already piqued his interest in

Eastern religions. But he found himself being drawn back to the Bible and Christianity.

Noting that everything he read about spirituality stressed the importance of finding "quiet time, time to reflect," Charles gradually set up an important morning ritual, one that took the place of the drink he had once needed to "calm his nerves" and help him unwind after a rough day. "I rise at five A.M.," he explains, "and spend some time reading the Bible and praying, which provides a quiet focusing on my inner needs and objectives. Then I lift some weights and run several miles, using headphones to focus on music. Finally I spend fifteen to twenty minutes meditating." He describes his meditation as "getting a clear mind — sometimes it's trying to not think about anything; other times I might sit and just watch a flickering candle." To him, these activities are "all one and the same — finding time to calm and center yourself, while in the past, alcohol was the ritual that allowed the centering."

Charles believes it is important to establish such new rituals in sobriety, to replace the tradition of drinking and whatever it brought the drinker. "Now I go to work in a less antsy way at nine o'clock instead of rushing off at seven-thirty, and I come home less stressed. I use the practices of my rituals to put problems out of my mind, and I can now handle all the issues that used to press every button in my body and lead me to drink," he affirms.

Another mainstay at this point in his sobriety is participating in his weekly SMART Recovery group, although Charles does not necessarily see himself attending meetings for the rest of his life. As for the role of spirituality, he explains, "Without a doubt, religion is important to my recovery. But my relationship with God is not one of humility and restitution — I'm more in the realm of 'God helps those who help themselves.' My feeling is that you've got to meet God halfway." He adds, "SMART has enabled me to take control of my life, change habits and rituals, and remind me of the consequences if I ever go back to using alcohol again. I feel good, and I am in control of my own life and destiny!"

The Masters and Spirituality

Charles G.'s story intrigued me not only because it illustrates how important spirituality is to many drinkers who have resolved their problem, but because he employs a number of spiritual techniques — "pillars of sobriety," as he calls them — that many other masters use. His is not the traditional twelve-step kind of spirituality that is captured in AA member Michele D.'s view that you should "make spiritual contact with a 'higher power' than yourself . . . admit that you are not the one in control." But both Charles and Michele are among the numerous masters who indicated that spirituality is central to their recoveries.

Comments related to spirituality were among the five most frequent responses to open-ended questions about key things the masters did to get sober and stay sober. More than half of traditional masters gave such an answer, while just 14 percent of nontraditional masters did so. Clarence C. (twelve years), who dropped out of AA early in his recovery, for example, lists "religion" and "seeking God's guidance for my life" as critical to his recovery, and he has become a regular churchgoer.

Looking back, Clarence says, "I never felt accepted until I started drinking. With God, I am always accepted as I am. I don't have to change, and I like that!" He adds, "I'm just a guy who is trying to live from day to day, who finds strength in the Lord rather than a meeting to discuss my latest problem with alcohol. I go to God and ask His forgiveness and guidance through the tough times, and He always comes through for me."

A handful of other masters who were not involved with AA told of dramatic conversions. Marie E., sober for twelve years, said she went through "seven years of hell" with drinking, "during which I would make vows, cry, and pray — but nothing would work." The turning point came one night when "I went to

The AA Way of Spirituality

"AA is a spiritual program and a spiritual way of life." So opens *Came to Believe . . .* , an AA book documenting individual members' spiritual experiences in the program. The suggestion in this book is that at AA, "spiritual" is not to be confused with "religious" — AA is not bound by theological doctrine and is meant to represent a "rich diversity of convictions implied in 'God *as we understood him.*'"

This is not to say that the AA program lacks religious influences. Its own *Twelve Steps and Twelve Traditions* states that the group's principles were "borrowed mainly from the fields of religion and medicine," and weekly meetings commonly open and close with prayers such as the Lord's Prayer.

Belief in something transcendental — a "higher power," outside of the individual — is part of the program, and prayer and meditation are seen as the principal means of conscious contact with this "higher power." The idea is not so much to pray to God for help in finding a way out of an alcohol problem; it has

the church, got down on my knees, and prayed with the pastor's wife. I gave it all to God. The next morning I woke up, and all desire was gone — I have never had a drink or cigarette again — not even one!" Today, she says, "I pray, read the Bible, and meditate every day to stay close to God. He is my strength."

Sandy V., now sober for more than twenty years, drank heavily for years after her daughter was diagnosed with a rare form of cancer and died. One night she had what she calls "kind of an out-of-body experience, and God let me see what I was doing to myself and my other children." From that point on, she never abused alcohol again, and she remains devoutly religious despite many more setbacks and personal medical problems.

Close to 40 percent of the masters indicate that they use prayer to help them avoid drinking — a technique much favored by people with traditional recoveries. And one quarter use some form of meditation to help them avoid drinking. For some this means using formal meditative techniques, but others meditate more to do with *humility* — "cleaning house" so that the "grace of God can enter us and expel the obsession." Members are urged to take stock of their shortcomings and "make amends" to people they've harmed, and to "pray rightly," *not* imploring "Grant me my wishes" but instead saying, "Thy will be done."

AA's *Twelve Steps and Twelve Traditions* stresses that AA does not demand belief in anything: "All of its Twelve Steps are but suggestions." Yet step three says that the effectiveness of the whole AA program rests on how well and earnestly members have "tried to come to 'a decision to turn our will and our lives over to the care of God *as we understood him.*'" And although the steps themselves state, "You can, if you wish, make AA itself your 'higher power,'" they go on to discuss how the doubter who considers his AA group the "higher power" will come to "love God and call Him by name." Consequently, it's difficult for some people not to view AA as a religious program, though others — including some masters who are atheists or agnostics — feel comfortable with the program and have found a way to make it work for them.

using recovery literature, such as AA publications. SOS member Becky H. says, "I pray and meditate every morning in order to focus myself, have a few moments of serenity, and 'refill my well.'" AA member Borden S. states, "I meditate on the meaning of life and on how other people deal successfully or unsuccessfully with their lives. I seek simplicity in what I perceive as complex." WFS member Kathryn N. does yoga and meditates regularly, adding, "I still have the habit of first thing in the morning going to my corner to read some positive ideas for the day."

Quite a few masters adhere to a less traditional type of spirituality, holding beliefs more like Richard D.'s: "I feel very close to our universe." WFS member Nancy B. describes her spiritual growth in recovery this way: "I am still an atheist, but I seek out peace and tranquility."

Some masters make a distinction between religion and spirituality. Long-time AA member Lilith V. says, "Religion answers none of my questions, eases none of my burdens, soothes none of my sorrows. *Spirituality,* however, is my mainstay." She goes on, "While I don't regularly make AA meetings, I continue to practice the principles of twelve-step recovery. I continue to seek a spiritual path, a path of growth, of coming closer to this 'God of my understanding.'" For her, spirituality has more to do with a process of "becoming whole" and finding "new truths" in life than in practicing a formal religion.

However you define it, there is strong evidence that spiritual or religious involvement is associated with a lower risk of alcohol and drug use, problems, and dependence, according to Dr. William Miller, who reviewed the relationship between spirituality and alcohol and drug problems in the journal *Addiction.*

Eight Different Ways in Which Spirituality Has Helped the Masters

To understand the very different shapes and forms spirituality can take and the ways in which it can help resolve drinking problems, consider the ways in which eight masters describe their spirituality.

From a self-described "nonfanatical" AA member

Marie S. (five years) maintains, "I have tried to adopt from AA what works for me, like the part about spirituality in my life. While I was drinking, I was a proclaimed atheist. Not anymore. Although my going back to church is very unlikely, I do believe in God and make spirituality an important focus in my life. Prayer and meditation are essential — they have opened up the inside, helped me to discover more beauty in life and in our collective existence."

From a master who had a Christian "spiritual awakening, rebirth experience"

Zoe A. (ten years) went to AA for the first five years of her recovery, finding that it helped her bridge from "alcoholic chaos to spiritual peace." With time, however, she felt a need for "a more focused, clearer spiritual relationship with God." She explains, "That is when I gave my life over to Jesus Christ and became a born-again Christian. Now a personal relationship with Jesus Christ is what keeps me sober."

From an AA member with a nontraditional concept of a "higher power"

George M. (five years) wrote, "I had no spiritual life before. I think I was looking for spirituality in a bottle. Now it is the most important part of my life. I still carry a great deal of resentment about my Catholic upbringing, and I have struggled to find a concept of a 'higher power' that I can apply in my life. What I have come up with is a distant memory from my childhood when I was sitting on my parents' living room floor. The sun was pouring in, lighting up the patterns in the carpet and spraying everything with a dazzling brilliance. Suddenly I was conscious of being conscious; I perceived my aliveness-of-being with a powerful certainty. That, to me, was a moment of 'God consciousness.' This power keeps me alive and sober today."

From a master who recovered with the help of counseling, WFS, and a sixteen-step empowerment group

Maddie M. (eight years) says, "I believe my drinking problem was due in large part to my loss of my connection with God — my 'higher power' — whatever word you want to use. Now I attend the Catholic Church and believe in many of its teachings. I also practice centering prayer, which is a form of meditation. I open myself to God's presence."

From an agnostic Unitarian who recovered with the help of AA

Jackie D. (ten years) maintains that AA helped her get in touch with a faith and spiritual life, which she defines "not as 'God' but as a sense about nature and an order in the world. I am consciously aware of nature and the earth being larger than me, and it helps me keep my life in perspective."

From a master who goes to AA frequently but who has explored many spiritual avenues

Denise T. (fourteen years) says, "Over the years, especially while drinking, I lost contact with myself and God. When I was exposed to the twelve steps, it made perfect sense that I needed to regain my connection to God and my spiritual self. Now I pursue various paths drawn from Christianity, Eastern religions, and New Age thought. My spiritual path has been most important in resolving my drinking problem. It has helped me realize I am not alone, that there is help from an entity more powerful than myself, and that I possess creative, healing power to assist in my own recovery."

From an AA member who sees herself as spiritual but not necessarily connected to any religious group

Marie F. (seven years) says, "My 'higher power' is more of an energy that is beyond all definition — all I know is that ever since I've tried to connect with this energy, my whole life has changed. With that connection has come a deepening experience of the infinite kindness, growth, and love that this power has to offer us all."

From a master who rejected AA's "higher power" concept, in part because she needed a more empowering type of spirituality

Marisa S. (seven years) says, "I'm not religious, and I don't believe in a God. But I believe very strongly in the sanctity of life and of the planet and the universe. Personally, I don't need humbling as much as I need emboldening. For me, spirituality is key in cultivating health, happiness, and sobriety — spirituality in the sense of believing in myself and in all that is good in the universe."

For Some, Spirituality Is Not the Key

A number of masters gave no indication that spirituality had played any role in their recoveries, and some stated that it played no role at all. In fact, the most common reason that masters who rejected AA did so was that they did not subscribe to a "higher power" concept or they disliked what they saw as AA's religious or spiritual orientation.

SOS participant John C., who tried AA early in his recovery and has been sober for eighteen years, says, "Spirituality played no part in my recovery. Rather, I had to fight to be a one-step person in a twelve-step world. The prevailing concept of spirituality during my early sobriety was a hindrance to promoting my personal strength and rebuilding my self-esteem. Since I was a humanist, personal responsibility for my recovery was the primary source of strength. I immersed myself in the literature of recovery and took everything that seemed practical and intelligent to me to bolster my ability to maintain sobriety." He adds, "The greatest model for me was the presence of other people who had recovered without a god or spirituality. They sort of found me at agnostic AA meetings and confirmed my belief that recovery required a very personal plan and personal responsibility."

Even some AA members admit that spirituality is not a big factor in their recoveries. Jane R., an AA member for nineteen years, states, "I tried to have a religious or spiritual experience but never did. Spirituality is not the central focus of my recovery — I'm too much of a scientist. I go to church once every couple of years and find it a pleasant experience, but that's it. I assumed that a religious experience would redefine who I was; it would be an emotional catharsis, and from then on God would help me out of the mess that was my life. None of that ever happened." Now Jane indicates that she pays "lip service" to AA's "higher power" by saying thank you at night when she remembers to do so. "That's it," she states. "I'm going through the motions.

And when things aren't going well, I try to imagine that 'God' has other plans for me. That's just to make myself feel better."

Rick N. (twenty-one years), a SMART Recovery leader, says, "The term 'spirituality' is so broad as to have little meaning. As such, I dislike this term." He adds, "When most people use the term 'spiritual,' I think they are really describing a feeling rather than some entity that has an existence all its own. It is the feeling of awe that overtakes us when we behold a sunrise or sunset, a starry sky at night, the cycle of birth and death, the rhythmic changing of the seasons, or the implacable forces of nature. When I contemplate these things, I feel connected with the universe in a very real sense. But I definitely do not think that recovery requires the experience of a 'higher power.' Twelve-step philosophy suggests that individuals do not possess the ability, the power to succeed, and that this power must come from outside themselves. Many people, religious or otherwise, simply cannot accept this abdication of self. There is no way I would have recovered if recovery required me to turn my life and will over to some benevolent deity or magical force which I do not believe exists."

It's obvious that many masters view spirituality as important to their recoveries. For some that means "turning it over" to AA's "higher power"; for others it's more of a oneness with nature and the universe. Some masters are religious, but they place more power in the hands of the individual. Finally, some make it clear that it is entirely possible to get sober and stay sober without religion, a "higher power," or spirituality in any sense of the word.

12

There's *Nothing* Missing

How the Masters Find Joy Without Alcohol

When most of the people around you can drink without having a problem, when movies and billboards glamorize fine liquor, and when advertisements make you feel like you're missing out on something if you can't have an ice-cold beer, how does someone who once got great pleasure from alcohol make up for the loss? Having accepted that the pleasures of their drinking days aren't worth the costs, don't the masters often have the feeling that things just aren't much fun anymore — that something is missing in their lives?

On the contrary, not drinking doesn't seem to be the hardship you might expect. Rather, the masters seem joyful about the richness and fullness of their sober lives: they get high on life without abusing alcohol and find fulfillment and pleasure in its absence.

Marisa S.'s Story

Compared with most other masters, thirty-four-year-old Marisa S. has a tale of youthful alcohol recovery. Nevertheless, her problem was serious and took a long time to resolve. First she cut back markedly for three years, and then she became abstinent, which she has remained for the past seven years. After exploring many avenues for recovery, Marisa says, "Gradually I learned that when I care enough about myself and pay attention to what's right for me, I don't drink. It became important for me to seek out the people whom I enjoy and who are good for me — and to stop feeling compelled to listen to those who don't fall into this category. I found that it's very important for me to trust my instincts and to let myself revel in the things that I enjoy." The recurrent themes in Marisa's story of recovery concern trusting her instincts, figuring out what in life really gives her joy and fulfillment, giving herself permission to do those things, and getting rid of the "shoulds" that determined so much of her past behavior and fueled her abuse of alcohol.

Marisa was the older of two daughters in what she describes as an "alcoholic" home. An outstanding student, she says of herself, "I was the good girl who held things together. I always had to do things right." Her "one way to rebel" was with alcohol. By her junior year in college, it wasn't unusual for her to drink every night and also to have a drink or two before daytime classes. That year she flunked out of college. Concerned, her friends talked with Marisa's parents, and they all confronted her about her drinking.

To prove she really didn't have a problem, Marisa decided not to drink for a while. She found, however, that it was unexpectedly difficult to stay away from alcohol, so she sought counseling and went into treatment. Afterward, she says, "I was dedicated to staying sober, became a good little AA 'do-be.' I went back to college and graduated with honors."

Marisa began a highly successful career in the fast-paced computer industry, in a very lucrative job that she hated. Gradually she drifted back into drinking. "I drank about a pint of vodka a day — I always had vodka nips in my purse, so I would never be seen drinking more than two or so drinks socially. I always had to worry about who could smell alcohol on my breath and about rotating my liquor stores, since I generally made daily or twice-daily trips."

"Screw the rules — I'm going to do what *I* think is right"

During this period Marisa met and married her husband. A combination of problems in this new relationship and a second drunk driving arrest led her to realize that she had a serious drinking problem and needed to strive for abstinence. She began a three-year whirlwind of not drinking and drinking again, going in and out of treatment programs, and seeing various counselors. Everyone and everything kept directing her to AA meetings. After her driving arrests, she notes, "AA was absolutely and stringently required." Of this time, she says, "I really wanted to be sober and did what I was told to do: I went to daily AA meetings and had a sponsor whom I talked with every day. But everything I was doing to get sober was feeding into my issues — needing to be perfect, doing what others were saying. At AA meetings, I was told, 'Sit down, shut up, and listen; don't trust yourself or your intellect.' The twelve-step philosophy fed my deep belief that I wasn't good enough — wasn't a good enough daughter, wife, employee. What I needed was to trust myself and my own feelings and to stop looking for others' approval."

At one point Marisa felt helpless, hopeless, and suicidal, but instead of giving up, she said to herself, "Screw all the rules. I don't care what anyone else thinks — I'm going to do what *I* think is right." Turning to an article her mother had given her previously about Women for Sobriety, Marisa proceeded to contact the group for its materials, went to the library to read books written by its founder, and took part in its pen pal program. In addition, since there was a SMART Recovery group in her area, she attended its meetings. "At AA, I had been told that my alcohol problem was cunning and baffling and that I had to pray to a 'higher power' to overcome it. I liked the fact that with WFS and SMART, I could establish my own path."

"I learned to revel in small pleasures each day"

Long before she gave up drinking for good, with the help of a therapist, Marisa began breaking away from the "shoulds" that haunted her and engaging in fulfilling activities that would eventually take the place of alcohol. She says, "Early on, I had been embarrassed by my passion for gardening and by the fact that it was such a homebodyish sort of hobby. Over time I learned to stop making apologies for who I am and to stop worrying so much about what other people thought. Outdoor activities, physical activities, and quiet time in nature all helped me to connect with myself."

Marisa also began to exercise rather than turn to alcohol when she was under stress. She explains, "If I planned to exercise, I couldn't drink much beforehand, and after exercising, I never had any desire to drink. Even things as simple as a walk outdoors were sometimes helpful in this respect — but serious exercise like on a NordicTrack was pretty well foolproof."

Marisa eventually qualified to become a WFS group leader and started a WFS group in her community, which she led for five years. She continues to garden "passionately," has good relationships with her husband and extended family, and is "ridiculous" about her two cats. On her list of pleasures in sobriety are "brunch outings with girlfriends; occasionally tossing aside my list of 'to do's' and curling up with a book or lounging by the pool; travel — my husband and I make it a point to go on one big trip each year." But Marisa notes that she also takes time to appreciate "the small things in life," like sunsets, the beauty of a flower, taking a warm bath on a cold night, being silly with her husband, and having a nice dessert now and then. "When I was drinking," she reflects, "I did some of these things, but I couldn't appreciate them. Now I try to be aware of the many small gifts and pleasures each day and to revel in them."

Building a Life with No Room for Alcohol

Marisa S. is far from alone in her positive portrayal of sober life. One after another, the masters shared stories of renewal. As their experiences unfolded, it became clear that most of them have built lives that have no room for alcohol. In other words, they seem to have made a conscious effort to create lives in which abusive drinking has no place. Their lives are filled with new sources of gratification as well as meaningful endeavors.

When I asked them how they seek pleasure now that their alcohol problems are resolved, they mentioned many leisure activities.

Reading

One in four masters stressed the importance of reading. Marisa S., who says she couldn't concentrate enough to read when she had "an alcohol-addled brain," now reads almost every night. When Ralph C. first quit drinking, he "filled up the time formerly spent in bars by returning to a former passion to fill the time: reading — fiction, nonfiction, recovery literature." He recalls, "I had gotten away from reading as my drinking progressed — no time, blurred words, couldn't remember what I'd read five minutes earlier." Now he goes through ten to fifteen books per month.

Hobbies and the arts

Many people mentioned how much they enjoy hobbies such as crafts, artwork, time on the computer, and home improvement, as well as attending plays and concerts. Billy H. crochets for a hobby. Sixty-two-year-old Sheri L. enjoys writing as a hobby and just started taking a course in children's literature. Married masters Clare J. and Cal T. note that one of their major sources of pleasure in sobriety is going to the ballet, opera, and art museums.

Travel and vacations

Marisa S. says, "Vacations are a wonderful thing for the soul!" Heath M., a self-described "gay senior," says of himself and his companion of thirty-five years, "We travel constantly, for we're both afraid that we might enter into real seniority without having climbed, tasted, or savored something in some remote corner of the world."

Nature and the outdoors

Quite a few masters mentioned their enjoyment of gardening, pets, hiking, being outside, and nature in general. Sarah N. maintains that one of the top ways she stays motivated to remain sober is by pursuing "my interest in living things and the environment. It's both a spiritual connection and a 'good fight' to occupy me." Rebecca M. says, "I go outside whenever possible, because I have a greater appreciation of nature, colors, smells, and sounds."

Food and eating well

One of life's great pleasures for a number of masters — one in ten — is food. Rebecca M. says that food is one of her principal pleasures in sobriety: "It tastes better, so I arrange to have more dinners with friends and family." For Ann T., "A big slab of chocolate cream pie is about the most pleasurable thing I can think of."

Actually, I would have guessed that the masters would make far more comments than they did about the importance of food and nonalcoholic beverages, given prevalent ideas about sugar cravings and caffeine addiction among "recovering alcoholics." I also thought that more masters would have been influenced by popular books promoting nutritional approaches to recovery, such as low-sugar diets and megadoses of nutritional supplements. However, very few said anything about special diets or supplements, and almost none mentioned caffeine and sugar cravings or "addictions." (Despite claims to the contrary, there is little or no scientific evidence that dietary changes or nutritional supplements have anything to do with resolving alcohol problems. Nor could I find scientific explanations for reported caffeine and sugar cravings, which appear to have more to do with hearsay than with physiological needs.)

Many masters did state that in general, they eat more healthfully than they did when they were drinking, eating more fruits and vegetables and having more regular meals. Marisa S. became a vegetarian, as did seven other masters. Karen M. declares, "I eat much healthier foods now. I want to be the best I can be."

Today, Marisa S. sees the important role that taking care of her physical needs plays in sobriety. She explains, "I learned long ago that when I'm actively paying attention to my overall health and well-being — feeling good about myself and my life — alcohol doesn't have any power over me. For me, it's very important to try to do the best I can for myself by watching what I eat, making sure I'm getting exercise and fresh air, getting enough sleep, and treating myself to the occasional massage."

Finding Fulfillment Through Fitness

One of the big surprises was the extent to which the masters emphasized the importance of exercise in their sobriety. Exercise was the second most common way in which they seek pleasure in their lives, behind only their relationships with loved ones. Exercise was also one of the masters' ten most frequent responses to my question about how they keep themselves from going back to problem drinking.

Exercise even figures in the spiritual dimension of life for some masters, like Richard D., who remarks, "My spirituality and exercise go hand in hand. One without the other is empty. Many times when I run, ride, hike, or whatever, I find joy and thankfulness in having been given the ability, motivation, and time to enjoy myself in this way."

Handling Weight Changes in Sobriety

When people quit drinking, their weight can go up, down, or stay the same, depending on the individual. Putting on some pounds can be a plus for an underweight person in recovery, but it can be troublesome for others, like Elise C., who was somewhat overweight when she went into treatment and suddenly gained ten pounds. She explains, "I told the physician that I was craving sweets, and he told me there was a very good reason for this. I was thrilled, waiting for the detailed medical explanation. After a pause, he looked me straight in the eye and told me it was because I was feeling sorry for myself. He also told me not to worry about it — that my weight was of little consequence compared to my need to focus on learning to be sober. It was great advice, which I remembered when I quit smoking later." Between quitting drinking and quitting smoking, Elise gained quite a bit of weight, but she then lost most of it. She now says, "I'm still overweight, based on the charts. However, I feel okay about it. Maybe it's age, maybe it's acceptance — but being a size twelve to fourteen seems right for me."

When George M. first became sober, at a weight of 150 pounds and a height of six feet, he was actually malnourished — so much so, he says, that he

Although little research has been conducted on the value of exercise in resolving drinking problems, one small study conducted years ago under the University of Washington's Dr. Alan Marlatt and reported in 1986 compared the impact of exercise (running) and meditation on two groups of college-age men who were heavy drinkers. The men were told that the experiment was a study of the effects of nonchemical ways of getting high. Those who exercised drank less than those who meditated, and both groups consumed less alcohol than the members of a control group with no instruction to meditate or exercise.

The following comments from the masters about the role of exercise in their recovery support many of the known benefits of physical activity:

had done permanent damage to his eyes. Within six months, however, his weight shot up to 210 and he became concerned. "I went from never eating to always eating," he explains. "The feeling seems to be that once a person puts down the bottle and starts working on the emotional and/or spiritual issues, the body will take care of itself. I believe that more emphasis should be placed on the care of the body." Now, he says, "I try to exercise, and am constantly having dietary battles: the right foods, the right amount of food. I know my blood pressure and cholesterol count. I eat three square meals a day now, try to eat healthy food, and watch my weight. I actively work at my health."

But not everyone gains weight in sobriety. Some masters who were overweight while drinking garnered the strength to slim down in sobriety. And some just naturally lost weight when they quit drinking. Heather F. says, "Whenever I drank, I let down my guard with food and would eat foods and quantities that I would never eat when I wasn't drinking. When I gave up alcohol, even though I gave myself permission to eat pretty much what I wanted to make things easier, I still lost about eight pounds, because I was no longer going on my drunken food binges." Similarly, Marisa S., who is just under five feet four inches tall, says that she lost about twenty-five pounds over the course of her recovery and has maintained a weight of about 110 pounds for ten years now.

◆ "Exercise has become much more important in recovery — both for the high and to cope with feelings." — Jane R. (nineteen years, AA member)

◆ "I exercise to relieve stress, improve mood, maintain weight, increase circulation and endurance — all of which keep me stress-hardy, thereby helping me be less vulnerable to the wiles of temptation." — Zoe A. (ten years, religious recovery)

◆ "When I first quit drinking, walking and bicycling were among the most important things I did. I figured endorphins* would replace the alcohol, and they did." — Cal T. (eleven years, quit on his own)

◆ "Exercise is one of the ways I seek pleasure in sobriety. Being fit has made me confident in a way that nothing else has." — Stanley K. (twenty-two years, AA member)

◆ "I walk regularly, often with a sponsor, and chose a job that includes physical work outdoors as part of the package. As one of my sponsors says, 'When you exercise, you feel better. And when you feel better, you think better.'" — George M. (five years, AA member)

◆ "I exercise at the time of day I used to start drinking — after work. Working out provides a great transition between my job and our busy family dinner hour." — Heather F. (nine years, eclectic recovery)

Some people who were exercisers long before they quit drinking, like Richard D., have eased up on the intensity of their exercise. He told me, "As my years of sobriety increase, the urgency of my exercise has diminished. I find that skipping a day or two is okay." He still sets competitive goals each year, but adds, "I am definitely less obsessive." Similarly, Herbert Z. says, "Oddly enough, I exercise less now than when I drank. When I was drinking, my denial mechanisms drove me to demonstrative excesses of athleticism, such as running marathons, cycling two hundred-mile-per-day and longer races, and generally pretending to be a monster of good health. Now I'm more relaxed."

It all seems to come back to the idea of establishing balance in

---

* Endorphins are morphine-like proteins produced by the body are involved in pain relief and possibly in controlling mood and to stress. There is speculation that endorphins may be responsi so-called high sometimes experienced when runners run long dista

life, as indicated by Heath F., who ran six marathons and never deviated from a seventy-mile-a-week running schedule when he was drinking. Although he still exercises and finds that "it reinforces whatever you do in life," he notes in the same breath that "balance is important."

Enjoying Small Pleasures

"lowers — growing them, cutting them for my home ice, just walking around and bending over to smell s Marisa S., illustrating one way in which she appreciapleasures in life, a sentiment expressed by many masters er for nine years, SOS member Becky H. declares, "I began to do what I think of as weaving a tapestry of sobriety. I *notice* things, positive things, and revel in them — a raindrop sliding down a leaf, my baby's giggle, the cat's paws twitching in her sleep, the smell of the gardenia. These are the threads of the tapestry that I work on every day." As Dorothy W. states, "Big things are no longer necessary. Small stuff seems enough."

Take a moment to come up with your own list of small pleasures — things you tend to take for granted but that, if you let them, really give meaning to your life. Make an effort — and give yourself permission — to enjoy, appreciate, or engage in at least one of th se activities e ry day.

Finding Fulfillment by Helping Others

Among the top ten ways in which the masters seek pleasure is helping others. Given AA's philosophy of carrying its message, it should not be surprising that masters with traditional recoveries are more likely than those with nontraditional recoveries to believe in the importance of reaching out to others with alcohol problems. But the general theme of helping others seems to be important to a number of nontraditional masters as well — many emphasized volunteer work, community service, or being involved with civic organizations. Trevor B. seeks pleasure through involvement in a rehabilitation and detox association as well as by volunteering for an emergency medical service; Evan J. enjoys helping people who wish to become sober, primarily through the SOS e-mail group.

Nolan H. mentions that one of his pleasures is spending time doing volunteer work related to his children's sports. He finds that "it's nice to have a hobby that gives me personal satisfaction, but by the same token I'm doing some good for the community and the kids." SMART Recovery member Rick N. says he devotes "a significant amount of time to causes and ideas outside of myself — i.e., environmental, political, social."

Some masters have found greater meaning in life by switching to careers in which they help others. During Dorothy W.'s sobriety, sh   clinical so-five spot on the list of how the masters seek pleasure in their lives was "through employment."

◆ Lilith V. says, "I've come from being a high-school/college dropout, topless dancer, minimum-wage worker to a respected career professional, earning $80K this year — legally!"

◆ After quitting drinking at the age of forty-six, Roxi V. went back to school, got an M.S. degree, and became a vice principal of a junior high school.

◆ Paul V. has quadrupled his income since he became sober nine years ago.

Not everyone defined professional betterment in sobriety as climbing the career ladder and making more money. Marisa S. declares, "I used to define myself in terms of my success at work, and I considered it good and virtuous to be entirely consumed by my job. Now my work is primarily something that I do to support other, more important aspects of my life. It's still very important to me to work to the best of my ability, but I'm no longer willing to be consumed by this."

Likewise, Herbert Z., a lawyer, states, "I've become more relaxed about my work. This has its good side and its bad side. As a drinking alcoholic, I had a highly compulsive personality and was driven to maintain an appearance of being superbly organized. Now that my drinking is behind me and I have some self-esteem back, I no longer feel the drive to be such a superman. This has made me a nicer person to deal with. But since my office is not so buttoned down as it used to be, I have occasionally missed deadlines that I would never have come close to missing before."

Enjoying and Enhancing Relationships

By far the most common response to how the masters seek pleasure in sobriety is through relationships with their families, loved ones, and friends. More than half of both traditional and nontraditional masters listed enjoying or appreciating family or friends as one of their top three ways to seek pleasure, making comments like "being with my family," "time with friends and family," "loving my husband, friends, and family," "spending time with my adult children."

When I asked the masters how their relationships have changed in sobriety, more than nine out of ten stated that relationships with others have changed largely for the better. Many indicated that their associations with others are more open, more honest, deeper, and/or more trusting. Here are some specific responses concerning these changes:

◆ "I am very open and honest with everyone. My nineteen-year-old daughter and I communicate well. Also, my wife and I communicate and enjoy our time together. I give people more of a chance." — Richard D.

◆ "My relationship with my parents has really healed — we love and respect one another tremendously and we have fun together." — Rosa L.

◆ "I no longer feel that relationships 'just happen.' I am an active participant in building my friendships, my relationship with my husband and children." — Carolyn J.

◆ "I had estranged myself from my family when drinking. When sober, I reestablished all ties, especially with my father, who passed away last year. He was my biggest supporter, never failing to mention his pride in my recovery and remembering my sobriety date as well as I do." — Ralph C.

Renewing Life in the Bedroom

Although some masters revealed that they have had trouble with sexual intimacy since becoming sober, far more went out of their way to make comments about how their sex lives have improved. Some indicated that they are more present or conscious during sex, while others said that they have become more creative sexually. In addition, quite a few masters indicated that they are no longer promiscuous.

◆ "Sex in sobriety is a much purer, more real thing." — Marisa S.

◆ "Reaching orgasm is easier!" — Lev W.

◆ "My sex life is great, but sober sex was initially a big adjustment." — Camille G.

◆ "Since I became sober, I am unafraid to initiate sexual times with my spouse and speak freely about what pleases me." — Doris O.

◆ "My sex life is much better. I also remember it in the morning!" — Perry C.

◆ "My present sexual experience at seventy is the best of my life." — Lester H.

Fixing Family Relationships

Marisa S. notes that one of the greatest difficulties for her in early sobriety was "working out problems with my husband. The problems were mainly around trust — lots and lots of broken trust, as a result of my continually relapsing. Every time I drank again, he shut down. For a considerable stretch of time, my husband lived with the fear that he might get a call from the police, which actually happened a few times, or that I might turn up dead at some point."

Since couples and families often lack the skills to manage such problems, it is not uncommon for marriages and families to break up within the first year or two of recovery. Even when relationships have been good, initiating sobriety can cause tension for a family or a couple. Marisa says, "Unfortunately, there was nothing I could do to fix our problems in early sobriety. We did have some couples counseling along the way, but basically it just took time."

Here are some ways in which the masters have improved their family relationships:

◆ Heide M.'s marriage broke up around the time she became sober, leaving her alone to raise four small children. She maintains that because of family counseling and communication classes, she and her children can now get through anything. "We are a very close family and are always there for each other."

◆ Thomas V., who is married to master Roxi V., says, "Roxi and I used to have two or three arguments a week and physical fights a couple of times a month when we were drinking. Since we've been sober, we've had no fights and very few arguments. My relationship with Roxi has grown as we have grown. We communicate better and share our sobriety efforts." (They go to both AA and SOS meetings together.)

◆ Richard D. went to personal improvement seminars that led him to try to correct past mistakes with his ex-wife and his daughter. He told me, "I wrote my ex-wife a letter thanking her for all she had done for me and our daughter. I apologized for all that I could not do for her and all of the hurts that I caused in our marriage. Also, I apologized to our daughter for my drinking, not being around more, and not being my best for her and myself." Today he feels that he has a very loving relationship with his daughter.

Finally, it's important to be prepared for the fact that relationships do not always get better in sobriety. Jessica C. explains, "The hardest part in the beginning was my relationship with my husband. He wanted me to be sober but not to change in other ways. However, to stay sober, I had to care about myself more — be more assertive and not put up with his criticisms of me and his attempts to sabotage my sobriety. I refused to take total blame and responsibility for the marriage, and after one year I insisted we go to marriage counseling. It turned out to be divorce counseling, because he wasn't interested in making any changes in himself."

For Carolyn J., it was important to end a destructive relationship with her father. "It wasn't worth the price I paid emotionally to be in it," she concludes. "Two events — quitting drinking and severing my relationship with my father — were twin liberating experiences. I could not have done one without the other." She did, however, heal her relationships with her husband and daughters in sobriety.

Treasuring Sobriety

When I asked Randall N. how he seeks pleasure now, he responded, "Usually I feel that sobriety itself is enough of a reward for me. In fact, it's more than a reward to me — it's a priceless treasure." Tammie A. adds, "When I drank, I always had a deep, dark secret, and I felt shameful. Now I get enormous pleasure out of being proud of who I am and how I live my life. I am so much happier sober that I am motivated to continue the growth." *As these masters attest, it's as if sobriety has become an end in itself — it's evident that they treasure being free from alcohol's grip.*

Phil Q. boasts, "Last week, when a doctor whom I hadn't seen in a long time asked me how long it had been since I'd had a drink, I sure loved answering his question with 'Oh, about fourteen years or so.' That was pretty nice." In Kerry G.'s words, "Sober life is a gift, and I'm basically a happy person today. I'd have to be nuts to throw that away for the hell and despair of booze. I'll be honest: I like being thirty-six and having fifteen years of sobriety. I take pride in it and wouldn't throw it away. I had no life when I was drinking; I'd sit on a barstool and talk about all the things I was going to do someday. Today I do them. I found myself when I put down the drinks."

Echoing Randall N., Marisa S. says, "I treasure my sobriety. I remember each day that I choose not to drink and why I choose this. I'm grateful for my sobriety because it gives me choices, gives me life, gives me the chance to be happy, to enjoy people, to have my husband, family, and friends. Without it, I don't have anything that matters. I truly believe that in sobriety, all things are possible. I can be who I want to be, live the way I want to live, and do anything and everything that is important to me."

With so much to stay sober for, who would ever want to go back?

Appendix: A Consumer Guide to Recovery Options

Selected References

Index

Appendix: A Consumer Guide to Recovery Options

Inclusion of any resources in this book does not necessarily constitute endorsement. Neither does exclusion necessarily signify lack of endorsement for any particular recovery option. The following list is by no means exhaustive.

Quitting Drinking on Your Own

People who want to try resolving alcohol problems on their own — without going into treatment, seeking counseling, or attending a recovery group — may be interested in the following books. The Web sites listed at the end of this appendix may also prove helpful for solo recovery, as can materials from recovery groups.

Changing for Good, by Drs. James O. Prochaska, John C. Norcross, and Carlo C. DiClemente (New York: William Morrow, 1994).

Coming Clean: Overcoming Addiction Without Treatment, by Drs. Robert Granfield and William Cloud (New York: New York University Press, 1999). Primarily for professionals, but has an appendix for lay people.

Managing Your Drug or Alcohol Problem: Client Workbook, by Drs. Dennis C. Daley and G. Alan Marlatt (San Antonio, Tex.: Psychological Corporation, 1997).

Problem Drinkers: Guided Self-Change Treatment, by Drs. Mark and Linda Sobell (New York: Guilford Press, 1996). Designed for professionals who work with people who want to quit drinking with minimal intervention, but can be used by sophisticated lay people.

Sex, Drugs, Gambling, & Chocolate: A Workbook for Overcoming Addictions, by Dr. A. Thomas Horvath (San Luis Obispo, Calif.: Impact, 1998).

Take Control, Now!, by Marc Kern, Ph.D. (Los Angeles: Addiction Alternatives, 1994). To order, write to Addiction Alternatives, Beverly Hills Medical Tower, 1125 South Beverly Drive, Suite 401, Los Angeles, CA 90035. (Also available at this Web site: http://www.AddictionAlternatives.com.)

The Truth About Addiction and Recovery: The Life Process Program for Outgrowing Destructive Habits, by Dr. Stanton Peele and Archie Brodsky (New York: Fireside Books, 1991).

When AA Doesn't Work for You: Rational Steps to Quitting Alcohol, by Drs. Albert Ellis and Emmett Velten (New York: Barricade Books, 1992).

Achieving Sobriety with Individual Counseling

What to look for in a mental health professional

If you decide to deal with an alcohol problem through individual counseling, it's important to start by asking questions about credentials. According to A. Thomas McClellan, Ph.D., director of the Treatment Research Institute at the University of Pennsylvania, "Virtually anybody can advertise as an addiction therapist. Private individual therapy for alcohol problems is unstudied and unregulated." Be aware too that some people who specialize in addiction counseling and treatment refer to themselves as "addictionologists" or "addictionists," but these labels do not reflect any recognized, standardized credentials.

Start by making sure that the person is a licensed psychologist, social worker, or psychiatrist in your state. Each state has its own laws regulating the practice of psychologists and social workers. In some states there are strict laws about who can call himself or herself a counselor or a therapist; in others there is little or no regulation. It is wise to seek out someone who has met certification criteria from a longstanding professional organization with licensing requirements that have been established and are monitored by a state board. (For information about chemical dependency counselors, see the section on treatment programs, beginning on page 286.)

Although this is not an exhaustive list, you should look for a counselor with a degree such as Ph.D., Psy.D., M.D., or M.S.W. — any one of which should have been granted by an accredited institution of higher education. The next question is whether the therapist in question has any special training or expertise with alcohol problems. (Some professional organizations offer specialty certification in addictions, as indicated below.) Before you go to see a private therapist, be sure to check your health insurance to determine coverage.

What about the popular notion that people who have never had a drinking problem lack the necessary "credentials" for counseling those troubled by alcohol? Studies consistently show that counselors who have themselves recovered are neither more nor less likely to help problem drinkers get better. In general, research has found that the most effective therapists for alcohol problems are those who have an empathetic style that demonstrates respect for the client. This is in contrast to the confrontational, rather aggressive approach, which is now used much less frequently than in the past, to "break down denial" by confronting the person about being an "alcoholic" and insisting on the need to quit drinking (as opposed to letting the person arrive at his or her own conclusions). Research on confrontational approaches has failed to yield a single study showing a positive outcome for problem drinkers.

Certainly the counselor you choose has to be someone you feel comfortable with — not necessarily all the time, because much of what you are dealing with is by nature uncomfortable stuff. But there needs to be a certain chemistry of trust and understanding between you. If you don't click with the first person you try, don't let this dissuade you from trying another counselor.

Resources for finding a mental health professional

Word of mouth is one of the best ways to find a good therapist. Although a drinking problem is certainly a personal issue that is not always easy to address or get others to talk about, you can get ideas from others who have been through counseling. (Again, check out the recommended therapist's credentials.)

Association for Advancement of Behavior Therapy (AABT) is a membership organization for mental health professionals (primarily psychologists) who specialize in cognitive and behavioral therapies. AABT offers a Clinical Directory and Referral Service, which is a list of members (from the United States, Canada, England, Brazil, and Switzerland) who subscribe to the directory and who have met certain criteria established by the organization. (Note, however, that not everyone with expertise in this area is a member of AABT, and not all AABT members subscribe to this directory.) You can find the list by going to AABT's Web site (http://www.aabt.org), which allows you to search for clinicians by their specialty area (including alcohol abuse) and location. Or you can call 212-647-1890 for a list of clinicians in your area. You can also ask for the list in writing: Association for Advancement of Behavior Therapy, 305 Seventh Avenue, 16th floor, New York, NY 10001.

The **American Psychological Association (APA)** offers a public education information line (800-964-2000) for referrals to state psychological associations, which will provide names and numbers of licensed psychologists who are their members. (Note, however, that not all licensed psychologists are members of APA or their state associations, so don't rule out all other psychologists.) You can ask for a referral to a psychologist who has expertise with alcohol problems and/or who specializes in cognitive-behavioral approaches or brief intervention for alcohol problems. But you may just be given names of clinics with licensed providers, in which case you will have to call each clinic yourself and ask if anyone with expertise in these areas is on the staff.

The APA also offers certification to psychologists who have experience with alcohol and drug treatment and who pass a qualifying exam. You can ask psychologists if they have this certification, officially called the Certificate of Proficiency in the Treatment of Alcohol and Other Psychoactive Substance Use Disorders (APA-CPP Substance Use Disorders). Since this is a rather recent program, not every psychologist who has expertise in this area will have this certification (and not every qualified psychologist will choose to take this exam). To find out if any psychologists in your area are certified by this program or if a particular psychologist is certified, you can contact APA's certification program by phone (202-336-5879) or by e-mail (apacollege@apa.org).

SMART Recovery has a Web site that lists state-by-state e-mail addresses and phone numbers for its advisers (http://www.smartrecovery.org — click on its national meeting list). These advisers have "(PA)" listed after their names, meaning that they are professional advisers to SMART Recovery. Most PAs are licensed behavioral health professionals; some of them have private practices, and you can try calling for an appointment. If you do not have access to the Internet, you can call SMART Recovery headquarters at 440-951-5357 for a referral to a PA if there is one in your area.

Board-certified addiction psychiatrists are physicians who are already certified in psychiatry who go on to get subspecialty certification in addiction psychiatry, which is granted by the American Board of Psychiatry and Neurology (a member of the American Board of Medical Specialties). A board-certified addiction psychiatrist has completed a prescribed training program and passed a subspecialty examination in addictions. To find out if a psychiatrist has this credential, visit the Web site of the American Board of Medical Specialties at http://www.certifieddoctor.org. To locate a psychiatrist with this certification, you can turn to the *Official ABMS Directory of Board Certified Medical Specialists,* which is available at some large public, university, and medical libraries. (All psychiatrists who are qualified to treat addictions do not have this certification.)

The **American Psychiatric Association** can help you locate one of its member psychiatrists through its toll-free number: 888-357-7924, then press 0. When you call that number, you will be provided with the phone number of a district branch, which in turn can give you names of members in your area who treat alcohol problems.

The **National Association of Social Workers (NASW)** is the largest organization of professional social workers. It offers professional credentials in the following areas: ACSW (Academy of Certified Social Workers, a generalist credential); QCSW (Qualified Clinical Social Worker, an entry-level clinical credential); DCSW (Diplomate in Clinical Social Work, an advanced clinical credential). The association also offers specialty certifications, one of which is an advanced clinical practice certification in addictions: Alcohol, Tobacco, and Other Drugs Certification (ATODC). The NASW Register of Clinical Social Workers contains the names of QCSW and DCSW clinical social workers across the country and can be sorted by zip code, specialty, language, client group, and practice. Practice specializations listed include addictions/substance abuse. The register is accessible through NASW's Web site (http://www.socialworkers.org) or is available in book form or on CD-ROM by calling 800-227-3590.

The **American Society of Addiction Medicine (ASAM)** is a national society of physicians and medical students who are dedicated to improving the treatment of alcohol problems and other addictions. More than three thousand of its members have participated in its certification program. To be certified in addiction medicine, a physician must have at least one year of involvement in the field and receive ongoing continuing education related to the treatment of alcohol and drug dependence. About 30 percent of ASAM-certified members are psychiatrists, but physicians in any medical specialty can be certified. ASAM does not have a referral service, but a listing of its members is available at its Web site: http://www.asam.org. To verify someone's certification, you can visit the certification pages on the Web site or call ASAM at 301-656-3920 (ASAM's e-mail address is Email@asam.org.).

Recovery Group Meetings:
The What, Where, and When

Alcoholics Anonymous (AA)

About AA meetings
Procedures. Meetings of AA fall into several general categories, including beginners', open, and closed meetings. Beginners' meetings are open to anyone who thinks he or she might have a drinking problem and are often held before larger AA meetings. In some places these meetings provide newcomers with information about "alcoholism," recovery, and AA; other beginners' meetings are question-and-answer sessions. As their name implies, open meetings are open to anyone, whether or not that person has a drinking problem. At most open meetings, a chairperson gives a description of AA. Then one or more AA members act as speakers, telling personal stories, sometimes called "drunkalogs," about their drinking past and possibly their interpretation of AA. Closed meetings are limited to people with a drinking problem and can follow a number of different formats. Some are "speaker meetings," followed by a discussion, while others are held primarily for member discussion. Discussion meetings may be step meetings, in which one of the twelve steps is singled out for discussion, with members sitting around a table, commenting or sharing one at a time. (Typically, members introduce themselves by first name, saying, "I'm an alcoholic." You don't have to say this, and you can pass on discussion if you want.) According to AA's 1998 membership survey, 85 percent of members belong to a home group

that they go to regularly, which allows members to maintain close contact with each other. Members in this survey attended an average of two AA meetings a week.

It may not be clear to an AA newcomer that participants often adhere to a "no-cross-talk" custom at meetings. That is, they do not comment on or interrupt another person's monologue with questions or advice. Typically, meetings include time for announcements relevant to AA members as well as for presentation of medallions to commemorate participants' anniversaries (months or years), marking the date when they quit drinking. (If someone has a slip or a relapse and then quits drinking again, typically he or she starts with a new anniversary date and the count of sobriety time begins anew.)

AA meetings often open with a group prayer or recitation and might close with all members standing and holding hands while reciting the Lord's Prayer. AA does not charge any fees to members. Local groups cover expenses for rental of meeting places, refreshments, and literature by passing the hat at meetings.

Meeting frequency, location, and leadership. AA meetings are typically held in public locations such as churches, universities, hospitals, and correctional facilities. Members of any particular AA group decide how often to get together — usually once or twice a week for an hour to an hour and a half — and how they will run meetings. Typically, members elect a chairperson, secretary, and other officers. Members who lead groups do not need to have any credentials or training.

Privacy. Anonymity is encouraged by using first names only during meetings, keeping others' attendance at meetings confidential, and not discussing your AA membership with the media, though some people choose to disclose their membership publicly. In addition, some groups close their meetings with a reminder that what has been discussed, as well as who was present, should not be mentioned outside of the meeting.

Finding an AA group
One of the advantages of AA is that you can find a meeting just about anytime, anyplace, anywhere. According to AA World Services, Inc., there are about 51,000 AA groups, with almost 1.2 mil-

lion members, in the United States alone. Canada has more than 5,000 AA groups, and close to 40,000 groups exist outside of the United States and Canada. Worldwide, nearly 2 million people in more than 98,000 groups are members of AA. The number of AA groups in correctional facilities in the United States and Canada is almost 2,500. In these two countries, look for Alcoholics Anonymous in the white or yellow pages of any telephone directory. Some communities also have regional AA "intergroups," or clubs that hold AA meetings and can provide referral information. You can also consult daily event listings of local newspapers, which commonly list when and where AA meetings take place. Or contact AA headquarters (see below).

Sometimes groups with special interests form their own AA meetings — for instance, for women, lesbians, gays, or young people only. There are also AA groups for "impaired" professionals, such as physicians, nurses, attorneys, and members of the clergy. Some areas have meetings geared toward atheists and agnostics. Local AA offices may have information about how to locate some of these special groups.

Internet access

There are a number of twelve-step Internet meetings and chat rooms. Master Camille G., who goes to a women's AA meeting on the Internet, explains: "Every month someone picks a topic, which is e-mailed to the group. People respond and also discuss problems. Anniversaries are also celebrated." In this way, the Internet can be a great resource for people who can't get out — say, for young parents at home with children, older folks, or disabled people.

AA publications

AA offers many publications, which can be obtained through its national headquarters and often at local meetings. Two books typically provided to AA newcomers are *Twelve Steps and Twelve Traditions* and *Alcoholics Anonymous*, more commonly referred to as the "Big Book." (Some groups donate the books; others may charge.) *Twelve Steps and Twelve Traditions* provides a comprehensive description of the twelve steps and twelve traditions of AA. *Alcoholics Anonymous* presents personal stories of members from all walks of life. A new edition of this so-called Big Book was recently released. AA also publishes a monthly magazine, *AA Grape-vine*.

For more information about Alcoholics Anonymous

AA World Services, Inc.
P.O. Box 459
Grand Central Station
New York, NY 10163

Phone: 212-870-3400
Web address: http://www.alcoholics-anonymous.org

Twelve-step resources with a religious orientation
People interested in a Christian emphasis in a twelve-step program may want to contact or visit any of the following:

- Alcoholics for Christ: 800-441-7877; http://www.alcoholicsforchrist.com
- Alcoholics Victorious: 800-624-5156; http://www.av.iugm.org
- Calix Society (for Catholics): 800-398-0524; no Web site available
- Institute for Christian Living/Renewed Life Services: 763-593-1791; no Web site available
- Overcomers Outreach: 800-310-3001; http://www.overcomersoutreach.org

To explore alcohol and drug addiction resources for Jewish people, you can contact a group known as JACS (Jewish Alcoholics, Chemically Dependent Persons and Significant Others). Call 212-397-4197, or visit the Web site: http://www.jacsweb.org.

Women for Sobriety (WFS)

About WFS meetings
Procedures. Rather than introducing themselves as "alcoholics," participants open WFS meetings by saying something like "I'm Sue, and I'm a competent woman." After introductions and a brief program overview, the discussion usually focuses on a particular topic regarding problem drinking or something culled from WFS literature. WFS recommends that groups consist of no more than six to ten women, to enable all women to participate in discussions, which

are like conversations in the round. (Members can pass if they want.) Cross-talk (back-and-forth dialogue among members) is encouraged. At the end of the meeting, members join hands and recite the WFS motto. Some count time in sobriety, but the practice varies from group to group and woman to woman. There is far less focus on the past at WFS than at AA — the focus is on moving on. However, members are encouraged to maintain contact with their group so they have a place to return to if sobriety becomes difficult. Newcomers to WFS are often invited to arrive at meetings early (or to stick around afterward) so the moderator can talk to them privately about what to expect in the group. There are no fees for attending WFS. At meetings, donations are often collected by passing the hat.

Meeting frequency, location, and leadership. WFS meetings are typically held in such places as hospitals, churches, and women's health centers and are usually held once a week for no longer than an hour and a half. They are led by moderators — members with at least one year of sobriety under their belt, who know the WFS program, philosophy, and literature (and use them in their sobriety), and who have read Jean Kirkpatrick's book, *Turnabout*. (Women who state that they meet these criteria fill out a several-page application form; there is no formal training.)

Privacy. At meetings, WFS members typically use first names only. WFS asks members to keep confidential the identities of those who attend meetings as well as all that takes place there.

Finding a WFS group

Worldwide, more than one hundred WFS groups exist, most of them — surprisingly — in rural areas of the United States. (WFS also has fifteen groups in Canada as well as groups in Australia, New Zealand, England, and Northern Ireland.) WFS does not list group locations or phone numbers on its Web site, so the best way to find out if there is a group near you is to e-mail or call headquarters. Sometimes WFS meetings are listed in phone books. WFS also has a pen pal program, either by regular mail or by e-mail, whereby moderators and members can reach out to one another, particularly to new members. WFS headquarters knows of a small number of treatment facilities offering WFS groups, and some others give out WFS literature and referrals to their clients. (Since the 1980s the organization has been offering literature for Men for Sobriety [MFS] groups, based on the

WFS program, but currently there are only two MFS groups in existence, both in Canada.) For more information about any of these options, contact WFS headquarters or visit the Web site. If you or someone you know would like to start a new group, contact headquarters for information about the application process.

Internet access
On the Internet, WFS has its own chat-room meetings and a message board.

WFS publications
WFS offers a wide variety of literature, including books, booklets, workbooks, and audiocassette tapes. All members are advised to obtain a copy of "The Program Booklet," a purse-size publication by Jean Kirkpatrick that details the thirteen "Statements of the 'New Life' Program," for which there is a $3.00 charge. WFS also recommends that members eventually read *Turnabout: New Help for the Woman Alcoholic,* the story of Dr. Kirkpatrick's journey from problem drinker to founder of WFS. In addition, WFS encourages members to subscribe to its monthly newsletter, *Sobering Thoughts.*

For more information about WFS
Women for Sobriety, Inc.
P.O. Box 618
Quakertown, PA 18951-0618
Phone: 215-536-8026
e-mail address: NewLife@nni.com
Web address: http://www.womenforsobriety.org

SMART Recovery

About SMART Recovery meetings
Procedures. Those who attend SMART Recovery meetings usually start by going around the room with self-introductions of their own choosing (attendees do not call themselves "alcoholics") and giving individuals the opportunity to share how the past week went. Four to twelve people per meeting is typical. Since SMART Recovery is a relatively new program, it is still experimenting with different formats. Generally, meetings open with the coordinator or another member making a brief statement describing the SMART Recovery program, stressing confidentiality, and reviewing the mee

agenda. Next the leader asks if a member will share something he or she has done or learned from SMART Recovery during the past week. This is followed by setting an agenda for the meeting; during this time, the coordinator asks each person if he or she has had a particularly bad week and needs extra time. (Attendees can pass if they want.) Next comes the heart of the meeting, during which members share and discuss a strategy from the SMART Recovery "4-Point Program" (see page 125). During this portion of the meeting, "drunkalogs" are discouraged; sharing and open discussion (or cross-talk) is encouraged. In closing, the group typically considers a homework project, such as identifying a particular way to cope with urges to drink during the upcoming week. At the end, ten minutes are devoted to socializing.

SMART Recovery encourages members to attend the group for as long as they keep deriving benefit from it, which for most people is months or years rather than a lifetime. At these meetings, you're much less likely than at AA to hear people count time in sobriety. When a relapse does occur, members are reminded that recovery is still possible and that perseverance is what really counts. Newcomers are invited, but not required, to participate in meetings. Some groups host meetings just for newcomers or invite new members to meet with the coordinator before the meeting. At the end, the hat is passed — a donation is suggested but not required.

Meeting frequency, length, and leadership. SMART Recovery meetings are usually held once a week in such places as hospitals, churches, libraries, offices of treatment professionals, and an increasing number of correctional facilities. Most SMART Recovery groups meet weekly, with sessions lasting about ninety minutes. Meetings are led by "coordinators," volunteers who have achieved sobriety through any means and who believe in the SMART Recovery principles; they can also be people who never had a drinking problem. (Most coordinators are lay people, but a good number of them are mental health professionals.) Coordinators are assigned to a "professional adviser" (PA) — a volunteer who is typically a licensed mental health professional with training in addictive behavior. The PA is available to advise the coordinator on any issues that arise in the groups. There is no mandatory formal training of coordinators, but SMART Recovery offers yearly training sessions that coordinators are encouraged to attend.

Privacy. Most SMART Recovery members do not use their last names in groups. One of the ground rules is that all participants agree to confidentiality for all that is said and done at meetings. It is not permissible to tell anyone outside the group who attended or what was said in any way that would identify an individual. Violation of confidentiality is grounds for removal from the program.

Finding a SMART Recovery group

Currently more than 325 SMART Recovery groups are found in the United States (SMART Recovery also has a small number of groups in Canada, Australia, Scotland, and Sweden). To locate a meeting near you, contact SMART Recovery's central office or visit its Web site. In some larger metropolitan areas, SMART Recovery meetings may be listed in the phone book. For people who do not have access to a local group, headquarters will send information on how to start one, including advice on finding a location, arranging publicity, and recruiting a PA. A small number of treatment programs are affiliated with SMART Recovery, which means that the program uses a cognitive-behavioral approach and is "in keeping" with SMART Recovery program principles. (Call headquarters or go to the SMART Recovery Web site for a listing.)

SMART Recovery publications

SMART Recovery has put together a recommended reading list with eight core books. These include the *SMART Recovery Member's Manual* as well as *The Small Book*, the original Rational Recovery guidebook written by Jack Trimpey. SMART Recovery also recommends six other books deemed useful for members, as well as a quarterly newsletter called *News and Views*. All SMART Recovery publications, plus some of the recommended and core books, can be ordered through the organization's central office.

Internet access

SMART Recovery now has quite a few daily on-line meetings. It also hosts a chat room; information about it is available on the Web site. The group runs a list service called SMARTREC for those who want to share daily e-mail consisting of ideas, conversations with others on the list, and encouragement. To subscribe, send the following message to listserv@maelstrom.stjohns.edu:

subscribe SMARTREC yourfirstname yourlastname

For more information about SMART Recovery
SMART Recovery Central Office
7537 Mentor Avenue
Suite #306
Mentor, OH 44060
Phone: 440-951-5357
e-mail address: SRMail1@aol.com
Web address: http://www.smartrecovery.org

Secular Organizations for Sobriety (SOS)

About SOS meetings

Procedures. SOS tells groups to run their meetings any way they want to, as long as the group is structured around SOS foundations: secularity, sobriety, and self-help. Attendance at meetings generally is about a dozen people. SOS meetings usually open with a statement about the foundations of SOS and a reminder that what goes on in the meeting is confidential. Next, many meetings allow time for newcomers to introduce themselves and for people to announce special events, such as births or new jobs. Although the group's "Suggested Guidelines for Sobriety" advise members to acknowledge that they are "alcoholics" or addicts, they do not have to introduce themselves in any particular way at meetings. The heart of the meeting is usually a discussion about a particular subject, which may be introduced by a chairperson whose job it is to come up with a topic and possibly lead the meeting. (The chair position is supposed to rotate from week to week.) Other meetings are looser, allowing for more open-ended discussion. The amount of cross-talk allowed varies with the group. Many meetings devote about three quarters of the time to sharing and the rest to cross-talk. SOS also encourages members to share "soberlogues," during which they focus on their sobriety rather than dwell on the past.

Some members may choose to count time in sobriety and have their anniversary dates of sobriety recognized at an SOS meeting. If someone relapses, however, SOS does not hold to the idea of counting sobriety time all over again. As the group's founder, James Christopher, says, "At SOS, we stick to the facts. If someone has five years sober, then relapses and stops drinking again, that's how it is: five years sober with a relapse. All the time away from alcohol is 'good time.'"

Most meetings end without ceremony, though in some groups members wish each other a sober week or applaud each other for another week of sobriety. Some groups go out for refreshments after the meeting, a practice designed to foster a sense of community among members.

Members are encouraged to go to meetings as long as they feel comfortable doing so. Accordingly, some choose not to attend meetings forever, and their sobriety is viewed as equally valid as anyone else's. SOS groups do not charge members a fee to join, though most pass a basket for voluntary contributions. Each meeting is financially self-supporting, and the group treasurer usually sends some of the meeting revenue to the International SOS Clearinghouse to support its activities.

Meeting frequency, location, and leadership. You can find SOS meetings most often in community buildings such as libraries and park and recreation buildings, as well as in Unitarian fellowship halls. According to Christopher, SOS is also offered in some prisons, particularly in the state of Texas. Typically, meetings are held weekly and last for an hour to an hour and a half. Friends and family of SOS members are welcome to attend meetings. Most SOS groups have at least two leadership roles, which rotate among members: secretaries (sometimes called convenors), who do everything from setting up the meeting room to keeping the discussion focused, and treasurers, who carry out financial duties such as paying room rental fees. Most members who serve as leaders have been sober in SOS for at least six months and are elected by group consensus, though these guidelines are not set in stone. No formal training is available for leaders.

Privacy. At SOS, it is assumed that participants prefer anonymity unless they state otherwise. Although some groups use name-and-number sign-up sheets to track meeting attendance and use as telephone resource lists, most people use only their first names and last initial, as is the case in discussions.

Finding an SOS group

There is no official count of SOS groups. In addition to its groups in the United States, SOS has a small number of groups in Canada, England, Belgium, France, and Venezuela (new groups are anticipated in Ireland and Spain at this writing). To locate one nearby, contact headquarters. Sometimes, however, SOS groups are listed in phone books. People interested in starting an SOS group locally should contact headquarters. In some locations, SOS has special groups, such as those for women or gay people.

Internet access
SOS chat rooms and bulletin boards can be accessed via its Web sites.

SOS publications
SOS's founder, James Christopher, has written three books detailing the philosophies and workings of SOS, all of which are available through the SOS International Clearinghouse: *How to Stay Sober: Recovery Without Religion; SOS Sobriety: The Proven Alternative to 12-Step Programs;* and *Unhooked: Staying Sober and Drug-Free.* SOS also puts out a group leaders' guide booklet. In addition, Christopher edits the *SOS International Newsletter,* a quarterly publication. Contact the SOS Clearinghouse to subscribe. SOS provides other literature, including booklets, brochures, videotapes, and audiocassettes.

For more information about SOS
Secular Organizations for Sobriety (SOS)
4773 Hollywood Boulevard
Hollywood, CA 90027
Phone: 323-666-4295
e-mail address: SOS@CFIWest.org
Web address: http://www.cfiwest.org/sos
SOS also has a European Web site: www.sossobriety.org

LifeRing Secular Recovery

For more information about LSR, the name that some former SOS groups have adopted, as well as locations of LSR groups nationally and internationally
LifeRing Secular Recovery Service Center
1440 Broadway, Suite 1000
Oakland, CA 94612-2029
Phone: 510-763-0779
e-mail address: service@lifering.org
Web address: http://www.unhooked.com

Groups, Programs, and Resources
for Moderate Drinking

Moderation Management

Moderation Management (MM) is a national nonprofit self-help group started by Audrey Kishline, a woman with alcohol problems who had been through traditional treatment and discovered on her own that she was able to drink moderately with no problems. She came up with MM in 1993, after doing a great deal of research on scientific methods for controlling drinking and preventing relapse and on cognitive-behavioral approaches to drinking problems. Concerned about the many people who are misdiagnosed as "alcoholic" or who would never enter the abstinence-based traditional treatment system, Ms. Kishline wondered, "How many people would be motivated to do something about their drinking problem sooner if a support program were available that did not insist on total abstinence, a religious/spiritual program, or labeling them as 'alcoholic'?" So she designed such a support program, which in October 2000 had ten "face-to-face" groups in eight states. (Group locations can be found via MM's Web site or by calling its main phone number.)

In the spring of 2000, Kishline left the helm of MM (see pages 182–83), but MM is still an active organization with a board of directors consisting of three respected psychologists and four lay members providing oversight.

MM is meant for those who want to quit or cut down on their drinking before they experience serious consequences. It is not designed for alcohol-dependent people, for those who experience withdrawal symptoms when they quit drinking, for formerly dependent people who are now abstaining, or for people with drug or food problems. The group's guidelines suggest starting with a month of abstinence, followed by moderate drinking under specific conditions and with the support of a group as needed. (Typically, groups meet once a week and are led by someone who has been in MM for a while.)

The MM program offers a nine-step approach to help people live healthier, more balanced lives. According to MM board member Marc Kern, Ph.D., recent research suggests that about 30 percent of MM members elect and stabilize with moderate drinking, about 30

assumed to have relapsed, and about 30
stinence-based program. He adds, "However,
choose abstinence yet stay with MM because of
and nonjudgmental atmosphere."
are anonymous and free-of-charge. People who don't
MM group nearby can access the program through its
which lists on-line groups and has a chat room. For more
ation, contact

Moderation Management Network, Inc.
P.O. Box 3055
Point Pleasant, NJ 08742
Phone: 732-295-0949
e-mail address: moderation@moderation.org
Web address: http://www.moderation.org

DrinkWise

Like Moderation Management, DrinkWise is a program designed
for people with mild to moderate alcohol problems who want to
quit or cut down on their drinking. Developed in Canada by a psychologist named Martha Sanchez-Craig, Ph.D., DrinkWise is based
on more than twenty years of successful research at the former
Addiction Research Foundation in Toronto, Ontario. Most of
DrinkWise's clients choose moderate drinking, but some elect abstinence.

Unlike the self-help format of MM, DrinkWise is run with the help
of master's-degree-level counselors who have specialized training for
this program and involves the use of a handbook with weekly assignments. (You can also purchase a book by the founder of DrinkWise
to use by yourself; see below.) DrinkWise incorporates behavioral
self-control strategies and is offered in a number of different formats:
a group program, an individual program, a telephone-guided program, and a videophone program. Costs range from $395 to $700,
depending on the format, and there is an initial consultation fee,
which is included as part of the total cost if you decide to do the
whole program. (Unfortunately, according to DrinkWise, health insurance may not cover these costs.) There are also two follow-up sessions for which there is no additional charge.

The DrinkWise program in North Carolina is based at the address below. There is also a DrinkWise program at the University of Michigan, which can be reached at 800-222-5145. For more information, contact North Carolina DrinkWise:

DrinkWise
c/o Theresa Edmondson, Director
The Brody School of Medicine at East Carolina University
600 Moye Boulevard
Greenville, NC 27858
Phone: 888-316-2736
e-mail: DrinkWiseemail@ecu.edu
Web address: www.drinkwise.com

Books on moderate drinking

DrinkWise: How to Quit Drinking or Cut Down, by Martha Sanchez-Craig, published by the Addiction Research Foundation in 1995. Can be obtained from the Centre for Addiction and Mental Health, Marketing and Sales Services, 33 Russell Street, Toronto, Canada M5S 2S1, or by calling 800-661-1111.

How to Control Your Drinking, by W. R. Miller and R. F. Munoz (New York: Prentice-Hall, 1976); now available in a revised edition from Dr. Miller by sending an e-mail request to dyao@unm.edu or calling 505-768-0279.

Moderate Drinking: The Moderation Management Guide for People Who Want to Reduce Their Drinking, by Audrey Kishline (New York: Crown, 1994).

Internet resources on moderate drinking

The respected psychologist and alcohol researcher Reid Hester, Ph.D., has a Web site (http://www.behaviortherapy.com) at which he provides a list of North American psychologists who provide training in moderate drinking. In addition, Dr. Hester offers software for moderate drinking that has been shown to give positive results in a research study. The title is "Behavioral Self-Control for Windows," and it can be ordered at http://www.behaviortherapy.com/software.htm or by calling 505-345-6100.

Formal Alcohol Treatment Programs

Shopping for a treatment program

If you are anxious to get into treatment immediately and/or desperate to do something about your drinking, you might find it difficult to shop around. But it's worth it to ask questions and compare programs. (You might get a supportive friend or relative to help you.) A first consideration might be deciding whether you want to go far away or stay close to home. A disadvantage of choosing a local program is possible loss of anonymity. (Some might argue, however, that this could firm your commitment to stay sober.) An advantage of staying near home is easy access to follow-up care, which is particularly important if you don't plan to attend a recovery group or have none in your area to your liking. Although some people do not need much follow-up, others need a lot of help getting their lives back together when they're newly sober. In fact, in a study in which people who had been in residential treatment were assigned randomly to groups with no, voluntary, or mandatory outpatient aftercare (twelve weeks), those who completed the aftercare program had substantially lower relapse rates than those who did not. Thus, if you go to inpatient treatment far from home, it would be wise to ask the staff to help you find good aftercare — say, from a recovery group or therapist in your area — before you leave formal treatment.

Perhaps the easiest way to find out about alcohol treatment programs in a particular location is to turn to the U.S. government's Substance Abuse and Mental Health Services Administration (SAMHSA). You can locate treatment centers in your area by calling the organization or by accessing the Substance Abuse Treatment Facility Locator (see SAMHSA, on pages 293–94). You can also call your state or county alcohol and drug abuse agencies for information about publicly and privately funded treatment programs in your area. Many treatment programs have Web sites, so you can visit some of them on the Internet. You can also do some shopping with the phone book, calling around to local professionals and agencies that offer alcohol programs. (Look in the yellow pages under "Alcohol.")

You might also get some insights about treatment programs by checking with local hospitals, recovery groups, clergy, and people you know who have recovered. As with private counseling, be sure to check your medical insurance to see what your coverage is for alcohol treatment. You may find that your insurance company has an arrangement with a specific treatment program, which limits your choices.

Once you narrow down your range of options, contact the programs to see if they are compatible with your needs. If you prefer a non–twelve-step treatment program, you will have fewer choices. (If this is your preference, be careful to ask detailed questions and make your desires known; a psychologist I interviewed recently told me about a client who was informed by a treatment center that the program was not twelve-step–based, but when she got there, she discovered that it was.)

Here are some questions you might want to ask to see whether a particular program, be it inpatient or outpatient, accommodates your needs, desires, and philosophies:

- Orientation and philosophy: Is the program twelve-step–based? If so, what if someone does not want a twelve-step orientation? Does it offer any other options? Does it have a particular religious orientation? Does it offer cognitive-behavioral approaches? Does it use confrontational approaches? Do the counselors work from the disease model or from a behavioral standpoint?
- How will your alcohol problem be evaluated when you first go in, and what will immediate treatment entail? For instance, will you have to go into a detox unit? How does the information gathered translate into treatment options for you?
- How much can you be involved in planning your own program for resolving your drinking problem?
- What kinds of counseling does the program offer — individual, group, family, marital? How much time is spent in each of these areas? (It's wise to get a feel for how much the program is individualized.)
- What are the credentials of the counselors? Would much of your time be spent with licensed mental health professionals? Is a large percentage of the staff recovered people?
- Who are the other people who might be in treatment with you? If

you have preferences, find out if the program can accommodate any desires to be with more blue-collar or professional people, to be with your own sex, to be with others who have solely alcohol problems (not other addictions).

◆ What is a typical day like? Ask if you can see a schedule. How does the program vary from one week to the next?

◆ What is the continuing care program after you leave treatment? How often could/should you go to it? Whom will you meet with? Is there a group program and/or an individual program? Can you see a counselor on an ongoing basis? For how long?

◆ Does the program have a relapse prevention component? What if you have a slip or relapse? Is there a program for someone who needs a shot in the arm after a relapse, or do you have to start all over again?

◆ What is the program's success rate? And how does it define success? How many of the participants are return clients?

◆ Can you talk with some people who have been through the program?

◆ Are medications such as naltrexone or disulfiram (see pages 92–94) prescribed, and are psychiatric medications used if needed? (Some centers may ban psychiatric drugs, which is not in everyone's best interest. However, you don't want to go to a place where everyone is put on the same medications.)

Before going to a residential facility, you should check into how much freedom you have to come and go and see how easy it is to check yourself out if you decide it's not for you. You may also want to investigate whether and how treatment will become part of your permanent medical record.

What's a CD counselor?

A number of masters told me they had worked with chemical dependency (CD) counselors in the process of recovery. Typically, you would encounter a CD counselor in an inpatient or outpatient treatment program. According to A. Thomas McClellan, Ph.D., director of the Treatment Research Institute at the University of Pennsylvania, "CD counselors are simply therapists with a specialty in addiction. Typically they have a B.A., an M.A., or an M.S.W. and some experience with addiction — personal and/or professional."

Since there is no recognized definition of a CD counselor and licensing guidelines vary from state to state, it would be wise to look into the training of anyone you're considering seeing. A 1998 report from the U.S. government's Center for Substance Abuse Treatment (CSAT) suggests that historically, CD counselors have been trained in programs that were often developed by treatment agencies rather than at academic institutions. As such, their training varies greatly. Some of them are people who have been through the program themselves but received limited academic training. (Until just a short time ago, in my state just about anyone could call himself or herself a CD counselor; now guidelines are in place, but there are a number of exemptions. For instance, CD counselors at hospitals — as well as at federal, state, and local government treatment facilities — do not have to meet the guidelines.)

In 1998, CSAT published a comprehensive document that details for the first time who is qualified to treat people with addictions. The document identifies competencies that training programs should include and that future addiction counselors should be able to prove they have. For instance, a CD counselor is supposed to be familiar with multiple approaches to resolving substance-use problems. A number of states (including Virginia, California, Wisconsin, Oregon, New York, Texas, and Delaware) have modified their certification standards to use these competencies, and some colleges and universities are using the document to develop and revise their curricula for training CD counselors.

To be a savvy consumer, ask counselors under consideration about their educational background. Do they have any college courses in alcohol treatment? What kind of on-the-job training do they have? In this training, have they had formal supervision by an expert? Are they certified by your state, and what does that mean? Are they certified by any professional organizations, such as the International Certification & Reciprocity Consortium/Alcohol & Other Drug Abuse, Inc. or the National Association of Alcohol and Drug Abuse Counselors (NAADAC)? If so, what level of certification do they have? It seems safe to say that it's not uncommon for CD counselors to favor traditional twelve-step approaches to recovery, which is fine if that is what you're after. In his experience, Charles Bufe, the coauthor of *Resisting 12-Step Coercion,* says, "Having credentials as a chemical dependency counselor is an almost sure indication that a person has a twelve-step bias. I would ask a CD counselor if he or she is familiar with alternatives to AA and also ask them how effective AA is. A good and honest answer would be something to the effect of 'AA works for some people.'"

Internet Resources

A search of the World Wide Web for recovery options is mind-boggling but is truly one of the best ways to get a handle on the many different ways to get sober, whether you want to do it on your own or with help. The following Web sites are a sample of those with useful information.*

http://www.cts.com/crash/habtsmrt
HabitSmart is a Web site created and maintained by the licensed psychologist Robert Westermeyer, Ph.D. His site provides a great deal of useful content about addiction and recovery, including information about cognitive approaches, harm reduction, and moderate drinking. The Web site provides links to many other useful sites.

www2.potsdam.edu/alcohol-info
Easy to use, colorful, and entertaining, this fascinating Web site, called "Alcohol: Problems and Solutions," was developed by David J. Hanson, Ph.D., a professor of sociology at the State University of New York at Potsdam. The site provides general information about alcohol consumption and abuse, covers alcohol in the news, addresses alcohol and youth (often challenging conventional views), posts interviews with other experts, and has an extensive listing of other sites on alcohol, drinking, and recovery.

---

* I cannot vouch for the validity of information on Web sites mentioned in *Sober for Good* or on other Web sites to which they are linked. Because Web sites commonly go out of business or move without leaving a forwarding address, some of the Web addresses in this book may no longer be accessible. Be aware that on the Internet, your anonymity may not be fully protected. Also, be selective about information you receive in on-line groups, since in many cases there is no way of knowing whether the information given by people involved will be helpful or hurtful to you.

http://www.niaaa.nih.gov
This is the Web site of the U.S. government's National Institute on Alcohol Abuse and Alcoholism, a division of the National Institutes of Health. It has information about the organization, its publications, databases, press releases, research programs, and more. (The ETOH database, updated monthly, is the most comprehensive online bibliographic database, containing more than 100,000 records on alcohol abuse and alcoholism.)

http://www.drugnet.net
In his book *Recovery Options,* Joseph Volpicelli, M.D., Ph.D., refers to the link page of this Web site from the Drug and Alcohol Treatment and Prevention Global Network as "the mother of all addiction-links pages . . . a good one to bookmark for clicking onto other pages." (He notes that among the many links to organizations, some disreputable ones are listed.) There are links for college students, educators, family and friends, gay people, health professionals, and more.

http://www.peele.net
This is the Web site of the psychologist, attorney, and author Stanton Peele, Ph.D., who has devoted his career to addictions and unconventional resolution methods. At his comprehensive site, he expresses his opinion about controversial issues related to alcohol, answers personal questions, provides a library of his many publications and a bookstore of recommended books, addresses legal and forensic issues, and has extensive links to other resources on the Internet.

http://www.addictionsearch.com
The Addiction Search Web site was developed recently by Emil Chiauzzi, Ph.D., a clinical psychologist with experience in addictions. Dr. Chiauzzi set up his site as "a gateway to research-based addictions information — covering basic drug and alcohol information, prevention, harm reduction, social issues, treatment outcomes, statistical findings, and links to organizations." A major goal of this site is to offer links to the latest information from well-respected, reliable sources. The focus is on research, particularly the kind that

gives an overview of a key area, which allows you to review information efficiently.

http://www.darnweb.com

This Web site from the Drug & Alcohol Recovery Network (DARN) has a search engine for locating treatment centers with more than 12,000 facilities in its database. DARN also describes itself as a nationwide Internet directory of drug and alcohol treatment facilities, institutions, and health professionals.

http://www.well.com/user/woa

This Web site, named Web of Addictions, describes itself as "dedicated to providing accurate information about alcohol and other drug addictions." It provides links to other Internet resources related to addictions, contact information for a variety of groups, fact sheets about addictions (arranged by drug), and information about meetings and conferences on addictions.

http://www.med.upenn.edu/recovery

This is the Web site of the Internet Alcohol Recovery Center of the Treatment Research Center at the University of Pennsylvania. With information for both consumers and professionals, this site provides useful information about alcohol recovery, has a chat room, links you to other interesting sites, and has extensive information about the drug naltrexone. The center's addiction treatment program (in Philadelphia) is also described.

http://mentalhelp.net/selfhelp

This is the Web site for the American Self-Help Sourcebook On-line from the American Self-Help Clearinghouse. Its searchable database includes hundreds of support groups. All the user has to do is to enter keywords for a particular type of problem, such as alcohol abuse or depression. Under alcohol abuse, among its extensive listings are descriptions of and links to various twelve-step groups, including specialty groups (for pharmacists, dentists, etc.); support networks for academics, psychologists, and realtors who have or had alcohol problems; nontraditional recovery groups; and various religious alcohol recovery groups. This listing has groups not listed elsewhere. The site also provides ideas for starting groups.

http://www.cmhc.com
CMHC Systems describes itself as the industry leader in providing management information systems for mental health and substance abuse (among other topics) in the United States. At its Web site, under "Services," there is a link to its Mental Health Net, which is a guide listing many on-line mental health, psychology, and psychiatry resources, including some related to alcohol recovery.

http://www.crosswinds.net/~empower16/steps.htm
This is the site for "The 16 Steps of Personal Empowerment," which describes itself as "a positive, flexible, and holistic self-support alternative." Although the author is no longer personally involved with this Web site, the "16 steps" are taken from Dr. Charlotte Kasl's book *Many Roads, One Journey: Moving Beyond the Twelve Steps*. Quoting from this book, the site says that the steps encourage people to "celebrate our personal strengths, have choices, stand up for ourselves, heal our physical bodies, express our love for each other, and see ourselves as part of the entire community, not just the recovery community." The site includes the "16 steps of empowerment," ways to locate a 16-step group near you (although the developer of the site feels there are not many active groups), a link for participating in an "e-mail circle" (an on-line support group based on the 16 steps), and information about how to start a 16-step group and how to order Dr. Kasl's materials. This Web site also has extensive links to other recovery and support resources on the Internet.

http://www.christians-in-recovery.com
This is the site for Christians in Recovery, Inc., which provides information and resources for people with various addictions. This Web site has a directory of Christian treatment centers, support groups, and counselors, as well as links to other Christian Web sites.

Other Resources

Substance Abuse and Mental Health Services Administration (SAMHSA)
Room 12-105, Parklawn Building
5600 Fishers Lane
Rockville, MN 20857

SAMHSA is the federal agency charged with improving the quality and availability of services in order to reduce problems related to substance abuse and mental illnesses. It has a number of centers, including the Center for Substance Abuse Treatment and the Center for Substance Abuse Prevention. SAMHSA's services include its Substance Abuse Treatment Facility Locator and a mental health directory. (Its referral help line numbers are listed below.) SAMHSA's National Clearinghouse for Alcohol and Drug Information (NCADI) describes itself as the nation's "one-stop resource for the most current and comprehensive information about substance abuse prevention." The best way to explore SAMHSA's vast array of programs and resources is to visit its Web site. To access its directories of service providers and referral help lines, go to http://www.samhsa.gov/look3.htm.

SAMHSA's Web address: http://www.samhsa.gov
NCADI's Web address: http://www.health.org
Referral help line for locating substance abuse treatment in
your area: 800-662-HELP
Referral help line for referrals and publications concerning
mental health: 800-789-CMHS

Recovery Options Corporation
32234 Paseo Adelando, Suite C
San Juan Capistrano, CA 92688
Phone: 1-800-662-2873

This organization, founded by two men who saw the need for such a service, offers a national toll-free referral service for people seeking recovery services for any type of addiction. According to its description of its services, you can call and have a confidential conversation with one of the organization's crisis response counselors, who will then spend the time needed to help you — or family members of someone with a substance abuse problem — find a recovery approach that's personally right. Regardless of your financial situation, Recovery Options will help you find a therapist, a twelve-step group, a non–twelve-step group, or a treatment program. According to Recovery Options' director, Kirby Dean, "We help people find whatever they are searching for."

National Council on Alcoholism and Drug Dependence, Inc.
  (NCADD)
12 West 21st Street
New York, NY 10010
Phone: 212-206-6770
24-hour referral number: 1-800-NCA-CALL
Web address: http://www.ncadd.org

Founded by the first woman to stay sober in AA, NCADD provides education about alcoholism and drug addictions. It is a voluntary organization with a nationwide network of affiliates who provide information and referral for people seeking intervention and treatment as well as educational programs. NCADD has an informal relationship with AA and has a traditional, disease-oriented approach to alcohol problems and recovery. Its Web site has a comprehensive list of links to other resources and organizations.

Canadian Resources

Before I list some of the larger organizations that provide resources, a few comments are in order about the general differences between approaches to managing alcohol problems in Canada and the United States. According to Robin Room, Ph.D., the past vice president for research at the former Addiction Research Foundation in Toronto, twelve-step treatment programs are prevalent in Canada but not as dominant as they are in the United States. He notes, "In Canadian culture, more attention is paid to professional expertise for treating drinking problems, as opposed to life-experience expertise. Cognitive-behavioral approaches have thus made somewhat more headway." Dr. Room adds that in Canada there is less insistence than in the United States on abstinence as the only goal. As such, moderate drinking and harm reduction approaches are more accepted in Canada than in the United States for people with mild to moderate drinking problems. Arthur McCudden, a senior public information officer at the Centre for Addiction and Mental Health, says, "Typically, if someone doesn't want a twelve-step approach, he or she would work on a one-on-one basis with a professional in one of our treatment programs."

Benchley, Peter. *Rummies*. New York: Random House, 1989.

Dardis, Tom. *The Thirsty Muse: Alcohol and the American Writer*. New York: Ticknor & Fields, 1989.

Maxwell, Ruth. *The Booze Battle*. New York: Praeger, 1976.

McGoldrick, Edward J. *The Conquest of Alcohol: A Handbook of Self-Therapy*. New York: Delacorte, 1966.

Morris, Kokin, and Ian Walker. *Women Married to Alcoholics*. New York: William Morrow, 1989.

V., Rachel. *A Woman Like You: Life Stories of Women Recovering from Alcoholism and Addiction*. New York: Harper & Row, 1985.

Recommended Resources for Professionals

The masters listed some of these books as helpful to them as well.

Daley, Dennis C., and G. Alan Marlatt. *Managing Your Drug or Alcohol Problem: Client Workbook*. San Antonio, Tex.: Psychological Corporation, 1997.

———. *Managing Your Drug or Alcohol Problem: Therapist Guide*. San Antonio, Tex.: Psychological Corporation, 1997.

Hays, Kate F. *Working It Out: Using Exercise in Psychotherapy*. Washington, D.C.: American Psychological Association, 1999.

Hester, Reid K., and William R. Miller. *Handbook of Alcoholism Treatment Approaches*. Boston: Allyn and Bacon, 1995.

Horvath, A. Thomas. *Sex, Drugs, Gambling, & Chocolate: A Workbook for Overcoming Addictions*. San Luis Obispo, Calif.: Impact, 1998.

Institute of Medicine. *Broadening the Base of Treatment for Alcohol Problems*. Washington, D.C.: National Academy Press, 1990.

Johnson, N. Peter, ed. *Dictionary of Street Alcohol and Drug Terms*. Columbia, S.C.: School of Medicine, University of South Carolina, 1993.

Kurtz, Ernest. *Not-God: A History of Alcoholics Anonymous*. Center City, Minn.: Hazelden Educational Materials, 1979.

Marlatt, G. Alan, ed. *Harm Reduction: Pragmatic Strategies for Managing High-Risk Behaviors*. New York: Guilford, 1998.

Marlatt, G. Alan, and Judith R. Gordon, eds. *Relapse Prevention*. New York: Guilford, 1985.

McGrady, Barbara S., and William R. Miller. *Research on Alcoholics*

Anonymous: Opportunities and Alternatives. New Brunswick, N.J.: Rutgers Center of Alcohol Studies, 1993.

Miller, William R., ed. *Integrating Spirituality into Treatment.* Washington, D.C.: American Psychological Association, 1999.

Miller, William R., and Nick Heather, eds. *Treating Addictive Behaviors,* 2d ed. New York: Plenum, 1998.

Miller, William R., and Stephen Rollnick. *Motivational Interviewing: Preparing People to Change Addictive Behavior.* New York: Guilford, 1991.

Peele, Stanton. *Diseasing of America.* San Francisco: Jossey-Bass, 1995.

Peele, Stanton, and Charles Bufe with Archie Brodsky. *Resisting 12-Step Coercion.* Tucson: See Sharp Press, 2000.

Schuckit, Marc Alan. *Educating Yourself About Alcohol and Drugs.* New York: Plenum, 1998.

Tucker, Jalie A., Dennis M. Donovan, and G. Alan Marlatt, eds. *Changing Addictive Behavior.* New York: Guilford, 1999.

Vaillant, George E. *The Natural History of Alcoholism Revisited.* Cambridge, Mass.: Harvard University Press, 1995.

Volpicelli, Joseph, and Maia Szalavitz. *Recovery Options: The Complete Guide.* New York: John Wiley & Sons, 2000.

Selected References

Alcoholics Anonymous. 3d ed. New York: Alcoholics Anonymous World Services, 1976.

Alcoholics Anonymous Comes of Age: A Brief History of AA. New York: Alcoholics Anonymous World Services, 1985.

Alcoholics Anonymous 1998 Membership Survey. New York: Alcoholics Anonymous World Services, 1999.

American Psychiatric Association. *Diagnostic and Statistical Manual of Mental Disorders.* 4th ed. Washington, D.C.: American Psychiatric Press, 1994.

American Psychological Association, Division 50. "Special Issue: Spirituality in Addiction and Recovery." *Addictions Newsletter 6,* 1 (1998).

B., Hamilton. *Getting Started in AA.* Center City, Minn.: Hazelden, 1995.

Babor, Thomas F. "The Classification of Alcoholics." *Alcohol Health & Research World* 20, 1 (1996): 6–14.

Baumeister, Roy F. "Crystallization of Discontent in the Process of Major Life Change." In *Can Personality Change?,* eds. Todd F. Heatherton and Joel L. Weinberger. Washington, D.C.: American Psychological Association, 1994.

Bradley, Katharine A. "The Primary Care Practitioner's Role in the Prevention and Management of Alcohol Problems." *Alcohol Health & Research World* 18, 2 (1994): 97–104.

Bufe, Charles. *Alcoholics Anonymous: Cult or Cure?* 2d ed. Tucson: See Sharp Press, 1998.

Burman, Sondra. "The Challenge of Sobriety: Natural Recovery Without Treatment and Self-Help Groups." *Journal of Substance Abuse* 9 (1997): 41–61.

Came to Believe. New York: Alcoholics Anonymous World Services, 1973.

Carbutt, James C, Suzanne L. West, Timothy S. Carey, Kathleen N.

Lohr, and Fulton T. Crews. "Pharmacological Treatment of Alcohol Dependence: A Review of the Evidence." *Journal of the American Medical Association* 281, 14 (1999): 1318–25.

Cunningham, John A, Linda C. Sobell, Mark B. Sobell, and Janet Gaskin. "Alcohol and Drug Abusers' Reasons for Seeking Treatment." *Addictive Behaviors* 19, 6 (1994): 691–96.

Cunningham, John A., Linda C. Sobell, Mark B. Sobell, and Geeta Kapur. "Resolution from Alcohol Problems With and Without Treatment: Reasons for Change." *Journal of Substance Abuse* 7 (1995): 365–72.

Daley, Dennis C., and G. Alan Marlatt. *Managing Your Drug or Alcohol Problem: Therapist Guide.* San Antonio, Tex.: Psychological Corporation, 1997.

Dawson, Deborah A. "Correlates of Past-Year Status Among Treated and Untreated Persons with Former Alcohol Dependence: United States, 1992." *Alcoholism: Clinical and Experimental Research* 20, 4 (1996): 771–79.

———. "Symptoms and Characteristics of Individuals with Different Types of Recovery from DSM-IV Alcohol Dependence." *Journal of Substance Abuse* 10, 2 (1998): 127–42.

Donovan, Dennis M., and G. Alan Marlatt, eds. *Assessment of Addictive Behaviors.* New York: Guilford, 1988.

Dorsman, Jerry. *How to Quit Drinking Without AA.* Rocklin, Calif.: Prima, 1994.

Fanning, Patrick, and John T. O'Neil. *The Addiction Workbook.* Oakland, Calif.: New Harbinger, 1996.

Fingarette, Herbert. *Heavy Drinking: The Myth of Alcoholism as a Disease.* Berkeley: University of California Press, 1988.

Fox, Vince. *Addiction, Change and Choice: The New View of Alcoholism.* Tucson: See Sharp Press, 1993.

Gordis, Enoch. "The National Institute on Alcohol Abuse and Alcoholism." *Alcohol Health & Research World* 19, 1 (1995): 5–16.

Graham, Allan W., and Terry K. Schultz, eds. *Principles of Addiction Medicine.* 2d ed. Chevy Chase, Md.: American Society of Addiction Medicine, Inc., 1998.

Granfield, Robert, and William Cloud. "The Elephant that No One Sees: Natural Recovery Among Middle-Class Addicts." *Journal of Drug Issues* 26, 1 (1996): 45–61.

Grant, Bridget F., Thomas C. Harford, Deborah A. Dawson, Patricia

Chou, Mary Dufour, and Roger Pickering. "Prevalence of DSM-IV Alcohol Abuse and Dependence." *NIAAA's Epidemiologic Bulletin* 35 (1994): 243–48.

Hall, Sharon M., Barbara E. Havassy, and David A. Wasserman. "Commitment to Abstinence and Acute Stress in Relapse to Alcohol, Opiates, and Nicotine." *Journal of Consulting and Clinical Psychology* 58, 2 (1990): 175–81.

"Hard Proof About Cooking with Alcohol." *Tufts University Diet & Nutrition Letter* 8, 4 (1990): 1.

Hays, Kate F. *Working It Out: Using Exercise in Psychotherapy.* Washington, D.C.: American Psychological Association, 1999.

Heather, N., W. R. Miller, and J. Greeley. *Self-Control and the Addictive Behaviors.* New York: Maxwell Macmillan, 1991.

Hester, Reid K., and William R. Miller. *Handbook of Alcoholism Treatment Approaches.* Boston: Allyn and Bacon, 1995.

Horvath, A. Thomas. *Sex, Drugs, Gambling, & Chocolate: A Workbook for Overcoming Addictions.* San Luis Obispo, Calif.: Impact, 1998.

Horvath, Arthur T. "Alternative Support Groups." In *Substance Abuse: A Comprehensive Textbook,* ed. Joyce H. Lowinson, Pedro Ruiz, Robert B. Millman, and John G. Langrod. Baltimore: Williams & Wilkins, 1997.

Humphreys, Keith, Rudolf H. Moos, and John W. Finney. "Two Pathways Out of Drinking Problems Without Professional Treatment." *Addictive Behaviors* 20, 4 (1995): 427–41.

Institute of Medicine. *Broadening the Base of Treatment for Alcohol Problems.* Washington, D.C.: National Academy Press, 1990.

Irvin, Jennifer E., Clint A. Bowers, Michael E. Dunn, and Morgan C. Wang. "Efficacy of Relapse Prevention: A Meta-Analytic Review." *Journal of Consulting and Clinical Psychology* 67, 4 (1999): 563–70.

Johnson, Bankole A., and Nassima Ait-Daoud. "Medications to Treat Alcoholism." *Alcohol Research & Health* 23, 2 (1999): 99–106.

Johnson, N. Peter, ed. *Dictionary of Street Alcohol and Drug Terms.* Columbia, S.C.: University of South Carolina School of Medicine, 1993.

Kadden, Ronald M. "Cognitive-Behavioral Approaches to Alcoholism Treatment." *Alcohol Health & Research World* 18, 4 (1994): 279–86.

Kaskutas, Lee Ann. "What Do Women Get Out of Self-Help? Their Reasons for Attending Women for Sobriety and Alcoholics Anonymous." *Journal of Substance Abuse Treatment* 11, 3 (1994): 185–95.

Kasl, Charlotte Davis. *Many Roads, One Journey: Moving Beyond the 12 Steps.* New York: HarperPerennial, 1992.

Khantzian, E. J., and John E. Mack. "How AA Works and Why It's Important for Clinicians to Understand." *Journal of Substance Abuse Treatment* 11, 2 (1994): 77–92.

King, Michele Pukish, and Jalie Tucker. "Behavior Change Patterns and Strategies Distinguishing Moderation Drinking and Abstinence During the Natural Resolution of Alcohol Problems Without Treatment." *Psychology of Addictive Behavior* 14, 1 (2000): 48–55.

Kinney, Jean, and Gwen Leaton. *Loosening the Grip: A Handbook of Alcohol Information.* 5th ed. St. Louis: Mosby, 1995.

Kremer, David, Marjorie J. Malkin, and John J. Benshoff. "Physical Activity Programs Offered in Substance Abuse Treatment Facilities." *Journal of Substance Abuse Treatment* 12, 5 (1995): 327–33.

Kurtz, Ernest. *Not-God: A History of Alcoholics Anonymous.* Center City, Minn.: Hazelden Educational Materials, 1979.

Kurtz, Linda Farris. "Research on Alcohol Abuse and Recovery: From Natural Helping to Formal Treatment to Mutual Aid." In *The Addiction Process: Effective Social Work Approaches,* ed. E. M. Freeman. New York: Longman, 1992.

Lieber, Charles S. *Medical and Nutritional Complications of Alcoholism.* New York: Plenum, 1992.

Litten, Raye Z., and John P. Allen. "Medications for Alcohol, Illicit Drug, and Tobacco Dependence." *Journal of Substance Abuse Treatment* 16, 2 (1999): 105–12.

Living Sober. New York: Alcoholics Anonymous World Services, 1975.

Ludwig, Arnold. *Understanding the Alcoholic's Mind.* New York: Oxford University Press, 1988.

Margolis, Robert D., and Joan E. Zweben. *Treating Patients with*

Alcohol and Other Drug Problems: An Integrated Approach.
Washington, D.C.: American Psychological Association, 1998.

Marlatt, G. Alan, ed. *Harm Reduction: Pragmatic Strategies for Managing High-Risk Behaviors.* New York: Guilford, 1998.

Marlatt, G. Alan, and Judith R. Gordon, eds. *Relapse Prevention.* New York: Guilford, 1985.

Marsano, Luis. "Alcohol and Malnutrition." *Alcohol Health & Research* 17, 4 (1993): 284–91.

McCaul, Mary E., and Janice Furst. "Alcoholism Treatment in the United States." *Alcohol Health & Research World* 18, 4 (1994): 253–60.

McGrady, Barbara S., and William R. Miller. *Research on Alcoholics Anonymous: Opportunities and Alternatives.* New Brunswick, N.J.: Publications Division, Rutgers Center of Alcohol Studies, 1993.

Miller, William R. "Researching the Spiritual Dimensions of Alcohol and Other Drug Problems." *Addiction* 93, 7 (1998): 979–90.

———. "What Really Drives Change?" *Addiction* 88 (1993): 1479–80.

———, ed. *Integrating Spirituality into Treatment.* Washington, D.C.: American Psychological Association, 1999.

Miller, William R., and Nick Heather, eds. *Treating Addictive Behaviors.* 2d ed. New York: Plenum, 1998.

Miller, William R., Robert J. Meyers, and J. Scott Tonigan. "Engaging the Unmotivated in Treatment for Alcohol Problems: A Comparison of Three Strategies for Intervention Through Family Members." *Journal of Consulting and Clinical Psychology* 67, 5 (1999): 688–97.

Miller, William R., and Stephen Rollnick. *Motivational Interviewing: Preparing People to Change Addictive Behavior.* New York: Guilford, 1991.

Moos, Rudolf H. "Treated or Untreated, an Addiction Is Not an Island unto Itself." *Addiction* 89 (1994): 507–9.

Murphy, Timothy J., Robert R. Pagano, and G. Alan Marlatt. "Lifestyle Modification with Heavy Alcohol Drinkers: Effects of Aerobic Exercise and Meditation." *Addictive Behaviors* 11 (1986): 175–86.

National Institute on Alcohol Abuse and Alcoholism. *National*

Treatment Center Study: Summary Report. Washington, D.C.: U.S. Public Health Service, 1997.

————. *National Treatment Center Study: Summary Report (No. 3).* Washington, D.C.: U.S. Public Health Service, 1998.

————. *National Treatment Center Study: Summary Report (No. 4).* Washington, D.C.: U.S. Public Health Service, 1999.

O'Farrell, Timothy J., and W. Fals-Stewart. "Family-Involved Alcoholism Treatment: An Update." In *Recent Developments in Alcoholism.* Vol. 15: *Alcoholism Services Research in the Managed Care Era,* ed. M. Galanter. New York: Plenum, forthcoming.

O'Malley, Stephanie S., Adam J. Jaffe, Grace Chang, Richard S. Schottenfeld, Roger E. Meyer, and Bruce Rounsaville. "Naltrexone and Coping Skills Therapy for Alcohol Dependence." *Archives of General Psychiatry* 49 (1992): 881–87.

Orford, Jim, Edna Oppenheimer, and Griffith Edwards. "Abstinence or Control: The Outcome for Excessive Drinkers Two Years after Consultation." *Behavior Research & Therapy* 14 (1976): 409–18.

Peele, Stanton. *Diseasing of America.* San Francisco: Jossey-Bass, 1995.

Peele, Stanton, and Archie Brodsky. *The Truth about Addiction and Recovery.* New York: Fireside, 1991.

Peele, Stanton, and Charles Bufe, with Archie Brodsky. *Resisting 12-Step Coercion.* Tucson: See Sharp Press, 2000.

"Perspectives on Precipitants of Relapse." *Addiction* 91 (Supplement, 1996).

Project MATCH Research Group. "Matching Alcoholism Treatments to Client Heterogeneity: Project MATCH Posttreatment Drinking Outcomes." *Journal of Studies on Alcohol* 58 (1997): 7–29.

Schuckit, Marc Alan. *Educating Yourself about Alcohol and Drugs.* New York: Plenum, 1998.

Shute, Nancy. "The Drinking Dilemma." *U.S. News & World Report,* September 8, 1997, pp. 55–65.

Sobell, Linda C., John A. Cunningham, and Mark B. Sobell. "Recovery from Alcohol Problems with and without Treatment: Prevalence in Two Population Surveys." *American Journal of Public Health* 86, 7 (1996): 966–72.

Sobell, Linda C., John A. Cunningham, Mark B. Sobell, Sageeta Agrawal, Douglas R. Gavin, Gloria I. Leo, and Karen N. Singh. "Fostering Self-Change Among Problem Drinkers: A Proactive Community Intervention." *Addictive Behaviors* 21, 6 (1996): 817–33.

Sobell, Linda C., Mark B. Sobell, Tony Toneatto, and Gloria I. Leo. "What Triggers the Resolution of Alcohol Problems Without Treatment?" *Alcoholism: Clinical and Experimental Research* 17, 2 (1993): 217–24.

Sobell, Linda C., Tony Toneatto, and Mark B. Sobell. "Behavioral Assessment and Treatment Planning for Alcohol, Tobacco, and Other Drug Problems: Current Status with and Emphasis on Clinical Applications." *Behavior Therapy* 25 (1994): 533–80.

Swift, Robert M. "Drug Therapy for Alcohol Dependence." *New England Journal of Medicine* 340, 19 (1999): 1482–90.

———. "Medications and Alcohol Craving." *Alcohol Research & Health* 23, 3 (1999): 207–13.

Tate, Philip. *Alcohol: How to Give It Up and Be Glad You Did.* Tucson: See Sharp Press, 1997.

Trimpey, Jack. *The Small Book: A Revolutionary Alternative for Overcoming Alcohol and Drug Dependence.* New York: Delacorte, 1989.

Tuchfeld, Barry S. "Spontaneous Remission in Alcoholics." *Journal of Studies on Alcohol* 42, 7 (1981): 626–41.

Tucker, Jalie A., Dennis M. Donovan, and G. Alan Marlatt, eds. *Changing Addictive Behavior.* New York: Guilford, 1999.

Tucker, Jalie A, Rudy E. Vuchinich, and Julie Akiko Gladsjo. "Environmental Events Surrounding Natural Recovery from Alcohol-Related Problems." *Journal of Studies on Alcohol* (1994): 401–11.

Tucker, Jalie A., Rudy E. Vuchinich, and Michele M. Pukish. "Molar Environmental Contexts Surrounding Recovery from Alcohol Problems by Treated and Untreated Problem Drinkers." *Experimental and Clinical Psychopharmacology* 3, 2 (1995): 195–204.

Twelve Steps and Twelve Traditions. New York: Alcoholics Anonymous World Services, 1953.

U.S. Department of Health and Human Services, Public Health Service, National Institutes of Health, and National Institute on Alcohol Abuse and Alcoholism. *Alcohol and Tobacco: From Basic*

Science to Clinical Practice. NIH Publication no. 95-3931 (Washington, D.C.: Government Printing Office, 1995).

——. *Ninth Special Report to the U.S. Congress on Alcohol and Health*. NIH Publication no. 97-4017 (Washington, D.C.: Government Printing Office, 1997).

——. *The Physicians' Guide to Helping Patients with Alcohol Problems*. NIH Publication no. 95-3769 (Washington, D.C.: Government Printing Office, 1995).

Vaillant, George E. "A Long-term Follow-up of Male Alcohol Abuse." *Archives of General Psychiatry* 53 (1996): 243–49.

——. *The Natural History of Alcoholism Revisited*. Cambridge, Mass.: Harvard University Press, 1995.

Vaillant, George E., and Susanne Hiller-Sturmhöfel. "The Natural History of Alcoholism." *Alcohol Health and Research World* 20, 3 (1996): 152–61.

Watson, Amy L., and Kenneth J. Sher. "Resolution of Alcohol Problems Without Treatment: Methodological Issues and Future Directions of Natural Recovery Research." *Clinical Psychology: Science and Practice* 5, 1 (1998): 1–18.

Wells-Parker, Elisabeth. "Mandated Treatment: Lessons from Research with Drinking and Driving Offenders." *Alcohol Health & Research World* 18, 4 (1994): 302–6.

Westermeyer, Robert. "The Codependency Idea: When Caring Becomes a Disease." http://www.habitsmart.com/cdpnt.htm, 1996.

Wolfe, Brenda L., and Robert J. Meyers. "Cost-effective Alcohol Treatment: Community Reinforcement Approach." *Cognitive and Behavioral Practice* 6 (1999): 105–9.

Index

AA (Alcoholics Anonymous): and abstinence, 108, 173, 193; active involvement in, 228; and admitting powerlessness over alcohol, 85, 97; advantages of, 111–14; and anonymity, 109, 273; autonomy of AA groups, 109; combined with other recovery methods, 19; contact information on, 275; court-ordered attendance at, 14–16; and day-at-a-time philosophy, 75–76, 82–83; defined as only recovery method, 1, 12–14, 18, 21; discontinuing going to meetings, 226; drawbacks of and dissatisfactions with, 10, 77, 114–15, 226, 244, 245, 249; and drug problems and eating disorders, 105; and employee assistance programs, 14–15; finding an AA group, 273–74; as helpful to problem drinkers, xx, 3, 6, 7, 8, 12, 24, 52–53, 68, 71, 80, 83, 85, 88, 106–7, 122, 143, 180, 181; and helping others, 14, 258; and higher power, 10, 14, 107, 108, 132, 134, 235, 239–41, 242–46; history, background, and program overview of, 107–10; and "hitting bottom," 53–54; Internet meetings and chat rooms, 274; and label of "alcoholic," 37; lifelong need for, 18; meeting frequency, location, and leadership, 273; meeting procedures in, 109, 272–73; as not helpful for everyone, xx, xxi, 10, 12–14, 16, 19–20, 21, 23, 77, 86, 97, 114–15, 116, 132, 249; number of AA groups worldwide, 23, 273–74; personal story of, 106–7; persons attending, 16, 19, 20, 21–22, 24, 52–53, 62, 68, 69, 71, 75, 77, 80, 83, 85, 87, 88, 106–7, 137, 143, 149–50, 174–75, 180, 181, 196, 205, 206, 211–12, 226, 228, 237, 242–45, 262; publications of, 274–75; and regular meeting attendance, 109, 145, 225–26; research on, 23–25; role models in, 87; for smoking cessation, 89; and spirituality, 107–9, 235, 240–41; sponsorship in, 109–10, 111; statistics on dropouts from, 25; success stories of, 24–25; and treatment programs, 141; twelve steps of, 108–9, 110, 142; Web address for, 275; and women, 111–12, 116, 117. *See also* Recovery methods

AABT. *See* Association for Advancement of Behavior Therapy (AABT)

AADAC. *See* Alberta Alcohol and Drug Abuse Commission (AADAC)

Abstinence: and AA, 108, 173, 193; and alcohol traces in specific foods and drinks, 189–91; choice

130, 202, 203, 205; for bipolar disorder, 169; containing alcohol, 190; for smoking cessation, 90; for sobriety, 92–94, 137

Meditation, 203, 236, 237, 238, 240–41

Men for Sobriety (MFS), 276–77

Meyers, Robert J., 156, 157, 160, 162, 166–67

MFS. *See* Men for Sobriety (MFS)

Miller, William, 63, 143, 242

Minnesota model, 139–40

MM. *See* Moderation Management (MM)

Moderate drinking: characteristics of persons successful with, 176; choice of, versus abstinence, 185; commitment to, 81–82; and decreased risk of heart disease, 34; definition of "successful drinking," 177–78; and emotional well-being, 186; getting help with, 187–88; groups, programs, and resources for, 186–87, 283–85; personal stories of, 171–75, 188, 191–92; and problem with abstinence for all, 182–85; and "restrained drinkers," 178; statistics on, 173–74, 178–79; strategies for, 185–87; successful return to drinking for former problem drinkers, 82, 170–79; traces of alcohol in specific foods and drinks, 189–91; unsuccessful attempts at controlled drinking for former problem drinkers, 4, 11, 15, 46, 70–73, 176–77, 179–83. *See also* DrinkWise groups; Moderation Management (MM)

Moderation Management (MM), 18–19, 20, 23, 126, 175, 177, 180, 182–83, 185, 186, 187, 283–84

Moodiness, 202–3. *See also* Depression

Motivation: and alcohol at home, 230–34; and attendance at recovery group meetings, 225–26; and business situations with alcohol, 232; and celebrating sobriety, 222–24; dealing with temptations to drink, 226–34; and defining what to be sober for, 61–63; and drink pushers, 233; and drinking buddies, 229–30; and imagining sober life, 63–66; and past memories of problem drinking, 217–22; personal stories of, 218–22; and recovered or forever recovering, 224–25; and social functions involving alcohol, 228–29; and social pressure to drink, 233; and substitute activities for drinking, 228; and taking stock of drinking pros and cons, 57–61

Moyers, Bill, 13

NA. *See* Narcotics Anonymous (NA)

Nagging by family members, 147–48, 156–57

Naltrexone, 92–93

Narcotics Anonymous (NA), 105

NASW. *See* National Association of Social Workers (NASW)

National Academy of Sciences, 22

National Association of Social Workers (NASW), 271

National Council on Alcoholism and Drug Dependence (NCADD), 165–66, 295

I think Smart Recovery or moderation management might be useful.

Each of the Canadian provinces has its own agencies for dealing with alcohol and drug problems. To obtain a list, contact the Centre for Addiction and Mental Health, listed below. Also below are some of the larger organizations in Canada that provide local, national, and sometimes international resources.

> Canadian Centre on Substance Abuse (CCSA)
> 75 Albert Street
> Suite 300
> Ottawa, Ontario
> Canada K1P 5E7
> Phone: 613-235-4048
> Web address: http://www.ccsa.ca

One of the functions of this national agency is disseminating information on substance abuse. The best way to explore CCSA's many resources is to visit its Web site. By clicking on "Resources," then on "CCSA Databases," you can access its Directory of Addictions Organizations in Canada as well as its database of national substance abuse treatment services — both of which you can search by city or province. From "Resources," you can also connect to a "Virtual Clearinghouse on Alcohol, Tobacco, and Other Drugs," which can in turn link you to scores of organizations, both Canadian and international. (CCSA's Directory of Addictions Organizations in Canada is available in paper form for $49.95 Canadian.)

> Centre for Addiction and Mental Health (CAMH)
> 33 Russell Street
> Toronto, Ontario
> Canada M5S 2S1
> Phone: 800-463-6273 (in Ontario); 416-595-6111
> Web address: http://www.camh.net

CAMH describes itself as "the largest mental health and addictions facility in Canada." Created in 1998 through a merger of four organizations (including what was known as the Addiction Research Foundation), it is affiliated with the University of Toronto and operates inpatient and outpatient programs as well as research facilities in Toronto. It also runs twelve community offices across Ontario. CAMH's work focuses on the needs of Ontario, but it extends across the country and internationally. If you go to the Web site and click on "About Addictions," you'll find links to such resources as the Les/Bi/

Gay Program, the Women's Interest Network, and the Substance Abuse Network of Ontario. The CAMH library offers a wealth of resources, many of which can be accessed on-line. By phone, you can request a list of national and provincial drug agencies from CAMH's information center.

> Drug and Alcohol Registry of Treatment (DART)
> 232 Central Avenue
> London, Ontario
> Canada N6A 1M8
> Phone: 800-565-8603
> Web address: http://www.dart.on.ca

DART provides bilingual information and referral services in Ontario for both lay people and professionals trying to find addiction treatment for themselves, family members, friends, or clients. Its toll-free number puts callers in touch with staff members trained in offering education and guidance in finding addiction treatment in Ontario based on the individual's situation.

> Drugs Help and Referral
> Phone: 514-527-2626 (Montreal and surrounding areas); 800-265-2626 (outside of Montreal only)

This bilingual telephone service refers people with alcohol and other drug problems to the agency that provides the appropriate service. This service also answers questions about substance abuse and provides information for people concerned about a loved one. The service is available twenty-four hours a day, seven days a week.

> Alberta Alcohol and Drug Abuse Commission (AADAC)
> 6th Floor, Pacific Plaza Building
> 10909 Jasper Avenue
> Edmonton, Alberta
> Canada T5J 3M9
> Phone: 780-427-2837
> Web address: http://www.aadac.com

In the western part of Canada, this organization offers widely used informational resources and also delivers outpatient, training, and prevention services in many locations throughout Alberta. AADAC also offers crisis and residential treatment services at various locations. The main office can refer you to services in your area.

Addictions Foundation of Manitoba (AFM)
1031 Portage Avenue
Winnipeg, Manitoba
Canada R3G OR8
Phone: 204-944-6200
Web address: http://www.afm.mb.ca

With its twenty-six offices in three regions, AFM provides prevention, treatment, research, and educational services relating to alcohol and other addictions for residents of Manitoba. For help with an alcohol problem, call AFM's main number, which will refer you to a local office where counselors can help determine which program is right for you. AFM also has a library with comprehensive information about addictions.

The Canadian Psychological Association (CPA)
151 Slater Street, Suite 205
Ottawa, Ontario
Canada KIP 5H3
Phone: 888-472-0657
Web address: http://www.cpa.ca

Click on "Find a psychologist" on CPA's Web site to connect to a Canadian Register of Health Service Providers in Psychology, which allows you to search particular locations for psychologists. After each person's name there is a list of his or her areas of expertise and theoretical orientation (such as behavioral or cognitive). At this writing, no phone referral service is available.

Canadian Society of Addiction Medicine (CSAM)
P.O. Box 1873
Kingston, Ontario
Canada K7L 5J7
Phone: 613-541-3951
e-mail address: csam@kingston.net
Web address: http://www.csam.org

An affiliate of the Canadian Medical Association, CSAM is largely a physician-member organization, with some research scientist members as well. If you contact CSAM by phone or by e-mail, you can receive a list of names of member physicians in your area. (CSAM recently started a certification process for members who meet certain criteria.)

Self-Help Resource Centre
40 Orchard View Blvd, Suite 219
Toronto, Ontario
Canada M4R 1B9
Phone: 416-487-4355
Web address: http://www.selfhelp.on.ca

Among its many services, this organization has a directory of more than 450 self-help groups for a wide range of issues, including some for alcohol problems, in the greater Toronto area. The center can help you locate a group in your area by phone or through its directory or Web site. (A contact person at the center indicated that there are few self-help recovery alternatives to AA in Canada, but I was able to find a link to one Ontario alternative called Clean and Sober Thinking at the center's Web site.)

Books Recommended by the Masters

The following books were mentioned by various masters as being helpful in resolving their drinking problems. Some of the books may be available in other editions. Inclusion in this list does not indicate an endorsement; readers will need to assess whether books suit their circumstances.

Alcoholics Anonymous, 3d ed. New York: Alcoholics Anonymous World Services, 1976.

Alcoholics Anonymous World Services. *Twelve Steps and Twelve Traditions.* New York: Alcoholics Anonymous Publishing, 1996.

Bufe, Charles. *Alcoholics Anonymous: Cult or Cure?* 2d ed. Tucson: See Sharp Press, 1998.

Casey, Karen. *Each Day a New Beginning: Daily Meditations for Women.* Center City, Minn.: Hazelden, 1996.

Dorsman, Jerry. *How to Quit Drinking Without AA.* Rev. ed. Rocklin, Calif.: Prima, 1997.

Ellis, Albert, and Emmett Velten. *When AA Doesn't Work for You: Rational Steps to Quitting Alcohol.* New York: Barricade, 1992.

Fanning, Patrick, and John T. O'Neil. *The Addiction Workbook.* Oakland: New Harbinger, 1996.

Fingarette, Herbert. *Heavy Drinking: The Myth of Alcoholism as a Disease.* Berkeley: University of California Press, 1989.

Fox, Vince. *Addiction, Change and Choice: The New View of Alcoholism.* Tucson: See Sharp Press, 1993.

Hamill, Pete. *A Drinking Life: A Memoir.* New York: Little, Brown, 1995.

Kasl, Charlotte Davis. *Many Roads, One Journey: Moving Beyond the 12 Steps.* New York: HarperPerennial, 1992.

Kishline, Audrey. *Moderate Drinking: The Moderation Management Guide for People Who Want to Reduce Their Drinking.* New York: Crown, 1994.

Knapp, Caroline. *Drinking: A Love Story.* New York: Delta, 1997.

Living Sober. New York: Alcoholics Anonymous World Services, 1975.

McGovern, George. *Terry: My Daughter's Life-and-Death Struggle with Alcoholism.* New York: Plume, 1997.

Peck, M. Scott. *The Road Less Traveled.* New York: Simon & Schuster, 1998.

Peele, Stanton. *Diseasing of America.* San Francisco: Jossey-Bass, 1995.

Peele, Stanton, and Archie Brodsky. *The Truth About Addiction and Recovery.* New York: Fireside, 1991.

Pluymen, Bert. *The Thinking Person's Guide to Sobriety.* New York: St. Martin's, 1999.

Ragge, Ken. *The Real AA: Behind the Myth of 12-Step Recovery.* Tucson: See Sharp Press, 1998.

Tate, Philip. *Alcohol: How to Give It Up and Be Glad You Did.* Tucson: See Sharp Press, 1997.

Trimpey, Jack. *The Small Book: A Revolutionary Alternative for Overcoming Alcohol and Drug Dependence.* New York: Dell, 1996.

Wegscheider-Cruse, Sharon. *Another Chance: Hope and Health for the Alcoholic Family.* Palo Alto, Calif.: Science & Behavior Books, 1989.

Woititz, Janet Geringer. *Adult Children of Alcoholics.* Deerfield, Fla.: Health Communications, 1990.

Out-of-Print

The following out-of-print books may be available in various editions from libraries or used and rare book dealers, or over the Internet.